THE LIBRARY OF WORLD AFFAIRS

Editors:

GEORGE W. KEETON

and

GEORG SCHWARZENBERGER

Number 2

CHINA MOULDED BY CONFUCIUS

BY THE SAME AUTHOR

Rules of Private International Law Determining Capacity Capacity to Contract (Stevens & Sons, Lond.)

Laws of China (contributed to *The Lawyers Directory*, Cincinnati, Ohio)

Civilization and Art of China (William Clowes & Sons, Lond.)

Translation from Chinese into English:

First Draft Civil Code

Supreme Court Decisions

Prize Court Judgments, etc.

PORTRAIT OF THE AUTHOR

CHINA
moulded by
CONFUCIUS

THE CHINESE WAY
IN WESTERN LIGHT

by

CHENG TIEN-HSI, LL.D. LOND.

Of the Middle Temple, Barrister-at-Law; Quain Prizeman in Public International Law; Fellow of University College, London; Judge of the Permanent Court of International Justice; Formerly Professor of Law in the University of Peking; Senior Member of the Law Codification Commission; Judge of the Supreme Court; Vice-Minister and Acting-Minister of Justice; Special Commissioner of the Chinese Government for the Chinese Art Exhibition in London, 1935, &c.

Published under the auspices of
THE LONDON INSTITUTE OF WORLD AFFAIRS

HYPERION PRESS, INC.
WESTPORT, CONNECTICUT

Library of Congress Cataloging in Publication Data

Chêng, T'ien-hsi, 1884–
   China moulded by Confucius.

   Reprint of the 1946 ed. published by Stevens,
London, which was issued as no. 2 of The Library
of world affairs.
   Includes bibliographical references.
   1. China—Civilization. 2. Confucius.
I. Title. II. Series: The Library of world
affairs, no. 2.
DS721.C48 1973   915.1'03   73–869
ISBN 0–88355–064–4

/49041

Published in 1946 by Stevens & Sons, Limited, London, England

First Hyperion reprint edition 1973

Library of Congress Catalogue Number 73-869

ISBN 0-88355-064-4

Printed in the United States of America

孔子模型之中國人
（華道西光）
鄭天錫

To the Loving Memory of
MY PARENTS
This Book is Respectfully
Dedicated

'When the *Great Principle* (the ideal social order that Confucius had in his mind) prevails, the world is like one home common to all; men of virtue and merit are to be elected to be rulers; sincerity and amity pervade all dealings between man and man; people shall love not only their own parents and own children, but also those of others; the aged, the young, the helpless widows and widowers, the orphans, the destitute, the incapacitated, and the sick shall be well provided for and well looked after, while the able-bodied shall exert themselves in their aid; men shall be appropriately employed and women suitably married; one detests that things are abandoned or wasted on earth, but, when gathered or stored up, they are not to be retained exclusively for oneself; one detests that exertion does not proceed from oneself, but its fruits are not to be regarded exclusively as one's own. Thus there will be no, and no cause for, conspiracy, robbery, theft, or rebellion, and no need to bolt one's outside door. This is a true Commonwealth.'—Confucius, *Book of Li*, Bk. XXI, Title *Li Yun*, Ch. 9.

FOREWORD

It is no small measure of consolation to be able to feel that one's time is not idly spent, when others are 'doing their bit' in a tormented world. It is with this feeling that I look back on my few years' quiet existence in Geneva during the Second World War; for, profiting by an existence without the usual daily routine, I have been able to put in a concrete shape a few reflections that have cropped up during a long period of years. My sojourn in the West has covered a good part of my life, and I always cherish a happy memory of it both in things I have learned and in persons I have met. For years I have deemed it an agreeable duty to try in my small way to introduce into my country what I have learned abroad, and thus to contribute, as best I can, directly and indirectly to a better understanding between the East and the West. But understanding requires mutuality, and so I feel it also my duty to try to bring in return to the West some of the ideas and ideals that my country and my countrymen have treasured for centuries. In this attempt I need hardly say that I express my views and thoughts simply as a private individual, wholly independent of any public capacity that I may possess or have possessed. One thing, however, I may say. While the treasures of a country, in the form of works of art like those which a few years ago I had the honour, as Special Commissioner of my Government, to bring over for exhibition in London, and which have attracted world-wide attention, can be seen by the eye, those, in the form of wisdom of the sages like those which will be unfolded in this book, such as what is said about 'noiseless music, formless manners, and badgeless mourning',[1] appeal rather to the soul.

To be exact, part of this work consists, by way of illustrations, of translation, with comments, of selected passages from the ancient Classics, including under this term the doctrines of Confucius and other sages, and, as a supplement to literature, a chapter of a well-known historical romance. In the translation of the Classics, and, particularly, of the

---

[1] *Book of Li*, Bk. LI, Title *Confucius at Leisure*, No. 29. These words used poetically in praise of certain rules of benevolent government may be interpreted to mean that the best music which a ruler may give to his people is harmonious tranquillity through good administration, the perfect manners which a ruler may set to his people are dignified serenity, and the deepest mourning which a ruler may show to his people afflicted by death is sympathetic succour.

doctrines of the sages, I have tried to be as faithful as possible to the original, as a slight inaccuracy might modify its real sense, if not its apparent meaning, and, in order that my readers may judge the meaning for themselves, to keep as close as possible to the literal sense of the text, as deviation from it would defeat the purpose. But as the Classics are mostly worded in a language proper to the ancients, and as translation often involves interpretation, [1] too literal a translation would be worse than useless; because it not only would be unintelligible, but even might convey a wrong idea of the original. In other words, while a free translation is undesirable, a translation that is too literal is impossible. To try to bring out, in accordance with the spirit of this observation, what I believe to be the correct meaning of the text has been my task; but no little difficulty has been experienced in the attempt. The translation of certain words and certain phrases, in particular, has necessitated much research and meditation. For instance, in translating the passage from Confucius quoted in the front page of this work, I had, in order to make the sense of the text clear, to say '*helpless* widows and widowers', as it really means, instead of 'widows and widowers', as it literally appears to be; for, without adding the word 'helpless', the phrase would be open to the observation that there is no reason why a widow, who might have inherited a large fortune from her husband and have grown-up children, or a widower, who might have come by a handsome estate through the death of his wife and himself be still able-bodied, should, merely on the strength of being such, be treated in the same way as the incapacitated or the sick. Instances like this are many and, in consequence, I have had in a number of cases to add words to the sentence in order to complete the sense; but, in order to indicate that the added words are mine, I have as a rule put them in brackets. Moreover, as this book is intended to be readable not only in the cloister but also in the club, as it were, for which reason part of the work has been written in a lighter vein, the choice of materials has likewise absorbed much labour. I wish I had more time at my disposal to do justice to my attempt; but one must not expect too much in a lifetime. Happily, consciousness of fidelity to one's task is always a form of consolation for its imperfect execution. It may be added that I have taken care to set out the exact reference of every passage

[1] In interpretation, as distinguished from comment, I follow strictly, at least in spirit, the orthodox commentary, *if any*, unless I have good reasons for deviating from it, in which case I always set out the reasons. Interpretation of an ancient text, without regard to the commentary universally accepted for centuries and without giving reasons for disregarding it, would be like navigation without the compass, and would lead not only to uncertainty but even to the abuse of interpreting it according to one's caprice or to suit one's purpose.

from the Classics and, especially, of every saying quoted from the sages. This is, in my opinion, a detail of some importance, particularly when the quotations are worded in a foreign language and make the very subject of comment or discussion. As to references to English literature they are meant not for the average reader, because they would be superfluous, but only for those whose mother tongue is not English, and who, in consequence, may not always be familiar with it.

Lastly, I take this opportunity to express my thanks to Dr. Hu Tien-She, Director of the Sino-International Library, Geneva, for having kindly lent me many Chinese books for consultation and a few pictures for illustration. My children, by helping me, in the course of the preparation of this work, either in fetching volume after volume from the library or in typing page after page at home, have also facilitated my task. Their services are affectionately acknowledged.

F. T. CHENG

Geneva,
December 1945

CONTENTS

8. LITERATURE   *page* 211
PART I

PART II
Fragments from the 'Three Kingdoms'

9. ART   245

10. CONCLUSION   257

Index   259

LIST OF ILLUSTRATIONS

CHAPTER I

INTRODUCTION

WHAT mankind owes to the Second World War is a lesson[1] and a better world to be reconstructed.[2] What the Chinese owe to what has been known as the 'Sino-Japanese Incident', prelude to the second world catastrophe, is millions of dead and that the world has, quite apart from international politics, taken a remarkable interest in China and things Chinese. Several years' unbroken resistance,[3] during the greater part of which she fought single-handed, with practically no navy or aeroplane, and sometimes, to use the words of Generalissimo Chiang Kai-Shek, 'with little more than bare flesh',[4] against invasion by one of the strongest modern naval and military Powers, has awakened in the hearts of all peace-loving men a profound sympathy for her and her people with the additional surmise that there must be something in her civilization. On the occasion of the second Japanese withdrawal from Changsha, in 1941, the London *Times* said in its editorial: 'By her unflinching and effective resistance China has earned an honourable place among the nations leagued together to withstand the world-wide aggression of the Axis Powers.'[5] This comment is the more significant, as China then was still alone in the field and not yet a member of the United Nations. Since then even more generous words have been expressed, particularly by people of English-speaking countries. The following instances are typical:

1. 'From the outbreak of war between China and Japan in 1937 until the attack on Pearl Harbour, America lived on borrowed time. We owe China for providing these years of grace, which we can never repay. Our cities, our homes, and our sons were spared during those long years, while China was being ruthlessly destroyed.'[6]

[1] This will be appraised by the historian.
[2] 'Man never *is*, but always *to be* blest.'—A. Pope: *Essay on Man*, Epistle I, L. 96.
[3] It is in its eighth year at the date of writing.
[4] Press *communiqué* from *Chengtu*, 2nd June 1942.
[5] *The Times*, 3rd October 1941.
[6] By Dr. James L. MacConaughty, President of Wesleyan University, on the occasion of his election as President to the United China Relief Inc.; see Press *communiqué* from *Chengtu*, 13th September 1942. As this was transmitted by wireless, omissions and clerical errors are possible.

2. 'Sun Yat-Sen demonstrated to the world how a great man, inspired by no other thought than the determination to bring reforms and benefits to his country and people, can succeed in laying in a few years the foundation of a new era.' (Lord Teviot.)

'In recent years the whole people of Great Britain watched, with admiration and sympathy, the high patriotism and inflexible decision to his public duty of your leader, Generalissimo Chiang Kai-Shek. We recognize under his leadership your party has given political unity to the Chinese Republic and inspired through his example the brave people of China to withstand for five years the superior mechanical power of the Japanese aggressor.' (Captain Scrymgeour Wedderburn.)

'It is impossible to find words adequately to express our admiration for those who had wisdom, unity, and courage to face a powerful enemy under most appalling conditions. You saved China and in doing so rendered a great service to the world, as history will testify.' (Mr. J. J. Lawson.)

'As a sailor I should like to express the intense admiration wherewith the armed forces of Great Britain watched the epic struggle of their Chinese Allies against the invader under inspiring leadership. They recognize in China the pioneers of successful resistance to ruthless aggression, and they pay homage to her and her forces accordingly.' (Lord Ailwyn.)[1]

To these should be added the following comments made in the Anglo-American press on the seventh anniversary of the 'Incident':

1. 'During the past six years, the Chinese people have suffered unspeakable hardships and cruelties. Wide regions of their teeming countryside have been devastated, and their inhabitants subjected to the extreme of violence and extortion. Yet their resistance grows stronger, and their armies fight on. The people of China have never lost their reasoned confidence in ultimate victory. Their courage, their endurance, and their single-hearted refusal to compromise with aggression have made all free nations their debtors.'[2]

2. 'The world is in China's debt. It owes China for suffering alone and, as it turns out, to our benefit . . . though belatedly, the debt will now be discharged.'[3]

[1] Spoken respectively by members of the British Parliamentary Mission in addressing the Tenth Plenary Session of the Kuomintang, 16th November 1942; see Press *communiqué* from *Chengtu*, 16th November 1942. As this was transmitted by wireless, some omissions and clerical errors are possible.
[2] The London *Times*, 8th July 1943.
[3] The *New York Times*. See Radio Bulletin, No. 161, of American Legation in Switzerland, 8th July 1943.

Lastly, a scroll, presented by President Roosevelt on 23rd June 1944, to the City of Chungking and accepted by President Chiang Kai-Shek with the words 'Representing the people of Chungking I accept this scroll as a priceless symbol which they will hold for ever in gratitude and reverence', is phrased as follows:

'In the name of the people of the United States of America, I present this scroll to the City of Chungking as a model of admiration for its brave men, women and children. Under blasts of terror from the air, even in the days before the world at large had known this horror, Chungking and its people held out firm and unconquered. They proved gloriously that terrorism cannot destroy the spirit of people determined to be free. Their fidelity to the cause of freedom will inspire the hearts of all future generations.' [1]

Generosity is found not only in words but also in deeds. The numerous aids given by America and England in various forms to China and the Chinese people, culminating in their voluntary abolition, which was followed by other countries, of their extra-territoriality rights in China, kindle in the Chinese heart a deep sense of gratitude. Since then, too, everywhere one finds that knowledge of things Chinese is eagerly sought, and Chinese people are highly popular. Indeed, the very word 'China' seems to mean a great deal more. China, as the world knows, has lost millions of her gallant sons, without counting millions of men, women, and children of the civil population, who have directly or indirectly contributed their lives to the common cause. Writing even on 3rd October 1941, the London *Times* said: 'It is estimated that two hundred million Chinese have been affected by the war, and that nearly a third of that number have become casualties or refugees.' Since then, millions must have swelled the list. The sacrifice is such as no people in history has ever been called upon to bear, and is so heavy that, perhaps, only a people who had built the Great Wall before the birth of science and the Burma Road almost with bare hands, is able to support its However, if a durable peace can thus be secured and her civilization, hitherto so imperfectly understood and so often misinterpreted, [2] is henceforth accorded its due—a fact that will not fail to be beneficial to mankind—the sacrifice will not have been made in vain. And when it is remembered that every fourth child born on this globe is a Chinese, one can well realize that Chinese civilization, which is

[1] *Department of State Bulletin*, Vol. XI, No. 262, p. 4, 2nd July 1944.
[2] See Chapter 2, General Survey, for various opinions quoted about the Chinese people.

one of the oldest but has survived all its contemporaries, cannot be a matter of indifference to the human race.

Hitherto, men have been so accustomed to regard physical force[1] as the sure sign of vitality that Chinese civilization, because it always aims at peace and harmony, has often been regarded as being short of that vitality essential in a 'mighty' world. Other causes of mis-understanding have also not been wanting. As a matter of historical interest, it may be said that the early contact of the West with China was based largely on gain. That alone suffices to point to the existence of various motives and conflicts of interest. 'China is waking up', says one author, 'too soon perhaps for the commercial interests of Westerners, who, if they were wise, would let sleeping dogs lie.'[2] It is also natural that one would be inclined to judge others by the beliefs which one has inherited, and by the habits of life to which one is accustomed. This is particularly likely to occur where the materialistic advancement of the one is manifestly behind that of the other; for temptation to judge things on the surface is great, because they are 'obvious', and first impressions are irresistible, unless one has the will and 'wit'[3] to go deeper.

Many books have been written on China and the Chinese; but a Chinese proverb[4] says:

'Error in a hundredth part of an inch to start
Ends in a thousand miles from truth apart.'

For instance, the Chinese are said to have the 'characteristics' of a 'talent for misunderstanding', 'intellectual turbidity', and what not.[5] This statement, and others of a similar nature, show how easily a people may be misunderstood by others. The Chinese, as my readers will find, are just as human as the rest of mankind, the only difference between them and others, as members of the human family, being, perhaps, that the Chinese possess a longer history. The mere fact that a nation is very old is of course no hallmark of vitality or of the possession of a high standard of civilization; but it does evidence the existence of a capacity for survival. So far as China

[1] 'Whereas other nations have depended upon physical force, the Chinese have depended upon moral forces. No student of history, no observant traveller who knows human nature, can fail to be impressed to the point of deep awe, with the thought of the marvellous restraining power which Chinese morality has exerted upon the race from the earliest times until now.' (Arthur H. Smith: *Chinese Characteristics*, 2nd ed., pp. 287-8.)
[2] The Rev. E. J. Hardy: *John Chinaman at Home*, p. 210.
[3] See Herbert A. Giles: *The Civilization of China*, p. 237.
[4] *Book of Li*, Bk. L, Title 26.
[5] Arthur H. Smith: *Chinese Characteristics*, pp. 58, 194, 242.

is concerned, her history has not grown on barren soil. She had her Shakespeares and Miltons several centuries before the *Battle of Hastings*, and has contributed no little to Western civilization by her invention of paper, printing, and the compass. [1] The saying 'within the four seas all are brethren' [2] and what is called the Golden Rule [3] and even something higher, as we shall see, [4] are among the teachings of her sages who lived six centuries before the Christian era.

'When I used', says an English author, 'to hear people who had just come to China saying to a servant: "Boy, boy", in contemptuous tones, and never thanking the boy for service rendered, I was tempted to ask: "Do you know to whom you are speaking? Are you aware that this boy belongs to a nation that was highly civilized when we were savages; to a nation that has probably forgotten as much as we ever knew?' [5] 'From the point of view of science', says an eminent sinologue, 'the Chinese are, of course, wholly out of date, though it is only within the past hundred and fifty years that the West has so decisively outstripped the East. If we go back to the fifteenth century, we shall find that the standard of civilization, as the term is usually understood, was still much higher in China than in Europe; while Marco Polo . . . has left it on record that the magnificence of Chinese cities, and the splendour of the Chinese Court, outrivalled anything he had ever seen or heard of. Pushing further back into antiquity, we easily reach a time when the inhabitants of the Middle Kingdom "held learning in high esteem, while our own painted forefathers were running naked and houseless in the woods, and living on berries and raw meat".' [6]

The writer himself, who has lived over two decades in Europe and had the mournful opportunity of witnessing the First World War on the spot, as it were, with the woeful memory of all its horrors, which, alas! have been surpassed by those of the Second, had in 1935 the honour of delivering at the *China Society* at Oxford, a lecture entitled 'The Civilization of China as illustrated by her Classics', [7] in the course of which he said: 'There you have Chinese civilization in a nutshell. It points to a certain direction; but the world to-day

---

[1] See James Harvey Robinson: *The Ordeal of Civilization*, pp. 212, 217, *note*, 714; see Thomas F. Carter: *The Invention of Printing in China and its Spread Westward*, pp. 85, 93, 183, 184, 185.

[2] By Disciple Tze Hsia. See Confucius: *Lun Yu*, Pt. XII, Ch. 5, Sec. 4.

[3] Confucius: *Lun Yu*, Pt. VI, Ch. 28, Sec. 2.

[4] See *post*, p. 74.

[5] The Rev. E. J. Hardy: *John Chinaman at Home*, p. 212.

[6] Herbert A. Giles: *The Civilization of China*, p. 117.

[7] This has been published with another lecture under the title *Civilization and Art of China* (William Clowes and Sons, London).

seems to be heading for another. In the light of world events that
have taken place in recent years and are taking place at the present
moment, no seriously-minded person can look forward with indifference or without apprehension. As men sow, they will reap. In
Chinese we would say: "If one grows melons, one will get melons.
If one grows beans, one will get beans".' Looking back, and meditating on these words. I cannot help sadly feeling that I have been
an unwilling prophet. Now, I am the more convinced that, as war
is, after all, made by men, men must first be made peace-loving
and peace-minded before war can be made impossible, and that, in
this, Chinese civilization, as it has made the Chinese people peace-
loving and peace-minded, may have something to offer.

With this in view my task in the following pages is to try to give
a glimpse of the soul of my country and, incidentally, to explain
certain institutions, customs, and aspects of life, with the hope that
the civilization and culture of a people who have benefited the world
by their invention of paper, printing, and the compass, not to mention
the many treasures that shine in museums in the four corners of the
earth, may be better understood. My aim, moreover, is to clear in
a small way the path for a deeper and closer understanding between
the East and the West, the realization of which will, in the light
of the following words of a well-known philosopher, not fail to be
of mutual benefit to both:

'Instinctive happiness, or joy of life, is one of the most important
widespread popular goods that we have lost through industrialism
and the high pressure at which most of us live; its commonness in
China is a strong reason for thinking well of Chinese civilization.
In judging of a community, we have to consider not only how
much of good or evil there is within the community, but also what
effects it has in promoting good or evil in other communities, and
how far the good things which it enjoys depend upon evils elsewhere. In this respect, also, China is better than we are.' ¹ 'The
tolerance of the Chinese is in excess of anything that Europeans
can imagine from their experience at home. . . . I think contact
between East and West is likely to be fruitful to both parties. They
may learn from us the indispensable minimum of practical effici-
ency and we may learn from them something of their contemplative wisdom which enabled them to persist while all the other
nations of antiquity have perished. When I went to China, I went
to teach; but every day that I stayed I thought less of what I had
to teach them and more of what I had to learn from them. Among

¹ Bertrand Russell: *The Problem of China*, p. 12.

Europeans who had lived a long time in China, I found this attitude not uncommon. . . . I wish I could hope that China, in return for scientific knowledge (*and, let it be added, many others which the West can teach the East and which thousands of Chinese students are seeking yearly abroad*),[1] may give us something of her large tolerance and contemplative peace of mind.'[2]

Lastly, because the whole Chinese social system, or rather what may be called Chinese civilization and culture, as described in this book, is saturated with the teachings of Confucius and those of Mencius, the sage next to him and the most brilliant exponent of his doctrines, I give it the title:

CHINA MOULDED BY CONFUCIUS

And because the illustrations of its contents, in order to be readily intelligible to my Western readers, have been largely drawn from Western literature, I also give it the sub-title:

The Chinese Way in Western Light

[1] These words are mine.
[2] Bertrand Russell: *The Problem of China*, pp. 197-8.

CHAPTER 2

GENERAL SURVEY

THE average Chinese finds life agreeable,[1] though he may be poor, and, rightly or wrongly, thinks himself a reasonably-minded creature. Although the latter part of the statement seems to be a bold claim, I have not yet met anybody of any country in my life who thinks himself an unreasonably minded fellow. It would be presumptuous on my part to attempt to speak for the sanity of mind of others, which may be presumed; but to my countrymen I owe a duty to do so. The Chinese expects others only to be human, and this is the standard of conduct that he himself would profess to observe. He would say, for instance:

'The kingly way (i.e. the royal or standard conduct of man)[2] does not go beyond being human';[3] or
'What cannot be prevented from happening, if judged by the standard of being human, even a sage would not condemn';[4] or
'Conduct that is far from being human is rarely not an instance of dangerous hypocrisy.'[5]

As it is human to disagree, it is only to be expected that this self-estimation of the Chinese is not always shared by others. For instance:

'I have often talked with the most eminent and candid sinologues', says an author, 'and have always found them ready to agree with me as to the impossibility of a conception of Chinese character as a whole. . . . The Chinese has made himself a factor in the affairs of many lands. He is seen to be irrepressible; is felt to be incomprehensible. He cannot, indeed, be rightly understood in any country but China, yet the impression still prevails that he is a bundle of contradictions who cannot be understood at all.'[6]

[1] See *ante*, p. 22 and *post*, p. 94.
[2] The phrase in Chinese is called *Wang Tao*, meaning the Way of Reason, opposite to *Bar Tao*, the Way of Force.
[3] A well-known saying.
[4] Saying of Yang Whun of *Han* dynasty (206 B.C.–A.D. 196).
[5] Saying of Soo Shun, father of the poet Soo Tung Po of *Sung* dynasty (A.D. 960–1277).
[6] Arthur H. Smith: *Chinese Characteristics*, pp. 10-11.

Apparently the said author has not talked with the well-known sinologue, Professor Herbert A. Giles, who says:

'There is a very common statement made by the persons who have lived in China—among the people, but not of them—and the more superficial the acquaintance, the more emphatic is the statement made, that the ordinary Chinaman, be he prince or peasant, offers to the Western observer an insoluble puzzle in every department of life. He is in fact a standing enigma; a human being, it may be granted, but one who can no more be classed than his unique monosyllabic language, which still stands isolated and alone. This estimate is largely based upon some exceedingly false inferences. It seems to be argued that because, in a great many matters, the Chinaman takes a diametrically opposite view to our own, he must necessarily be a very eccentric fellow; but as these are mostly matters of convention, the argument is just as valid against us as against him. . . . The principles of general morality and especially of duty towards one's neighbour, the restrictions of law, and even the conventionalities of social life, upon all of which the Chinaman is more or less nourished from his youth upwards, remain, when accidental differences have been brushed away, upon a bed-rock of ground common to both East and West; and it is difficult to see how such teachings could possibly turn out a race of men so utterly in contrast with the foreigner as the Chinese are usually supposed to be. It is certain that anything like a full and sincere observance of the Chinese rules of life would result in a community of human beings far ahead of the "pure man" dreamt of in the philosophy of the Taoist.'[1]

In order to understand the Chinese properly, it is necessary to bear always in mind that their country is larger than the continent of Europe, their population constitutes a quarter of the human race, and their history covers over four thousand years. According to the author of The Ordeal of Civilization, 'an Austrian physician is attributed to have shown recently that the black pox which afflicted Henry VIII plays a great part in English history during his reign down to the present; that the hardened arteries of Charles V had their importance in European history; that the manifold disorders of James I and the distaste of Frederick the Great for bathing are by no means negligible in estimating their careers'.[2] If it is true, and I think it is only good sense, that the personal peculiarities of the ruler of a powerful country may have such important consequences

[1] Herbert A. Giles: The Civilization of China, pp. 235-7.
[2] James Harvey Robinson: The Ordeal of Civilization, p. 742.

in the evolution of history, the three factors of China just mentioned cannot fail to have their effect on the outlook of life and the habits of thought of her people. Their history with its 'ample page rich with the spoils of time' [1] affords them many object lessons, while the multi-millions of their kin, bound together by one language, one literature, and, with minor exceptions, one faith and one philosophy, as well as their manifold customs which, though varied in form, are the same in substance, offer them unique opportunities in the study of men, events, and affairs. As a result, they have learned and believe, first, that in all lands and ages human nature has been and is more or less the same, for, as they would say: 'All human beings alike have the seven feelings, namely, "pleasure, anger, grief, fear, love, hate, and desire",' [2] or 'The plum trees of all countries bear the same blossoms'; [3] secondly, that one's real happiness consists not in the possession of things or gratification of desires, which know no bound, but in the pacification of the mind, for, as they would say: 'If you compare yourself with those above (i.e. those who are more fortunate), you may find that you have not enough; but if you compare yourself with those below (i.e. those who are less fortunate), you will find that you have more than sufficient'; [4] and, thirdly, that the law of nature being immutable and human nature being what it is and has been, history constantly repeats itself, though in ever changing forms. In consequence, while they are always eager to learn, because they are a people who always hold learning in high esteem, they have an intuitive distrust of things that are unnatural or contrary to human nature, and have no great passion for things that are not indispensable to real happiness. Above all, they are not easy to be unduly moved by what is, or is supposed to be, new; not that they are complacent or merely conservative, nor that what is claimed to be new may be only a new form of barbarism, or a new form of heresy, or a new form of massacre, or a new form of torture, or a new form of suicide, none of which is worth learning, but rather that almost everything seems to them to have had in substance a counterpart in the past. For instance, the periodical wars in Europe and the various forms of diplomacy associated therewith, such as alliances, balance of power, non-aggression pact, entente cordiale, and the like, recall to them a familiar chapter of the History of the Warring States (481-205 B.C.), the only difference that strikes them being, perhaps, that there seems to have been less sanctity of treaties in the present

[1] Thomas Gray: *Elegy Written in a Country Churchyard*, Ls. 49-50.
[2] *Book of Li*, Bk. XXII, Title *Li Yun*; Ed. *Sze Bu Bei Yao*.
[3] A common saying.
[4] A common saying.

century than in those primitive days, when, in inter-state relations, no ruler yet dared to be cynically indifferent to the opinion of the world or to the judgment of history.

In the matter of theories, doctrines, or 'isms', the Chinese are on an even richer soil. Ranging from Individualism (like the philosophy of Yang Chu) to Equal Love (like the philosophy of Moh Tze) and from Social Contract[1] to Anti-Aggression,[2] various forms of 'isms', numbered by the score, were preached several centuries before the Christian era. Writing to a great London daily (of which I have unfortunately lost the clipping) during the First World War, an eminent Englishman said *in effect* that it seemed to him that 'in fundamentals the West could teach little to the Chinese; because it was remarkable that, even in the matter of strategy, the principal teachings of Sun Wu Tze,[3] who lived six centuries B.C., were found still applicable in the war then in progress'. This is, of course, an exaggeration, at least in the opinion of the Chinese, who are sending hundreds of their sons and daughters to the West every year as students. But it is curiously true, as has been said to me by a contemporary sinologue, whose name need not be mentioned here, that the modern 'ism', which claims to establish a 'New Order', has in the light of Chinese history, taught nothing new. Its gospel, as he says, is in essence a reflection, but in conception falls short, of the political philosophy of Li Sze, the well-known Prime Minster of the First Emperor of the *Chin* Dynasty (221-206 B.C.), who, conceiving an everlasting empire for his Imperial master, counselled and initiated the policy of burning all the classics and drowning any scholar who ventured to criticize his 'New Order'. As recorded by the historian, the famous decree was *substantially* worded as follows:

'All that is not recorded by the *Chin* Dynasty, and all ancient books in private possession, with the exception of those herein specified, shall be surrendered and burnt. Anyone who henceforth dares talk about ancient books shall be put to death and his body exposed in the market place. Anyone who dares criticize the present by reference to the past shall be executed with his near relatives, and any official who knows of any such offender, but fails to denounce him to the authorities, shall suffer the same penalty. Those who

[1] See *post*, p. 114.
[2] See *post*, p. 34.
[3] Most celebrated military genius in Chinese history. His famous work on strategy, referred to in that letter, is known as *The Thirteen Chapters of Sun Wu Tze*. It is interesting that he should have chosen '13' as the number. Anachronically speaking, he may have thought that there should be no superstition in military affairs.

should, but fail to, burn their books within thirty days after the issue of the decree shall be condemned to forced labour.'[1]

In other words, the past shall be wholly wiped out, and history shall begin right from the *Chin* Dynasty. Surely, this surpasses in magnitude anything yet conceived in a modern 'New Order'. That 'history shall begin from me' throws in the shade even the oft-quoted expression of Louis XIV, *L'État, c'est moi*. But, it should be remembered as a lesson, the ambition of the *Chin* Dynasty lasted only fifteen years (221-206 B.C.), and the only things that remain to remind men of its once glorious and mighty existence are the Great Wall, built in 214 B.C. and a long poem entitled *Ah Fang Kung*[2] *Fu*,[3] written by the celebrated poet Tu Mook of the *Tang* Dynasty (A.D. 618-907). The one is familiar to the tourists, some of whom may have picked up and brought home fragments of a fallen brick as treasured souvenirs of their visit to the East, but how many of them, if any, would have realized that they were witnessing not merely the relics of a gigantic wall, but the Maginot Line of a classic dynasty and the ruins of an ancient 'New Order'? The other depicts the artistic beauty and the architectural ingenuity of the then Imperial palace, which occupied an area of about 100 square miles and could comfortably accommodate 10,000 persons. The poet, while he admired the triumph of art and architectural genius, could not forget or forgive that the palace was the last word in luxury and foremost in folly, and so he ended his long poem with these words of warning to posterity:

'The people of *Chin* were too occupied to have the opportunity of voicing their lamentations; therefore later generations lamented them. But these later generations lamented without learning a lesson from their lamentations; therefore they were in turn lamented by generations that followed.'[4]

It is an irony of Fate that it is not the Empire of *Chin*, or its 'New Order', that becomes everlasting, as originally conceived, but the long poem, written about a thousand years afterwards on its ruins, that has become immortal.

I must ask pardon of my readers. To use the words of the horse buyer in Oliver Goldsmith's *Vicar of Wakefield*,[5] who went out of his way to make a long discourse on the dotage of the world and its

---

[1] *History* by Sze Ma Chen, Title 'Biography of *Chin*, the First Emperor.'
[2] A grand palace built in 212 B.C.
[3] Long poem of a certain style.
[4] The poem is contained in *Collected Ancient Essays*.
[5] See Ch. XIV.

A VIEW OF THE GREAT WALL

cosmogony, 'I am straying from the question'. Now, let me resume. Of course, the aeroplane, the submarine, the radio, and the like are things of which the Chinese cannot recall any counterpart in their past as they could in the other cases; yet even this newness may not prevent them from thinking that these modern wonders seem to have been more or less anticipated or contemplated in the well-known romance, *The Diary of Travel to the West*, written in the *Yuan* (A.D. 1277-1368) or *Ming* (A.D. 1368-1644) Dynasty.[1] There is a story often told that when the first motor-car made its way proudly across the Chinese desert, a man whose attention was drawn to it by its noise rose from his seat to cast a philosophic glance at it, but almost immediately resumed his seat, as if nothing had happened. This may be just one of the stories invented to illustrate the alleged Chinese apathy or insensibility towards modern progress. But there are certainly men who attach more intrinsic value to some poems of the *Tang* or *Sung* Dynasty than to some of the modern inventions, wonderful though they are. Did not Wolfe, while rowing to the cove now named after him, repeat, in a low voice, to the officers in his boat Gray's 'Elegy Written in a Country Churchyard', saying: 'Now, gentlemen, I would rather be the author of that poem than take Quebec'?[2] There is, therefore, much to be said for the Chinese point of view. The works of Thomas Gray or Shakespeare or Milton are by all standards untarnished gains to the world. The aeroplane, the submarine, and the like, not to mention poison gas, can at most, in the light of the two World Wars, be mixed blessings.

A story often told at the beginning of the present century was that Ito, the well-known Japanese statesman, after he had negotiated peace with Li Hung Chang in the first Sino-Japanese War (1894-1895), said that during the negotiation he stood somewhat in awe of the Chinese plenipotentiary, who looked and spoke as if China had won the war, or something to that effect. This might be just a story originated, perhaps, with a sense of irony; but it is one that could be true. The Chinese envoy could very well have felt that, though Japan had, for the time being, beaten China in the game of war and incidentally displayed technical knowledge and physical courage, China having been the teacher of Japan in the past—which means much in the East—had still much to teach her former pupil, at least in the game of peace, in essential virtue and fundamental wisdom. As man to man he was also no less a match for his interlo-

---

[1] There is a controversy as to the date. The authorship is attributed to Li Tse Chang. Though the book cannot be said to have any scientific value, it may quicken imagination and turn one's mind to the realm of possibilities.

[2] David Hume: *History of England*, p. 603, Ed. 1880.

cutor. He might be ignorant of Greek and Latin or chemistry and physics; but, like all Chinese scholars of the day, he was trained in a system, the curriculum of which, to use the words of an English sinologue, 'may be fitly compared with such an education as was given to William Pitt and others among our own great statesmen'. [1] Another story told about him was that a Chinese diplomat who accompanied him on his tour in Europe wrote in the album of Queen Victoria a couplet consisting of highly appropriate, but isolated and well known, poetic phrases compressed into two lines. This may also be just one of those things that may safely be told at dinner parties without fear of immediate contradiction; for who can have it verified on the spot? But on account of the literary merit of the couplet, which, however, will be lost in the translation, it may be set out here to satisfy curiosity:

> 'In the Holy West, behold!
> Descends the Mother Empress. [2]
> From the East a *crimson halo* [3]
> Surrounds a city blest.'

An adequate understanding of the Chinese necessitates, moreover, a knowledge of three things which form the key to Chinese culture and mentality, viz.:

1. *Li* (禮), which is generally translated as 'propriety' but means more, and is what the Chinese are taught from childhood to observe and what largely shapes their conduct.

2. *Jiun Tze* (君子), which is generally translated as 'gentleman' but means more, and is the standard to which the Chinese are taught to conform and by which men are commonly judged in China.

3. *Ching* (情), which is generally translated as 'sentiment' but means more, and is what is most apt to influence the Chinese mind.

LI

Li (which, for the sake of convenience, will hereafter be called propriety or moral rules of correct conduct) is that body of rules or conventions, some of which existed before there was law properly so called, and which used to and still govern the conduct of men, particularly educated men, beside the law, and formed, in ancient days,

---

[1] Herbert A. Giles: *The Civilization of China*, p. 112.
[2] According to Chinese Buddhist mythology, the mother of the Emperor of Heaven dwells in the West of Heaven.
[3] This is associated with saintliness and prosperity.

the only rules that governed relations between States. As an instance
of the latter, the rule of *not killing an envoy* (*Buoo Sah Lai Schi*), which
in modern days is termed diplomatic inviolability, was a rule of *Li*.
Unfortunately, the word in its secondary sense also means ceremony, though to a Chinese this can never cause confusion or misunderstanding; for in that secondary sense it is seldom used alone
but more often with other words, e.g., 'to perform *Li*' or '*Li* of
marriage', or '*Li* of funeral'. When used alone, it is generally understood to mean a rule of correct conduct and not ceremony. However,
the decline of the political fortune of a country seldom fails to involve
a corresponding decline of the value of its institutions in the eyes of
others, and so, when China was predicted loudly about to be 'broken
and scattered', [1] and it was proclaimed proudly that her defences had
been 'battered and broken', [2] *Li*, which the Chinese deem as their
cultural asset, was regarded by others as mere ceremony, and
Confucius, whom the Chinese ancients revered as 'the man who
knows *Li*' (i.e. the guardian of the unwritten law of the day) was
called by others 'the man of ceremonies'. [3] But to regard what the
Chinese consider to be *Li* as ceremony would be like regarding the
English Constitutional Conventions as ceremony, and to call Confucius 'the man of ceremonies' would be like calling the Speaker of
the English House of Commons by the same term.

As a result of this misunderstanding the Chinese are often represented as a people who attach excessive importance to form and
ceremony. Such misunderstanding may well have been enhanced by
the fact that, in the ancient *Book of Li*, which deals with many subjects, there is a chapter containing a set of rules, such as:

'When you are in company with your teacher, do not go aside
of the road to speak to others. When you meet your teacher on
the road, run forward, and stand properly to salute him by raising
both hands grasped together. If the teacher speaks to you, answer
him respectfully. If he does not speak, retire. When you go up
to a city wall, do not point anywhere with your fingers. When you
are on the top of a city wall, do not shout. When you are a guest,
do not ask for things to which you may be accustomed (at home).
When you are about to enter the hall, you should make some
noise (in order not to cause a surprise to the people inside). When
there are two pairs of shoes outside the door of a room, [4] enter only

[1] Legge: *The Chinese Classics*, Vol. I, Prologomena, p. 109.
[2] Legge: *The Chinese Classics*, Vol. II, Prologomena, p. 79.
[3] Legge: *The Chinese Classics*, Vol. I, Prologomena, pp. 73-4.
[4] In ancient times people sat on mats, and so they took off their shoes and left
them at the doorway when they entered a room.

when talkings are heard. If no talking is heard, do not enter. When you enter the house with a guest, you should request him at every door to enter first; but when the guest arrives at the bedroom, you should ask permission to enter first to arrange the seats. When the seats have been arranged, you then come out to welcome him in. At this moment the guest should decline to enter first, and so you respectfully accompany him in.'[1]

All this and the fact that it was taught and practised by the Chinese in days long before the birth of Aristotle may indeed seem strange to the stranger, who may well be excused for saying: 'Surely, this is ceremony!' But as a mark of civilization, this is also surely more genuine than the gibbet, the sight of which on the beach drew from the shipwrecked sailors the exclamation: 'Thank God, we've reached a civilized country!'[2] In short, the Chinese may indeed readily subscribe to the principle of 'keeping up some mechanical forms of good breeding'[3] in social intercourse; but it would be incorrect to regard them as a people attaching more importance to form and ceremony than other civilized peoples. If we may base our opinion on the sagacious observation of Gibbon that 'the laws of a nation form the most instructive portion of its history',[4] the Chinese may even be found to be a people who, except in marriage,[5] attach comparatively less to form. No Chinese litigant would ever lose his suit, as the Romans did, if, instead of saying in his plea that the defendant had cut his *trees* as the law provided, he alleged that the defendant had cut his *vines* as a fact,[6] nor would a Chinese court set aside a verdict merely because the foreman spelled 'first' 'fist'.[7] In Chinese law a parol contract has always been binding and is not rendered unenforceable for being not in writing. No lawyer need be employed for a display of conveyancing genius in the sale of a simple plot of land. If you sell, you sell. You do not have to say, 'convey, assign, transfer . . .', but call a spade a spade. In the notable English trial, known as the 'Brides in the Bath Murder Case', the learned judge in his summing up said: 'Since last August all over

[1] Bk. II, p. 1; Ed. *Sze Bu Bei Yao.*
[2] Professor Kenny: *Outlines of Criminal Law,* p. 31; Ed. 1929.
[3] Oliver Goldsmith: *Vicar of Wakefield,* Ch. IV.
[4] *The History of the Decline and Fall of the Roman Empire,* Ch. XLIV; London, Bell, 1882; Vol. V, p. 3.
[5] See chapter on Marriage.
[6] See *Institutes of Gaius,* IV, 11.
[7] See Storey: *Reform of Legal Procedure,* p. 206. 'One man was convicted of murder in the first degree, and the verdict was set aside because the foreman spelled "first" "fist".

Europe, sometimes in England, sometimes on the sea, thousands of lives of combatants, sometimes non-combatants, have been taken daily, with no warning, and in many cases with no justification. . . . And yet, while this wholesale destruction of human life is going on, for some days all the apparatus of justice in England has been considering whether the prosecution are right in saying that one man should die.'[1] These ringing words cannot fail to make one think, on the one hand, how dear is the life of a human being and, on the other, how cheap it is when it is mown down in its prime, daily by the thousands, according to form, so much so that, in late years in certain countries, some married women have refused to bear children in order to spare themselves the painful thought that their blood and flesh embodied in their dear ones will one day be no more and no better than mere food for the cannon. This is no philosophy of the pacifist, but only points to the folly of those who, ignoring that 'Peace hath her victories no less renowned than war', seek glory in human slaughter rather than in human salvation, and to the fact that the resigned recognition of the 'right' to kill in war, however instituted, is, in essence, mere attachment to form. Realizing this fallacy at a very early date, a sage of the Confucian School, whose doctrines have for centuries formed part of the daily lessons of the schools, taught the notion of *unrighteous war* and condemned war in general:

'In the whole period of *Spring and Autumn*',[2] says Mencius,[3] 'there was not a single righteous war. There might indeed be cases where one was better than another.'[4] 'To make war, for the contentious acquisition of territory, thereby causing (so many) men to be killed that the plain is covered with corpses, or for the contentious acquisition of a city, thereby causing (so many) men to be killed that the city is covered with corpses, is said to make the land devour human flesh. The crime is so great that (even) the death penalty is inadequate for it.'[5] 'If there is any person who (with the view of encouraging war) says: "I am well versed in the disposition of troops (or) I am well versed in the conduct of campaigns," he is guilty of a great crime.'[6]

Apart from the Confucian School of philosophy, all others likewise condemn war. For instance, Lao Tze, founder of Taoism, who lived

[1] Eric R. Watson: *Trial of George Joseph Smith*, p. 268.
[2] 722-481 B.C.
[3] Born in 372 B.C.
[4] Mencius: Bk. VII, Pt. II, Ch. 2, Sec. 1.
[5] Mencius: Bk. IV, Pt. I, Ch. 14, Sec. 2.
[6] Mencius: Bk. VII, Pt. II, Ch. 4, Sec. 1.

in about the sixth century B.C., and Han Fei Tze, leader of the Juridical School, who lived in about the third century B.C., said: 'Soldiers (i.e. war) are instruments of evil.' [1] Moh Tze, founder of another school of philosophy, [2] which has some resemblance to Buddhism, has even written, in his works, a chapter entitled 'Anti-Aggression', in which he says, *inter alia*:

> 'The killing of a person is said to be wrong and punishable with death. According to this principle, the killing of ten persons must be ten times as wrong and punishable with a tenfold death penalty, and the killing of a hundred persons must be a hundred times as wrong and punishable with a hundredfold death penalty. All enlightened men of the world know this and condemn killing as wrong, and yet, in the case of the great wrong of waging war against States (thereby killing many persons), they do not condemn it and, on the contrary, applaud it as right. They do not really know (what is right and what is wrong). . . . (For) if a person, on seeing a little blackness, calls it black and, on seeing much blackness, would call it white, he does not (really) know the difference between black and white.' [3]

Similar in spirit to the words of Moh Tze is the following satire of the well-known Taoist philosopher Chwang Tze:

> 'He who steals a coin is hanged;
> He who steals a State is crowned.' [4]

To clothe this Eastern dictum in Western garb:

> 'Thou shalt not covet they neighbour's *property*, [5]
> In the plainest term the Lord commands.
> Yet how often times with holy glory,
> Men did covet others' crowns or lands.'

With this diversion let us resume our main theme. The origin and essential meaning of *Li* may be gathered from the following Classical authorities:

1. '*Li* means reason, marks the line between near and distant relations, settles questions of propriety, distinguishes what is the

---

[1] See *post*, pp. 107 and 118.
[2] See *post*, p. 113.
[3] *Moh Tze*, Bk. V, Title *Anti-Aggression*.
[4] *Chwang Tze* (who lived in about the fourth century B.C.), Ch. 10.
[5] 'Thou shalt not covet thy neighbour's house . . . nor *anything* that is thy neighbour's'.—Tenth Commandment.

same from what is not, and clarifies the distinction between right and wrong. . . . Sages made *Li* for the instruction of men, so that they may realize that they differ from lower animals.'[1]

2. 'Since ages past *Li* has proved to be the substratum of the State. The Sovereign issues orders and ministers carry them out; fathers are tender and sons are obedient; elder brothers are affectionate and younger brothers are respectful; husbands and wives are harmonious; mothers-in-law are tender and daughters-in-law are dutiful: these constitute *Li*.'[2]

3. 'Men have desires. When they do not obtain what is desired, they are bound to seek for it. In the seeking, unless there are rules regulating measures and demarcations, disputes cannot be avoided, and disputes would lead to disorder. The ancient sage Kings who detested disorder prescribed *Li*, which thus had its origin.'[3]

4. '(The fundamental principle of *Li* is) in fête, rather to be frugal (with earnestness) than to be extravagant (without it); in mourning, rather to be (excessive) in sorrow than to be (excessive) in formalities.'[4] 'Without knowing *Li* one will not know how to conduct oneself.'[5]

5. A man asked a disciple of Mencius whether, in the case of eating (conformity to) *Li* or the eating itself is more important. The disciple replied: '(Conformity to) *Li* is more important.' Then the man asked again: 'If one who must eat in conformity to *Li* will die from hunger, while one who eats not in conformity to *Li* will obtain what to eat, must he (still) conform to *Li* (in such circumstances)?' The disciple, being unable to answer the question, went next day to see Mencius, who said: 'When gold is said to be heavier than feathers, does this mean a single clasp of gold to be compared with a wagon load of feathers? If you take the case where the matter of eating is vital (Lit., weighty) and the matter of *Li* is of no consequence (Lit., light) and compare them together, why say merely that the eating is more important? (There can be no comparison in that case.) Go and answer the man with this question: "If, by twisting your elder brother's arm and snatching what he is eating, you will obtain what to eat, while, by not doing so, you will not obtain what to eat, will you twist his arm (in order to gratify your appetite)?" '[6]

[1] *Book of Li*, Bk. I, and Bk. XXXVII; Ed. *Sze Bu Bei Yao*.
[2] *Jaw Chuan* (History of *Spring and Autumn*, 722-481 B.C.), Bk. VI, Title *Yen Tze Discusses Li*.
[3] *Hsun Tze* (who lived in about the third century B.C.), chapter on *Li*.
[4] Confucius: *Lun Yu*, Pt. III, Ch. 4.
[5] Confucius: *Lun Yu*, Pt. XX, Ch. 3.
[6] *Mencius*, Bk. VI, Pt. II, Ch. 1.

What has been quoted shows clearly that *Li*, in its primary sense, means not ceremony but rules of correct conduct. As illustrations of the application of *Li*, the following passages from an English author may be of interest:

1. 'If you are mobbed in a Chinese town, you should look straight at one or two of the people and say: "Your parents did not pay attention to your manners; they did not teach you the rules of propriety (*Li*)." A remark like this will make the crowd slink away one by one, quite ashamed of themselves.'[1]

2. One wet day in Peking, 'I amused myself looking into shops and learning the customs of the people in their homes. When they saw that I was interested in them and was making overtures of friendship, they would invite me to come in, show me their things, and offer tea, cakes, a pipe or a cigarette. Imagine a Chinaman's reception were he to try and get into the houses of London people absolutely unknown to him by simple civility!'[2]

3. 'We admired much the silver ornaments that were sold in the shops at Kiukiang. As we were looking into one shop, we heard in the back part of the house festive sounds. It was a wedding celebration, and the people made signs to us to go in. We did so, and were most hospitably treated and shown everything.'[3]

The happy experiences recorded in the last two passages just quoted show that the saying, 'Within the four seas all are brethren', is to the Chinese not a mere precept but a practical rule of conduct. Hospitality to the stranger is a matter of *Li*, the teaching of which forms an essential part of Chinese education. Personally, I also had the following experience in Hongkong:

One midsummer day towards the evening, when the sun was slowly descending on the horizon, a stream of young girls was coming out of a school. As they emerged from the hall into the street, a crowd gathered on a bypath to witness what appeared to be an interesting sight. There were, however, a few ruffians among the crowd, who began to make remarks. Suddenly, an elderly man turned round and looked fiercely at them, saying: 'Don't you know *Li*? You should be ashamed of yourselves.' The few ruffians, thus rebuked, blushed visibly and disappeared one by one with their heads downward.

After these quotations and illustrations, if an attempt may be made to define the term in accordance with modern notions, taking

---

[1] Rev. E. J. Hardy: *John Chinaman at Home*, p. 263.
[2] Rev. E. J. Hardy: *John Chinaman at Home*, p. 38.
[3] Rev. E. J. Hardy: *John Chinaman at Home*, p. 74.

into consideration the fact that the more important part of human conduct and relations, public or private, is now largely governed by law and no longer only by *Li*, it may be defined as:

'Rules, partly defined and partly undefined, of correct conduct and good manners, based more on moral principles than on conventions, and enforced not by legal sanction but by social reprobation, varying in degree with the education and status of the offender.'[1]

THE 'JIUN TZE'

Almost from the dawn of history the Chinese have been wont to distinguish between two types of men: *Jiun Tze* (Lit., the sovereign man, i.e. the man of virtue or principles or the Noble Man) and *Siao Yun* (Lit., the petty man, i.e. the man of no virtue[2] or principle or the mean man); for the two terms were used as early as in the *Book of History*,[3] one of the most ancient Chinese books extant, concerning which Pauthier says: 'What must profoundly astonish the reader of this beautiful monument of antiquity is the lofty reason and the eminently moral sense that inspired it. The authors of this work and the personages, in whose mouths were put the sayings it contains, must, in such a remote period of antiquity, possess a great moral culture that it would be difficult to surpass even in our days.'[4]

These two terms are nowadays translated generally as 'gentleman' and 'non-gentleman'; but between 'gentleman' and *Jiun Tze* there is a shade of difference or rather what the French call a *nuance*. For instance, if Machiavel is to be judged by his *Prince*, which teaches that 'it is of great consequence to play the hypocrite well'[5] and other similar cynical practices, it is certain that he cannot be classified as a *Jiun Tze*, though he must be called a 'gentleman'. It is, perhaps, due to this *nuance* that certain early writers have translated the term as the 'superior man'. But as the word 'superior' might be misunderstood for class distinction, I purposely use throughout this book the term *Jiun Tze* in its original, hoping thus to introduce it into the Western world and, with it, to bring to the notice of the latter a prominent feature of Chinese culture. As the notion of the *Jiun Tze*

[1] In China the doctrine *noblesse oblige* strictly applies. A well-known saying is: 'A higher standard of conduct is expected from the worthy' (*Chun Chiu tsak bei sen jair*).
[2] See Confucius: *Lun Yu*, Pt. XIV, Ch. VII, where it is said: 'There has never been a *Siao Yun* who is yet virtuous.'
[3] See Bk. IV, Record of *Yu* (2205 B.C.).
[4] G. Pauthier: *Livres Sacrés de l'Orient*, Intro., p. x.
[5] See *Prince*, Ch. XVIII, p. 111; Trans. Morley's Univ. Libr.; Ed. Routledge.

is considered by the Chinese to be so important in the formation of
character, let us select from the Confucian Analects a few sayings
(apart from those quoted in other parts of this book) concerning,
first, the characteristics of the *Jiun Tze* and, secondly, the contrast
between *Jiun Tze* and *Siao Yun*.

CHARACTERISTICS OF THE 'JIUN TZE'

1. 'The *Jiun Tze* does not, even for the space of a single meal,
deviate from virtue. In moments of haste or pressure, he would
adhere to it; and, in hours of danger or confusion, he would adhere
to it.' [1]
    'The *Jiun Tze* (in all actions) makes righteousness as the basis,
performs them with propriety, manifests them with modesty, and
completes them with sincerity. Such a man is a *Jiun Tze* indeed!' [2]
2. 'The *Jiun Tze* first practises what he (intends to) say and then
says in accordance with what he has practised.' [3]

In other words, the *Jiun Tze* first practises what he intends to
preach and then preaches what he practises.

    'The *Jiun Tze* wishes to be slow in his words but swift in his
actions.' [4]
    The *Jiun Tze* is moderate in his words (lest they may exceed his
actions), but ardent in his actions (hoping that they may exceed
his words).' [5]
3. 'The *Jiun Tze*, towards the world, has no prejudice for or
against anything. What is right he follows.' [6]
4. 'The *Jiun Tze* has neither anxiety nor apprehension; . . .
(because) when inward-examination reveals nothing guilty, he has
nothing to be anxious about or to apprehend.' [7]
5. 'The *Jiun Tze* is afflicted for want of ability in himself, and
is not afflicted for not being known by others.' [8]

[1] Confucius: *Lun Yu*, Pt. IV, Ch. 5, Secs. 2-3.
[2] Confucius: *Lun Yu*, Pt. XV, Ch. 17.
[3] Confucius: *Lun Yu*, Pt. II, Ch. 13.
[4] Confucius: *Lun Yu*, Pt. IV, Ch. 24.
[5] Confucius: *Lun Yu*, Pt. XIV, Ch. 29. Shortly, the saying may be rendered as:
'The *Jiun Tze* says less, but does more.' It has, however, been interpreted in the
Imperial Ching Interpretation of the Sacred Books (Bk. XXI, p. 6) as: 'The *Jiun Tze* is
ashamed of his words exceeding his actions.' This interpretation is more literal,
but less grammatical, than the one adopted here, which follows the commentary.
[6] Confucius: *Lun Yu*, Pt. IV, Ch. 10.
[7] Confucius: *Lun Yu*, Pt. XII, Ch. 4.
[8] Confucius: *Lun Yu*, Pt. XV, Ch. 18.

6. 'The *Jiun Tze* does not promote a person (solely) because of his words, nor does he discard (good) words because of the person.'[1]

7. 'The *Jiun Tze* is rightly faithful and not simply faithful.'[2]

In other words, the *Jiun Tze* adheres firmly to what is right and does not adhere to a thing blindly.

8. 'The *Jiun Tze* guards himself against three things: in youth, when his physical conditions are still unsettled, he guards against being sensual; in the prime of his life, when his physical conditions are vigorous, he guards against being quarrelsome; in old age, when his physical conditions have declined, he guards against being avaricious.'[3]

9. 'The *Jiun Tze* gives earnest thoughts to nine things: in seeing, to see clearly; in hearing, to hear distinctly; in countenance, to be kindly; in demeanour, to be courteous; in words, to be faithful; in actions, to be careful; in doubt, to seek informations from others; in danger, to beware of (possible) difficulties; in sight of gain, to be righteous.'[4]

10. 'The *Jiun Tze* puts righteousness above all.'[5]

CONTRAST BETWEEN 'JIUN TZE' AND 'SIAO YUN'

1. 'The *Jiun Tze* is liberal and not narrow-minded; the *Siao Yun* is narrow-minded and not liberal.'[6]

2. 'The *Jiun Tze* clings to virtue; the *Siao Yun* clings to comfort.'[7]

'The *Jiun Tze* is imbued with (the sense of) righteousness; the *Siao Yun* is imbued with (the idea of) gain.'[8]

3. 'The *Jiun Tze* is equanimous and composed; the *Siao Yun* is always distressed.'[9]

4. 'The *Jiun Tze* would (by various means)[10] help others to accomplish what is good and would not (by any means) help others to accomplish what is bad; the *Siao Yun* acts to the contrary.'[11]

[1] Confucius: *Lun Yu*, Pt. XV, Ch. 22.
[2] Confucius: *Lun Yu*, Pt. XV, Ch. 36.
[3] Confucius: *Lun Yu*, Pt. XVI, Ch. 7.
[4] Confucius: *Lun Yu*, Pt. XVI, Ch. 10.
[5] Confucius: *Lun Yu*, Pt. XVII, Ch. 23. This was an observation made in answer to a question whether the *Jiun Tze* esteemed bravery.
[6] Confucius: *Lun Yu*, Pt. II, Ch. 14.
[7] Confucius: *Lun Yu*, Pt. IV, Ch. 11.
[8] Confucius: *Lun Yu*, Pt. IV, Ch. 16.
[9] Confucius: *Lun Yu*, Pt. VII, Ch. 36.
[10] Guidance, assistance, encouragement, and advice—orthodox commentary.
[11] Confucius: *Lun Yu*, Pt. XII, Ch. 16.

5. 'The *Jiun Tze* is sociable, but not servile (i.e., fawning or cringing); the *Siao Yun* is servile, but not sociable.'[1]

6. 'The *Jiun Tze* is easy to serve but not so easy (Lit., difficult) to please. If one tries to please him in a way that is unrighteous, he will not be pleased. In the employment of men, however, he takes into consideration the limits of their capacity. The *Siao Yun* is easy to please, but not so easy (Lit., difficult) to serve. If one tries to please him even in a way that is unrighteous, he may be pleased. In the employment of men, however, he expects them to be all capable.'[2]

7. 'The *Jiun Tze* is serene but not proud; the *Siao Yun* is proud but not serene.'[3]

The *Jiun Tze* progresses upwards; the *Siao Yun* progresses downwards.'[4]

8. 'The *Jiun Tze* (can) unswervingly[5] endure want; the *Siao Yun* when in want, allows his thoughts to run wild (and succumbs to temptations).'[6]

'The *Jiun Tze* demands of himself; the *Siao Yun* demands of others.'[7]

9. 'The *Jiun Tze* may not be known (i.e., show merits) in small matters, but he can be entrusted with tasks of great importance; the *Siao Yun* cannot be entrusted with tasks of great importance, but may be known (i.e., show merits) in small matters.'[8]

10. 'The *Jiun Tze* fears (i.e., has a reverential awe[9] of) three things: he fears the dictates of Heaven (i.e., the divine law of justice); he fears great men; he fears the words of the sages. The *Siao Yun* does not comprehend the dictates of Heaven, and so does not fear them; he is irreverent to great men; he derides the words of the sages.'[10]

Compare these words of Carlyle: 'We all . . . venerate and bow down submissive before great men: nay can we honestly bow down to anything else? Ah, does not every true man feel that he is himself made higher by doing reverence to what is really above him? No nobler or more blessed feeling dwells in man's heart.'[11]

[1] Confucius: *Lun Yu*, Pt. XIII, Ch. 23.
[2] Confucius: *Lun Yu*, Pt. XIII, Ch. 25.
[3] Confucius: *Lun Yu*, Pt. XIII, Ch. 26.
[4] Confucius: *Lun Yu*, Pt. XIV, Ch. 24.
[5] This follows the interpretation of Ching Tze.
[6] Confucius: *Lun Yu*, Pt. XV, Ch. 1, Sec. 3.
[7] Confucius: *Lun Yu*, Pt. XV, Ch. 20.
[8] Confucius: *Lun Yu*, Pt. XV, Ch. 33.
[9] See commentary.
[10] Confucius: *Lun Yu*, Pt. XVI, Ch. 8.
[11] *Heroes and Hero-Worship*; Lecture I.

Such is the conduct of the *Jiun Tze* that Mencius said: 'The conduct of a *Jiun Tze* is not expected to be comprehended by everybody.' [1] This will be readily understood, if, in place of the words 'the conduct of the *Jiun Tze*', are substituted the words 'the rule of *noblesse oblige*'. On one occasion, Confucius, dissatisfied with the conduct of the ruler of his native State, left it rather on a smaller ground, running the risk of exposing himself to misunderstanding, than on a larger ground, which would expose the ruler to the contempt of the people. [2] There is a well-known classical story told by Mencius of how a *Jiun Tze* had been taken to be a fool. In the period of Spring and Autumn (722-481 B.C.) there lived a man named *Tze Tsan*, who was Prime Minister of the State *Cheng*, and, according to Confucius, possessed (in a high degree) the qualities of a *Jiun Tze*. [3] One day someone sent him a live fish as a present. Being a kind-hearted man, he did not wish to make a meal of the fish, and so ordered his pond-keeper to set it free in the pond. The latter being a rascal, instead of obeying the order of his master, cooked the fish for himself, and had the audacity to report to his master in these words: 'Just after I had set it free, it still showed signs of embarrassment. In a while, it was fairly lively, and then swam away rapidly and joyfully.' Thereupon Tze Tsan said: 'It found its right place! It found its right place!' The pond-keeper, on coming out, said: 'Who says that Tze Tsan is a wise man? I had eaten the fish myself, and yet he said: "It found its right place! It found its right place!"' Referring to this story, Mencius observed: 'A *Jiun Tze* may be imposed upon by what appears to be right, but he cannot be deceived by what is wrong in principle.' [4]

The story related here and the conclusion drawn from it find an apt illustration in the *Vicar of Wakefield*, the hero of which, Dr. Primrose, a *Jiun Tze* in the correct sense of the term, was easily 'taken in' by Ephraim Jenkinson's concocted benevolence and learning, but would not disavow his principles even for the acquisition of a fortune, saying: 'If I am to be a beggar, it shall never make me a rascal' [5] In other words, a *Jiun Tze* may by some means be sinned against, but cannot by any means be induced to be sinning. What matters here is that the primary aim of education of a person in China is to make him a *Jiun Tze*, just as the first object of education of a person in English-speaking countries is, if I understand it

[1] *Mencius*, Bk. VI, Pt. II, Ch. 6, Sec. 6.
[2] See *ibid.*
[3] Confucius: *Lun Yu*, Pt. V, Ch. 25.
[4] *Mencius*, Bk. V, Pt. I, Ch. 2, Sec. 4.
[5] See Oliver Goldsmith: *Vicar of Wakefield*, Chs. II and XIV.

rightly, to make him a gentleman. This does not mean that every
Chinaman is a *Jiun Tze*. The fact that there are prisons in China, as
in other countries, shows that there are men of a very different type.
But it is true to say that, for centuries and at the present day still,
the *Jiun Tze* is the standard of conduct by which men are commonly
judged in China.

'CHING'

Ching is a word easier to comprehend than to define. It is generally
translated as sentiment, that is, a mental attitude prompted by a
feeling of the heart. This is substantially correct. But, as I understand
the word, it seems to denote a feeling composed, in various degrees,
of affection, benevolence, charity, clemency, gratitude, kindness,
love, magnanimity, sympathy, and tenderness of the heart mixed
together. In the familiar phrase '*Ching Lee*' (Sentiment and Reason),
which the Chinese almost daily employ, *Ching* is regarded as if it
were a desirable companion, or the 'better half', of Reason. 'Words
may be exhausted', says a famous scholar of the *Tang* dynasty, 'but
Ching never.' [1] The average Chinese is very apt to be swayed by
Ching more than by reason, and he is proud of being so; because he
thinks that this aptitude tends to make him more human and more
humane, if less logical, less realistic, and less practical. It is *Ching*
that breeds in him, in a pronounced degree, the love of harmony,
the spirit of moderation, and what is called humanity. There are
familiar phrases in the Chinese language, expressing the idea of not
going to the extreme, especially in the sense of showing mercy to
one who is down. One of them is *Liu Ching*, meaning literally 'Leave
some *Ching*'. It is *Ching* that makes past relation a powerful appeal
to the Chinese heart. Many would-be breaches of human relations
have been averted, and many disagreeable memories obliterated, by
the mere thought or reminder of the familiar saying: '*Gee yau gin
yit whaw biet yau down choo*', meaning 'if there were going to be the
(unpleasant) present, why should there have been the (pleasant)
past?' It is *Ching* that makes one think of one's less fortunate friend
or relatives by rendering them some timely aid: 'To send coal to
others in the midst of snow', as the Chinese say. It is *Ching* that
reminds one of others' 'little, nameless, unremembered, acts'. [2]
'When you drink water', says the Chinese, 'think of the source from
which it comes.' It is *Ching* that makes Chinese marriage and friendship durable, [3] and gives birth to the conception of renewed matri-

[1] A saying of Han Yu.
[2] Wordsworth: *Lines Composed above Tintern Abbey*, L. 35.
[3] See chapters on Marriage and Friendship.

mony or friendship between the same persons in the next life; because their conjugal relation is so happy, or their friendship so cordial, that they hope it will be renewed if ever they are to be reborn after death. [1] It is *Ching* that underlies the following well-known line of the poem, entitled 'The *Pi-Par'*, by the celebrated poet Bak Chu Yee:

'We meet, and why need we have met before?'

It means that, since Fate has enabled us to make our present acquaintance, that is enough. The fact that we have not met each other before is of no consequence and, therefore, should form no obstacle to our acquaintance being instantly ripened into friendship. All these instances are only some aspects of *Ching*, but none could give a better idea of it than the following two passages from Mencius:

1. 'In the most remote ages there were people who did not bury their parents. When their parents were dead, they simply lifted their corpses up and threw them in the valley. Some days later, when they passed by them, foxes and wild cats were (seen) devouring them and flies and gnats gnawing at them. Perspiration (forthwith) appeared on their foreheads, and they turned their eyes aside to avoid a direct unbearable sight. They perspired, not because (they were ashamed[2] of being seen by) other people, but because their hearts (were so affected that their afflictions) were revealed in their faces and eyes. Therefore they went home and returned with baskets and carts (of earth) to cover up the dead bodies. If this act was right, as indeed it was, it shows that the filial son and the benevolent man, who bury their parents (decently without grudging the expenses), must have their good reasons.' [3]

Here *Ching* was depicted in a graphic manner. It consisted in the form of a benevolent sentiment, natural to man, but lying dormant in the primitive mind until awakened by filial affection. Since its awakening, people would bury not only the dead bodies of their parents but also those of others; for if the distressing sight of the exposed bodies of their parents could have produced such a torment in their hearts even in those most primitive days, a similar sight of the exposed body of a fellow being, after that benevolent sentiment had been awakened, must have also, at least gradually, caused them pain, which is sometimes the seed but more often the symptom of benevolence.

[1] The idea of re-birth is derived from Buddhist religion.
[2] See *Correct Interpretation of Mencius*, Vol. III, Bk. XI, p. 22.
[3] *Mencius*, Bk. III, Pt. I, Ch. 5, Sec. 4.

2. 'Tao Ying (a disciple) asked Mencius: "Suppose, while Shun was Emperor and Kaou-Yau Chief Justice, Koo-Sow (father of Shun) had committed a murder, what would have (Kaou-Yau) done in that case?"

' "(Kaou-Yau) would simply have him arrested (according to the law)," replied Mencius.

' "But would not Shun have forbidden this?" asked again the disciple.

' "How could Shun have forbidden this? It was just (what Kaou-Yau had to do) according to the law entrusted [1] to him (which even the Emperor could not defy)," answered Mencius.

' "Then what would Shun have done?" pursued the disciple.

' "Shun," replied Mencius, "would have regarded the abandonment of the Empire like the abandonment of a wornout grass shoe. He would have secretly run away with his father on his back to live somewhere along the sea-coast cheerfully and happily for the rest of his life, forgetting his Empire." ' [2]

This passage must not be taken to mean that the Sage suggested in any way that a person, whose father had committed a crime, should try to rescue him even by defiance of the law. If so, the simplest thing for the Sage to say would have been that Shun, being Emperor, could (like James II) have the law dispensed with or suspended or, even more in accordance with judicial procedure, have his father pardoned. He suggested nothing of the kind. He was in fact wholeheartedly for the supremacy of law. What the dialogue has vividly brought out is this: As early as in the days of Mencius the majesty of law and the principle of judicial independence were fully recognized, and the Sage said enough of this in no equivocal terms. This is what it should be, and is called *Lee* (Reason). But when the Sage was unwittingly pushed to the logical and cruel conclusion of his answers, he would rather take upon himself the responsibility of interpreting the would-be sentiment of Emperor Shun than pursue the subject any further. This is called *Ching*. The attitude thus displayed by the Sage is the embodiment of *Ching* and Reason in perfect harmony—the ideal state of things according to the Chinese. It has been attributed to Macaulay, if I remember rightly, the saying that if he were ever called upon to name a book which he would stake as the best specimen of the English language, he would readily sug-

---

[1] This means that the law was received from Shun, the Emperor, himself, who could not himself violate it. See commentary in *Correct Interpretation of Mencius*, Vol. VIII, Bk. XXVII, p. 12.

[2] *Mencius*, Bk. VII, Pt. I, Ch. 35, Secs. 1-6.

gest Bunyan's *Pilgrim's Progress*, or something to that effect. I have often thought that if I were ever asked to point to a passage in our language that could comprehensively put Chinese temperament or characteristics in a nutshell, I would unhesitatingly refer to that passage of Mencius.

CHAPTER 3

RELIGION

THE Chinese are often represented by others as a people having no religion but only a system of ethics; because the teachings of Confucius which the bulk of the Chinese regard as their religion provide neither a priesthood nor any form of prayer; because Confucius whom they regard as the Founder of their religion spoke rarely about God but constantly about man or the duties of man, and never about a future world but only about future generations; and because Confucius never claimed to be superhuman, but always asserted himself to be no more than a mere mortal. In consequence, the Chinese have sometimes been called 'heathens'. In my student days abroad, attending a lecture on modern history, I had the pleasure of hearing the learned lecturer classify the Chinese among 'semi-civilized' peoples. The ground of this classification, however, was never very apparent to me, until many years afterwards I read, in one of the works of Professor Bertrand Russell, the following passage:

'The Chinese are a great nation. . . . They will not consent to adopt our vices in order to acquire military strength; but they are willing to adopt our virtues in order to advance in wisdom. I think they are the only people in the world who quite genuinely believe that wisdom is more precious than rubies. That is why the West regards them as uncivilized.' [1]

Personally, I do not mind that others should think that I have no religion so long as they do believe that I have good principles. Yet, in my opinion, what has been said about the Chinese in the matter of religion depends very much on the meaning that one ascribes to the word 'religion'. Lord Haldane, nursed in philosophy and writing in the maturity of his years, said, in the concluding chapter of his *Autobiography*: 'I do not mean that the particular creeds have satisfied me. They have appeared as at best symbolic of what is higher, but not more, and I will add that I think the sense of this has held me back from being looked on as in the ordinary sense a "religious man". That description imports as a rule a creed.' [2] One may also ask: Is religion essentially bound up with any outward form, and is it not

[1] *The Problem of China*, p. 225.
[2] Page 348.

that, even in religions of the most formal kind, a person may be pious without saying a prayer or seeing a priest? Nay, one may have in fact said prayers or played the part of the priest without oneself knowing it. He who sincerely wishes or teaches others good is, in substance, saying a prayer in silence or delivering a sermon in miniature. Moreover, what better evidence of the existence of a religion in a nation can there be than the fact that its sacred books teach people, as those of the Chinese do, to revere and obey God[1] and love their neighbour like themselves[2]—precepts which are in fact equivalent to the first and second great commandments given in the Bible?[3] Indeed, I often think that if a person presented himself for the degree of Doctor of Divinity and were asked to put his thesis in a short and simple sentence, he could do no better than say: 'Revere and obey God, and love your neighbour like yourself.' Anyhow, if millions and millions of intelligent beings of a common origin have, for centuries and centuries, commonly believed in Heaven (the Chinese word of which is in sense, as we shall see, equivalent to the word God) and in certain principles, which are eternally good for mankind, and for which many are ready to give up, and many have given up, their lives,[4]—well, if such a faith were not considered to be a religion, that word would indeed be beyond comprehension.

It is, however, true that China never had a religious war—a fact which is sometimes taken or mistaken by some for a sign of lack of religious fervour, but deemed by the Chinese as a proof of religious wisdom. In China, so long as you are morally good, nobody would question your religion, not that the people are indifferent to religion, but that they are indifferent to what religions others may have when their conduct is unquestionable. Everyone in their opinion is free to worship God as he pleases.

The Confucianists, by which term are meant persons who believe in the teachings of Confucius, whether they regard them as religion or ethics, form the bulk of the Chinese people; but if you ask the average Chinese what religions there are in China, you will be told that there are three forms of religion: *Yu Jiao* (Lit., religion of the scholar or educated man, i.e., the religion based on the teachings of Confucius), *Shih Jiao* (religion of Buddhism), and *Tao Jiao* (Lit.' religion of the Way or Reason, i.e., the religion based on the teachings of Lao Tze). In fact there are, in addition to these, more than twenty

---

[1] See *post*, pp. 49-51.
[2] See *post*, pp. 73, 75.
[3] See *St. Matthew*, Ch. XXII, 36-40.
[4] See Confucius: *Lun Yu*, Pt. XIV, Ch. 13, Pt. XV, Ch. 8; *Mencius*, Bk. VI, Pt. I, Ch. 10, Secs. 1-5. For texts see *post*, p. 67.

million Chinese, who adhere to the Mohammedan faith and more
than a million who adhere to the Christian faith. Buddhism, like
Mohammedanism and Christianity, came from abroad; but, as it has
taken a deep root in China and has in some way been adapted to the
life of the people, the masses have almost forgotten its origin. All
these religions exist side by side in an atmosphere of religious fraternity. If at times there have been incidents of antagonism, they
were due to collision between man and man [1] rather than between
religion and religion. The average man in China thinks that all
respectable religions, as they all teach the supreme duty of loving
one's neighbour, the greatest knowledge that man is mortal, and
the highest wisdom of acknowledging this with humility, are for the
good of mankind, though he prefers his own; for 'every man selects
the form of art and religion that appeals to him most'. [2] He sees
God as the supreme embodiment of love and justice and not the
exclusive patron of any particular sect; for he remembers that there
was a time when there was no religion, as understood to-day, and
yet, in his opinion, God, as the supreme embodiment of love and
justice, must have loved mankind no less then than now and since.
He therefore believes that it is by one's deed, rather than by one's
profession, that one can hope to win God's approval and affection.
Above all, one should first fulfil one's duties in this world before one
thinks of one's own happiness in the next. This does not mean that
'it matters not how a man dies, but how he lives', [3] but rather,
though not simply, that 'we have to think of how to live before we
can learn how to die'. [4]

Confucius, when he was asked how the spirits of the dead should
be served, said: 'As you are not yet able to serve the living, how will
you be able to serve the spirits of the dead?' [5] When asked about
death, he replied: 'As you know nothing yet about life, how can you
know anything about death?' [6] When asked about wisdom, he said:
'To devote oneself to the duties due to mankind and, while maintaining an attitude of reverence towards spiritual beings, to keep a
due distance from them may be said to be wisdom.' [7]

[1] i.e., due to a conflict of material interests, or to the tactless ways in which
   some people sometimes expressed their views as regards the religions of others.
[2] *Autobiography* of Viscount Haldane, p. 248.
[3] Boswell's *Life of Johnson*; Ed. G. Birkbeck Hill, Vol. II, p. 106.
[4] *Autobiography* of Viscount Haldane, p. 344.
[5] Confucius: *Lun Yu*, Pt. XI, Ch. 11.
[6] Confucius: *Lun Yu*, Pt. XI, Ch. 11. Compare: 'We know not at all what death is
   in itself.'—Bishop Butler: *Analogy of Religion*, Pt. I, Ch. 1, 'Of a Future Life,' II.
[7] Confucius: *Lun Yu*, Pt. VI, Ch. 20. This passage, as it can be seen, forms a
   whole and therefore should be read as such.

In other words, men should be concerned more in the duties pertaining to life than in what will happen after death. To do good and fulfil our duties to mankind is not a price that we pay for our happiness after death but a gift we willingly and gladly offer to our fellow men. Moreover, so long as we are living in this world, it can only be right and, therefore, must be wise that we should first of all fulfil our duties to beings of this world, which we actually know, and, if we do this, our duties to beings of the next world, of which we have only a sense of awe but no real knowledge, may be fulfilled by maintaining towards them an attitude of reverence. To do otherwise, that is to say, to neglect our duties that are immediate by absorbing ourselves in what are, after all, only remote, cannot be wisdom. Death, moreover, like life, being the result of the operation of the law of nature, should be accepted with resignation. That is why it was said by the sage, Mencius, that 'The *Jiun Tze* (i.e., Noble Man) observes the (natural) law (by doing his best) and resigns himself wholly to the will of Heaven (in regard to the result)'. [1]

The same trend of thought is noticeable in the following dialogue:

'Confucius being very ill, Tze Loo (a disciple) requested permission to pray for him. He asked: "Is there such a thing (as praying)?" Tze Loo replied: "There is. In eulogies one says: 'Prayers have been offered for thee to the spirits of Heaven and Earth".' The Master (then) said: "I have been praying for a long time".' [2]

In other words, Heaven may be more effectively moved by conduct than by mere words, that is to say, if divine favour may be obtained by prayers offered at a moment of need, it will be the more surely obtained by constant conduct conforming to the will of Heaven, such as the practice of virtue, the reform of faults, if any, and the fulfilment of duties to humanity. One, therefore, should not neglect the cultivation of such conduct, when special divine favour is not felt in immediate need, thinking that praying at a given moment will make sufficient amends for the neglect, but should try at all times to deserve such favour by cultivating such conduct, and this was what Confucius had always been doing and would recommend others to do.

All that has been said on the spiritual question may be summed up in one sentence: Do your duties in this world **and** leave everything to God. The Chinese expression equivalent to the word God

[1] *Mencius*, Bk. VII, Pt. II, Ch. 33, Sec. 3.
[2] Confucius: *Lun Yu*, Pt. VII, Ch. 34.

is Heaven (*Tien*, which also means sky or physical heaven). For example:

1. 'I respect the wrath displayed by Heaven,
   And dare not act with any levity.
   I respect the changes willed by Heaven,
   And dare not act with least audacity.' [1]
2. 'Always follow (Heaven's) Ordinances:
   You'll be blessed with so much happiness.' [2]
3. 'When Heaven showers down disasters,
   One may avoid them still.
   When one oneself creates disasters,
   One cannot hope to live.' [3]

This means that one may escape disasters that are due to natural or supernatural causes, but not those that are due to one's own folly or wickedness.

4. 'It is Heaven that ordains wisdom, blessings, scourges, or lastingness.' [4]
5. 'He who offends against Heaven has no one to pray to (for obtaining a pardon).' [5]
Compare: 'But if a man sin against the Lord, who shall entreat for him?' [6]
6. 'Death and life are determined by the will of Heaven; riches and honour depend on Heaven.' [7]

The first part of the saying gives a religious consolation to those who have suffered an irreparable loss, while the second means that

---

[1] *Book of Odes* (Mow Sche), Title *Da Yah, Sang Min;* Ed. *Sze Bu Bei Yao,* Bk. XVII, No. 4.
[2] *Book of Odes* (Mow Sche), Title *Da Yah, King Wen;* Bk. XVI, No. 1.
[3] *Book of History,* Bk. VIII, Records of *Shang,* Title *Tai Tsah,* No. 6; *Mencius,* Bk. II, Pt. I, Ch. 4, Sec. 6.
[4] *Book of History,* Bk. XV, Records of *Chow,* Title *Chao Ko,* No. 14.
[5] Confucius: *Lun Yu,* Pt. III, Ch. 13, Sec. 2. The commentary of the word 'Heaven' in this passage is sometimes misunderstood by foreign students, who take the commencing words of the commentary, 'Heaven (here) means reason', as identifying Heaven with mere reason. But the commentary continues to say: 'He who acts contrary to reason offends against Heaven.' This shows that the two are separate, though linked together, the commencing words of the commentary being merely elliptical.
[6] First Book of Samuel, Ch. II, 25.
[7] Saying of Disciple Tze Hsia. See Confucius: *Lun Yu,* Pt. XII, Ch. 5, Sec. 3. The words 'will of Heaven' translate the Chinese word *ming,* which, in the general theological sense, means 'will of Heaven' or 'willed by Heaven' rather than 'fate' or 'predestination'.

man should try his best to deserve what he desires and should not complain when he fails to obtain it.

7. 'Those who obey Heaven survive; those who disobey Heaven perish.' [1]

Sometimes the term *Shang Ti* (Lit, the Upper Emperor) is used. For instance:

1. 'The ancient (sage) Kings who constantly practised virtue with piety were able to conform to the will of *Shang Ti*.' [2]
2. 'Descendants of the (Dynasty of) *Shang*
   Numbered o'er a hundred thousand strong.
   Shang Ti having issued His decree,
   They all submitted to *Chow* (Dynasty).' [3]
3. 'Though a person may have been sinful, [4] yet if he rectifies himself, and (as an outward and additional sign of purification) fasts and bathes, he may offer sacrifice to *Shang Ti*.' [5]

Although the Confucianists have neither churches nor priests, they have, in their houses, altars for the worship of Heaven and, in their cities and towns, temples of Confucius, while the function of the priest, as guardian of morals, is discharged by the parents and, in some measure, also by the teacher. In China, family instruction counts for much, and parents are in general very conscious of this duty towards their children, as may be gathered from the remark of a missionary quoted in the preceding chapter. [6] A well-known story, which reminds parents of this duty and used to form the second page of the First Book taught in school, is one about the mother of Mencius, the sage second only to Confucius. She became a widow at a comparatively early age, having only an infant son as her comfort and a weaving loom as her means of subsistence. Conscious that it is a sacred duty of parents to bring their children up in a worthy way,

---

[1] *Mencius*: Bk. IV, Pt. I, Ch. 7, Sec. 1.

[2] *Book of History*, Bk. VIII, Records of *Shang*, Title *Tai Tsah*, No. 7.

[3] *Book of Odes* (Mow Sche), Title *Da Yah*, *King Wen*; Bk. XVI, No. 1. The Ode was quoted in *Mencius*, Bk. IV, Pt. I, Ch. 7, Sec. 1.

[4] The Chinese word is *Oug*, which means vicious, wicked, or sinful. Although the commentary says that it means 'ugly and deformed', yet as the commentary goes on to say that 'this chapter is to encourage men to reform', and as the subsequent clause speaks of rectification of oneself, it is submitted that the word 'sinful' is correct.

[5] *Mencius*, Bk. IV, Pt. II, Ch. 25, Sec. 2. It may incidentally be mentioned here that the tablet placed inside the Hall of the Temple of Heaven is inscribed with the words 'Emperor of Heaven, *Shang Ti*'

[6] See *ante*, p. 36.

she devoted herself piously and patiently to that task, and, convinced that 'it is the good morals of the neighbours that constitute the goodness of a neighbourhood',[1] she changed her residence several times during the infancy of her son in search of a desirable home. One day, finding him unwilling to learn, she broke, partly by way of reproach and partly in despair, a rod of her weaving implement, her principal means of livelihood—an incident in consequence of which he was instantly reformed, and which made a lasting influence on him. Her virtue and wisdom contributed much to his future greatness, and her example has ever since been a source of inspiration and model for Chinese women, being a familiar allusion in eulogies relating to good mothers.

The tie between teacher and pupil is sacred, the teacher ranking, in the scale of upper relations, only after the parents. In the early days of vicarious liability, the teacher was held even responsible in some way for the gravest crimes, such as high treason and parricide, of his pupils. Before the introduction of the new system of education to meet modern needs, he taught nothing but the doctrines of Confucius and the philosophy of the Confucian School. His position, as moral guardian of the pupil, has since been appreciably modified; but even in the present day the relation between teacher and pupil is still highly respected and often constitutes a bond lasting for life. 'As I take', says Goldsmith, 'my shoes from the shoemaker and my coat from the tailor, so I take my religion from the priest.'[2] The Chinaman, it may be said, takes his religion from his parents and, in the old days, also from his teacher.

Ancestral worship, which is deep-rooted in custom, forms part of the Confucian faith. In every home there is an altar for the worship of ancestors, who are represented, if near, by tablets with their names engraved on them, and, if remote, by a general tablet engraved with the words 'Ancestors of all generations', while in every village there are ancestral chapels for worship on certain days of the year. Ancestral worship is not due to superstition or meant to immortalize the ancestors, but is, in its essence, to foster filial affection, whereby other virtues may be attained; for filial affection being itself a virtue, its cultivation cannot fail to breed other virtues. It is believed that if men are taught to have an affectionate regard even for the dead, they will understand more readily the duty of having an affectionate regard for the living. The disciple Tseng Tze, apparently addressing an advice to reigning rulers of his day, said:

[1] Confucius: *Lun Yu*, Pt. IV, Ch. 1. The text for the words 'good morals' *literally* means 'virtue'. The translation follows the commentary.
[2] Boswell's *Life of Johnson*; Ed. G. Birkbeck Hill, Vol. II, p. 214.

'Perform thy last duties to thy parents with devotion, and commemorate them with reverence, even when they have long departed: (in this way) the virtue of the people will be heightened.'[1]

What that passage means may be thus explained. Death is apt to be considered as the end of things, and so one's sense of duty towards those who have passed away is easily liable to be affected. Has not Antony in *Julius Caesar* said: 'But yesterday the word of Caesar might have stood against the world; now lies he there, and none so poor to do him reverence?'[2] Confucius has also said: 'If a person, for three years (after the death of his father) does not deviate from his father's way (which he may or may not follow),[3] he may be said to have given proof of his filial piety.'[4] The two observations are indeed different; but the point in common is that the continuance of reverence or affection after death shows that it is voluntary and genuine. Moreover, between living persons distance of space may make the heart grow fonder; but between the living and the dead distance of time makes the memory grow fainter. If, however, those who govern set the example that death accentuates rather than attenuates one's sense of duty that is due, and that reverence or affection for another is not effaced by death, even with the lapse of time, the people in general, either by following their examples, or through their inspiration, cannot fail to acquire, in time and in various degrees, a deeper sense of the true meaning of human relationship and thus to befit themselves for the generation of a feeling of brotherhood towards their fellow men.

All this may sound extravagant to the modern ear; for men of to-day are apt to judge the past by the present and, consequently, to regard as primitive what was in fact the seed of culture and civilization, just as they are accustomed to call the Stone Age or the Bronze Age primitive, without realizing that these were marked stages of progress in the history of man. Similarly, man's advancement in morals or ethics also had its stages and beginning. Though according to Chinese philosophy, as we shall see in the next chapter, man's nature tends to good, yet it could not be expected that, from the very commencement of mankind, man was able to love his neighbour. As we have seen in the preceding chapter, even the practice of interment was only of a tardy growth, and it was filial affection, stirred by the terrible sight of the parental corpses being

---

[1] Confucius: *Lun Yu*, Pt. I, Ch. 9.
[2] Shakespeare: *Julius Caesar*, Act III, Sc. II, Ls. 124-6.
[3] See Commentary.
[4] Confucius: *Lun Yu*, Pt. I, Ch. 11.

devoured by wild animals, that gave birth to that practice, which seems to us to-day so simple and natural. This enables us to infer that the primitive man must have first practised the benevolent 'art' of saving his parents from death due to hunger, when they had ceased to be able to feed themselves on their own strength, before he ever did the same thing to the helpless strangers who lived in the neighbouring caves, for the love of one's neighbour being a wider love must have had its seed, in the remote days, in the love of one's nearest relatives. From the love of the nearest relatives, men have learned not only to love mankind in general but also to be kind (as distinguished from being capriciously sentimental) to animals; for kindness to animals is but a further development of that benevolent feeling bred in the love of one's fellow beings. The ancient sages, realizing this, saw in filial affection not only a virtue in itself but also the germ of other virtues, and so fostered it by various institutions, such as the doctrine of filial piety and ancestral worship, not merely as a virtue for its own sake but also as a means of advancing the happiness of mankind. That is why it is said that 'filial piety is the root (or first step in the cultivation) of virtue', [1] and that 'no sin is greater than conduct contrary to filial piety', [2] because it poisons the spring of nature.

It is, however, only to be expected that this idea of ancestral worship is not always understood, particularly by those to whom such worship is an alien institution. 'The system of ancestral worship', says an author, 'when rightly understood in its true significance, is one of the heaviest yokes which ever a people was compelled to bear. As pointed out by Dr. Yates, the hundred of millions of living Chinese are under the most galling subjection to the countless thousands of millions of the dead. "The generation of to-day is chained to the generation of the past.". . . And while the generations of those who have passed from the stage continue to be regarded as the true divinities by the Chinese people, how is it possible that China shall take a single real step forward?' [3]

But the living Chinese are no more 'chained' to the dead than the dead are 'chained' to the living. The fact that the Chinese visit their ancestral tombs once a year and worship their ancestral tablets at home a few times annually, if possible, does not, in their opinion, and cannot, in the nature of things, hinder in any way their progress —a fact that may be seen in their unflinching resistance against aggression in the Second World War.

[1] Book of Filial Piety, Ch. 1; Confucius: Lun Yu, Pt. I, Ch. 2, Sec. 2.
[2] Book of Filial Piety, Ch. 11.
[3] Arthur H. Smith: Chinese Characteristics, p. 184.

The doctrines of Confucius so far referred to, if they have a bearing on the duties of man, are more or less only of a general character. Before coming to those of a specific nature it may be helpful to give a short sketch of his life [1] and a bird's-eye view of his doctrines as a whole. Confucius was born 551 B.C. in that part of China, then known as *Lu*, now forming part of the Shantung province, famous after the First World War in the episode of the restitution of *Kiao Chau* by Japan to China. During infancy he showed extraordinary cultural tendency in the display of his toys. On reaching manhood he became a minor official and a public teacher. In the latter capacity he crystal-lized into principles the wisdom of the ancient sages and formulated the fundamental rules of conduct of man, which, thanks to his disciples, have been preserved to posterity. According to a legend, he went to *Chow* to consult Lao Tze (Founder of Taoism) on *Li* (moral rules of correct conduct), who on parting said:

'I have heard that the rich and the high-stationed make gifts to others in the form of property, while the virtuous do so in the form of advice. Though I cannot play the part of the rich or the high-stationed, may I assume for the moment the role of the virtuous and take the liberty of making you a gift in words? At the present day, men who are clever with deep discernment and yet put them-selves within the reach of death are those who are fond of finding fault with others; men who are eloquent with wide knowledge and yet put themselves in danger are those who are fond of divulging others' vices. A son should not consider his person as his own (when his parents are living); a minister should not wait to be dis-graced (i.e., should not cling to his post when his words are no longer listened to).' [2]

After his return from *Chow* the number of his disciples grew. At the age of thirty-six, when *Lu*, his native State, was in disturbance and its ruler fled to *Chi*, he went also to *Chi*, where he served again as an official. But subsequently, on account of an intrigue against him, he left *Chi* and returned to *Lu*. At the age of forty-three, when a power-ful minister of *Lu* usurped the authority of the State, he retired and,

---

[1] The narration that follows is partly based on the Preface to *Lun Yu*; Ed. *Sze Bu Bei Yao*.

[2] *Family Sayings of Confucius*, Bk. III, p. 1. The contents of this work are believed to have been chiefly recorded by the near descendants of Confucius, basing them-selves on traditions rather than on what Confucius was actually heard to say at the time as in the case of the Analects or the *Chung Yung*. This story is referred to because, apart from giving an indication of the philosophy of Lao Tze, it is generally regarded as a clue to the proximate date of his existence, which is in fact controversial.

with the view of purifying the past for the better enlightenment of
the future, devoted his time to the revision of the ancient Odes,
history, *Li* (moral rules of correct conduct) and cultural music, [1]
while his disciples further grew in number. At the age of fifty-one,
he was appointed Prefect of the Capital and, as a result of his good
administration, was rapidly promoted up to Minister of State. At
the age of fifty-six, he became Prime Minister. [2] After he had assumed this office for three months, the country was so well governed
that theft disappeared. The good government of *Lu* roused fears and
jealousies among neighbouring States, of which *Chi* sent to the
Duke of *Lu* a band of women musicians in order to make him indulge
in dissipations. The Duke fell a victim to the plot, with the result
that Confucius gave up his office and left for another State. Thence
onwards, he travelled from one State to another with a group of
disciples, continuing, without fear or fatigue, to preach his doctrines
to a deteriorating world which he hoped to save. In this long inter-
state journey, he was in danger twice. In different periods of his life,
though out of office, he was often consulted by rulers of various
States. Ultimately, he was recalled to *Lu*, his native State, when he
had reached the age of sixty-eight. But he no longer desired to be in
office, and so devoted his time and energy to the revision and editing
of the ancient Classics, hoping that the basis of a civilization and
culture that had been built up by the accumulated wisdom and virtue
of the past might thus be preserved for future generations. The number of his disciples had then reached three thousand, among whom
seventy-two were very learned and virtuous. At the age of seventy-
one, he wrote the history of his period, known as *Spring and Autumn*
(722-481 B.C.). When this work was completed, 'traitorous ministers
and treacherous sons were alarmed'; [3] because it put on record, and
would thus make known to posterity, the evil deeds of the time
coupled with the names of their authors. He attached so much importance to this work that he expressed the wish that he should be
known and judged by it. [4] As subsequent generations have understood it, he, in fulfilling the role of the impartial historian and
mouthpiece of righteousness, has, by the simple means of approba-

[1] See chapter on Art for reasons for which great importance was attached to music
in ancient days.
[2] *History* by Sze Ma Chien, Bk. XLVII, p. 8. Foreign students of Chinese history
should note that Dr. Legge's challenge to the fact that Confucius was ever Prime
Minister of his native State (*The Chinese Classics*, Vol. I, Prolegomena, p. 74) was
based on erroneous references, mistaking even the date of the Premiership, which
is the fourteenth year of Duke Ting.
[3] *Mencius*, Bk. III, Pt. II, Ch. 9, Sec. 11.
[4] *Mencius*, Bk. III, Pt. II, Ch. 9, Sec. 8.

先師孔子行教像

德侔天地道冠古今
刪述六經垂憲萬世

唐吳道子筆

PORTRAIT OF CONFUCIUS

tion or condemnation of certain deeds or events, cleared the path for
right and just thinking and judgment, revealing the light of truth
to the everlasting enlightenment of posterity. He died at the age of
seventy-three. How his death was lamented may be gathered from the
following bewailing words of the Ruler of his native State:

'Alas! Heaven has no pity on my State by not leaving it that
venerable man! Now, I am left alone on the throne like a sorrowful
sick man. Oh, my Reverend Father! There will be no one to guide
me!'[1]

All his disciples mourned for him for three years. One of them Tze
Kung, whose name is frequently mentioned in these pages, lived by
his tomb for six years.

He had one son named *Lee*,[2] who died before him, and one grandson named Tze Sze, who composed the well-known treatise, *Doctrine
of the Consistent (or Golden) Mean*, based on ancient doctrines as taught
by him and his disciples. This and another well-known treatise
called the *Great Learning*, which was based on his own doctrines but
composed by his disciple Tseng Tze, forming part of the school
text-books in the old system of education, may be said to be the
groundwork of the teachings of the Confucian School. Both works
are highly philosophic, and some idea of their contents may be
gathered from the following comments of Pauthier:[3]

1. Concerning the *Doctrine of the Consistent Mean*: '*On peut cer-
tainement le mettre à côté, sinon au-dessus de tout ce que la philosophie
ancienne nous a laissé de plus élevé et de plus pur.*'[4]

2. Concerning the *Great Learning*: '*Après avoir lu ce petit traité,
on demeure convaincu que le but du philosophe chinois a été d'enseigner les
devoirs du gouvernement politique comme ceux du perfectionnement de
soi-même et de la pratique de la vertu par tous les hommes.*'[5]

Before setting out the basic principles of the two doctrines, which
cover a wide field, an introductory explanation, first of all, of the
elementary meaning of the term Mean, or Consistent Mean as

---

[1] *Jaw Chuan*, Bk. VI, 16th year of Duke Aoi.

[2] *Lee* means carp. His son was so named because, on the birthday of the latter, he
received a carp from the Ruler of his native State. The name so given was a mark
of respect to the donor.

[3] See *Livres Sacrés de l'Orient*, Introduction, p. xiii; Ed. 1840.

[4] 'One may certainly place it by the side of, if not above, all that is the loftiest
and purest which ancient philosophy has bequeathed to us.'

[5] 'After having read this small treatise, one rests convinced that the aim of the
Chinese philosopher has been to teach the duties of political government like
those of perfecting oneself and of the practice of virtue by all men'.

adopted here, may be helpful. In Chinese the term is called *Chung Yung. Chung* (Lit., central or middle) means 'without being inclined to any side and without excess or deficiency' [1] and signifies 'the Right Path that should be pursued by all within the universe'. [2] *Yung* (Lit. ordinary or constant) means 'normal' [3] or 'invariable' [4] and signifies 'the Permanent Principle that governs all within the universe'. [5] From these it may be formulated that what is balanced, normal, and consistent is within the Right Path and accords with the Permanent Principle, as dictated by Nature, and what is unbalanced, abnormal, and inconsistent, even though it may have the semblance of goodness, deviates from both. However, the doctrine does not, as is sometimes supposed, teach *merely* the practice of moderation or the taking of the middle course or the adoption of the mean between two extremes, [6] which is only another way of saying the middle course, though, in its application, it may in certain cases coincidentally point to that direction. Still less is it like 'the doctrine of the Peripatetics, which placed all virtue in a medium between two opposite vices'. [7] Those who think so cannot be taken to *mean* seriously. Let us take the simple case of eating or dressing. The Mean does not lie between eating nothing and eating to bursting point, or between going naked like the Adamites and dressing up to the chin. That would be a mean between two extremes which are evils or opposite vices, though in these two instances the mean would accidentally be right. The proper Mean, according to the doctrine, however, is between underfed and overfed or between underdressed and overdressed.

Let us now vary the illustration. Generosity is a virtue. But one who is 'more generous to his friends than just to his creditors' [8] cannot be regarded as practising a perfect virtue; because that kind of conduct, though it is the fruit of good nature and rooted in virtuous soil, does, at least unintentionally, injustice to others. The Mean would be 'just to your creditors and generous to your friends'. Again, to be charitable is a virtue, and to help the needy is a charitable act. But the conduct of a millionaire who gives his whole

---

[1] Chu Tze, post-classical orthodox commentator of the Confucian Classics.
[2] Ching Tze, a great philosopher of the eleventh century, whom Chu Tze acknowledged as his master. He was one of the two brothers reverentially called 'the two Chings' and ranked with the ancient Worthies.
[3] Chu Tze.
[4] Ching Tze.
[5] Ching Tze.
[6] See *Mencius*, Bk. VII, Pt. I, Ch. 26, Sec. 3.
[7] Legge: *The Chinese Classics*, Vol. I, Prolegomena, p. 47.
[8] This was said of Goldsmith.

fortune to the first beggar he meets in Wall Street on going to his
office in the morning, though an extraordinarily charitable act, can
hardly be regarded as a perfect virtue; because it is eccentric, and
abnormal. If, instead of giving his whole fortune to the first beggar
he meets in the street, he were to give it to a board of trustees to be
administered for the benefit of the needy, the act would be different.
In other words, abnormality is a deviation from the Mean. Again,
politeness is good and impoliteness is bad. But the Mean is not to
be found between politeness and impoliteness or between good and
bad. To be impolite or bad is entirely out of the question. The Mean
lies between being not polite enough and being excessively polite,
either of which is a deviation; for the one may give the appearance
of discourtesy, while the other may be construed as servility or insincerity. Therefore either excess or deficiency is a mark of imperfection;
for 'to go beyond (a thing) is (off the right path) just as not to come
up to it.'[1] It is true that it is better to err on the right side than on
the wrong side; but this does not mean that one should err at all.
It is a principle to be invoked only when one is in doubt as to the
correctness of one's action. For instance, it is a maxim of the Chinese
that a judge should 'rather err in letting off a person who is guilty
than err in condemning to death a person who is innocent'.[2] However, if one errs, there is an error and the act or conduct cannot be
regarded as perfect. Hence, excess, like abnormality, is a deviation
from the Mean. But it must not be thought from this that the Mean
imposes a limit in all actions, as the word itself might seem to suggest. There is, for instance, no limit in doing good, and there are
occasions on which even life may have to be given up for the sake of
virtue.[3] Indeed, in order to be able to conform to the Mean, one
often has to exert oneself to the utmost, just as one has to learn many
complicated things in order to be able to do some simple thing simply;
for to be able to conform to the Mean often requires not only virtue
but also wisdom and courage. If someone's hat has been blown away
by a gale and you run half a mile to recover it for him, this is admirable; but if it had been blown into the sea, and you jumped over-
board, risking your life for it, this might be virtuous and courageous,
but would be lacking in wisdom, for it is out of all proportion and,
in consequence, deviates from the Mean. Therefore, the Mean implies due proportion and not mere moderation, though in certain
cases the one may coincide with the other. Briefly, it may be said

[1] Confucius: *Lun Yu*, Pt. XI, Ch. 15.
[2] *Book of History*, Bk. IV, Records of *Yu*, Title *Da Yu Mu*. This indicates that the
   maxim is more than 4,000 years old.
[3] See *post*, p. 67 for sayings of Confucius and Mencius on this point.

that conduct conforming to the Mean is to do the right thing in the right way. At least this is one aspect of the doctrine. It is difficult to attain; for the equilibrium of the mind is apt to be disturbed by various feelings, and, when that equilibrium is disturbed, actions deviate from the Mean.

By proportion is meant not merely a harmonious relation between act and acting but also a harmonious relation in the cultivation and combination of human qualities essential to the attainment of perfection or the highest achievement. For instance, knowledge, virtue, and courage are all admirable qualities; but none of them without the others can enable one to reach the peak of excellence. Virtue alone may, indeed, be as luminous as a star, but it is only when accompanied by knowledge and courage that it can shine like the sun, whereas either knowledge or courage, if not accompanied by virtue, may often bring about darkness. A philosopher has said: 'Courage is so essential to virtue that I admire it even when it is associated with vice.' In this he must have meant that virtue needs courage as its minister, while courage needs virtue as its mother. As to knowledge unassociated with virtue one has only to remember the Biblical story of the Garden of Eden in order to have a proper estimation of its worth on the day of its birth.

Lastly, the Doctrine combats conduct or doctrines that are fanatic, unnatural, or beyond human comprehenson; because, being such, they cannot be in accord with the dictate of Nature. Falsehood has always a semblance of goodness, which is a cloak that Falsehood has stolen from Truth and lends to Deceit; but Time will expose them both. That is why Confucius said: 'To indulge in researches of what is beyond human comprehension and practise what is abnormal (or fanatic) (hoping thus) to be honourably mentioned in after-generations (i.e., to fish for a name) is what I would not do.' [1] That is also why it is said that 'the rule of the ancient sage Kings [2] was essentially human, resorting neither to what is abnormal or whimsical as a pretension to exaltedness nor to what is inhuman or unnatural as a bait for popularity'. [3]

The teaching of The Great Learning may be summed up in one sentence: The moral improvement of one's own person is the root or starting point of all achievements. That virtue should be cultivated for its own sake is a principle that is self-evident. What may need elucidation is that even for achievements, it is necessary first of all to cultivate

[1] Doctrine of the Consistent Mean, Ch. 11.
[2] Lit., Yao and Shun (Emperors of the Golden Age) and The Three Kings (Founders of the Hsia, Shang, and Chow dynasties).
[3] Ou Yang Shiu, eminent scholar of Sung dynasty. See Collected Ancient Essays.

virtue, which alone can give one the moral guidance and strength essential to noble achievements, and the lack of which often brings about disaster in their attempts. There may be men who have accomplished much with little virtue, but there are more who have been ruined for the lack of it. Have there not been men who might have shone in life or in history but for their 'slips'? Even a genius like Francis Bacon could not escape from the operation of this moral logic, though, through the soothing influence of time, men are to-day interested more in his *Novum Organum* than in his impeachment. Achievements as such can never atone for the lack of virtue; though they may incline the world to be indulgent to it. What seems to have been atonement is really a case where great virtues in the form of achievements over-redeem or over-shadow certain vices or moral weaknesses. Therefore no truly great man is not great both in achievement and in virtue: he is great not merely in certain capacity or capacities but also as a man. Chinese sages, wanting to inculcate this truth on men, have been wont to place virtue before achievement. Thus the Book of *Great Learning*, in praise of King Wen, called in Chinese *Wen Wang*, virtual founder of the *Chow* Dynasty (1122-255 B.C.) and one of the noblest and most venerated personages in Chinese history, refers to his virtues rather than his achievements:

'In the *Book of Odes* it is said: "How vast and profound was the virtue of King Wen! What splendour he incessantly displayed in abiding by his goals!" [1] (For instance) as sovereign, he abode by benevolence; as subject, he abode by reverence (i.e., loyalty); as son, he abode by filial piety, as father he abode by parental tenderness; and in intercourse with the people, he abode by sincerity.' [2]

These are no empty words, as they concerned a man who lived more than three thousand years ago, when civilization in a great part of the world had hardly begun. With these preliminary explanations, the essential parts of the two works may now be set out.

THE DOCTRINE OF THE CONSISTENT MEAN

'What Heaven ordains is called nature (i.e., the natural law). What conforms to nature (i.e., the natural law) is called the Right Path. What regulates the Right Path (for men's guidance, such as various institutions) is called Instruction.

'The Right Path may not be departed from for any moment. What may be departed from is not the Right Path. Therefore the

[1] *Book of Odes* (*Mow Sche*), Title *Da Yah, King Wen;* Bk. XVI, No. 1.
[2] *The Great Learning*, Ch. 3, Sec. 3.

Jiun Tze (i.e., Noble Man) is (particularly) careful, when unobserved,[1] and is (particularly) apprehensive, when unheard,[2] (lest in such circumstances he might go astray).

'(In the moral sense) nothing is so evident as what is secret (because the more secret a thing is, the more evident it is to oneself or one's conscience); and nothing is so manifest as what is minute (because the minute is nevertheless the positive beginning). [In other words, no wrong is permissible, even though it may be concealed, and no wrong is so small as to be negligible.] For this reason the *Jiun Tze* (i.e., Noble Man) is (particularly) vigilant over what is known to himself alone (i.e., his thoughts and conduct that are known only to himself,[3] lest he might in these deviate from the Right Path).

'The feeling of pleasure, anger, grief, or joy[4] not being aroused, the mind is said to be in a state of equilibrium. Such feelings being aroused and reacting in a proper degree, the mind is said to be in a state of harmony. Equilibrium is the universal source (from which all natural feelings and reasons spring). Harmony is the universal path (through which all that conform to nature pass).

'When equilibrium and harmony reach the highest point, the whole universe is tranquil, and all things flourish.'[5]

The meaning of the last paragraph, so far as it applies to the individual, may be explained as follows: With mental equilibrium, one will be able to attain impartiality in judgment and, with mental harmony, one will be able to avoid error in action, and, with the two cultivated to perfection, so that all forms of selfishness and improper feelings are eliminated, one will be able to see all things in their proper order and find that the world is with, rather than against, oneself; for, to borrow the words of Milton,

'The mind is its own place, and in itself
Can make a Heaven of Hell, a Hell of Heaven.'[6]

[1] The text, literally, is in the active sense; but, put in the passive sense, it is more harmonious with the meaning of the next paragraph. The commentary does not restrict it to the active sense. Besides, to say 'to have seen nobody', as interpreted in the *Book of Li* (Bk. LII, Title *Chung Yung*, No. 31), is really equivalent to saying 'to have been seen by nobody', at least one would believe so.
[2] The text of this, like the other, is, literally, in the active sense, and it is for the same reasons as in the other that it has been put in the passive sense here.
[3] See *The Great Learning*, Ch. VI, and *Complete Works of Wang Yang Ming*, Bk. I, p. 18.
[4] It is possible that this enumeration is not meant to be exhaustive. The *Book of Li* speaks of 'seven feelings', which include love, hate, and desire. See *ante*, p. 26.
[5] These passages form the first chapter of the work, being the doctrine which Tze Sze, grandson of Confucius, expounds in the subsequent chapters.
[6] *Paradise Lost*, Bk. I, Ls. 254-5.

Not merely so. He who has attained to that perfection may, either by the principles he practises or by the example he sets, exercise a permanent salutary influence on the general course of things of the universe, such as the case of the sage or, it may be added, the case where, on account of the exceptional virtue of one person, the estimation of his whole race, even if not also its moral tone, is enhanced.

THE GREAT LEARNING

'The principle of *The Great Learning* (a book for adults, forming the gate through which one enters the avenue of virtue) consists in enlightening the moral sense (of oneself, which is received from Heaven and self-luminous, but may be darkened or clouded by human passions or materialistic desires); in renovating (i.e., reforming) others (by enlightening their moral sense); and in attaining (in both cases) the goal [1] of perfection. (In other words, what the Book teaches is to make oneself perfect and others perfect.)

'It is only when the goal to be attained is known that the aim is fixed. It is only when the aim is fixed that a calm and steady state of mind can be achieved. It is only when a calm and steady state of mind is achieved that the mind can be at ease. It is only when the mind is at ease that one is able to ponder with care. It is only when one is able to ponder with care that one will be able to reach the goal.

'Things (in their relative importance) have what is the principal (or root, i.e., object of the immediate aim) and the auxiliary (or branches, i.e., object of the mediate aim). Affairs (in their natural sequence or as cause and effect) have what is the beginning (i.e., the aim) and what is the end (i.e., the result). (Actions in their natural order have what is first and what is last.) Knowing what is first and what is last to pursue approaches the right way. [2]

'The ancients, wishing to enlighten the moral sense of the world, first governed well their own States. Wishing to govern well their own States, they first put their families in good order. Wishing to put their families in good order, they first improved morally their own persons. Wishing to improve morally their own persons, they first rectified their hearts. Wishing to rectify their hearts, they

[1] See commentary for words inserted in brackets. The word 'goal' is based on the commentary of the last word of the next paragraph.

[2] Lit., the text of the second sentence of this passages reads: 'Affairs have end and beginning.' The inversion of the words 'beginning' and 'end' was merely for the sake of euphony. The words inserted in brackets are necessary for clarifying the texts, which consist of pithy sentences. The illustration of the meaning of this passage will be found in the next.

first purified and made sincere [1] their thoughts. Wishing to purify and make sincere their thoughts, they first perfected their moral knowledge. The perfection of moral knowledge lies in the profound and conscientious study of (the true meanings and reasons of) things (and affairs).

'It is only when (the true meanings and reasons of) things (and affairs) have been profoundly and conscientiously studied that the moral knowledge can [2] be perfected. It is only when the moral knowledge has been perfected that the thoughts can be purified and made sincere. It is only when the thoughts are purified and made sincere that the heart can be rectified. It is only when the heart is rectified that the person can be morally improved. It is only when the person is morally improved that the family can be put in good order. It is only when the family has been put in good order that the State can be well governed. It is only when the State is well governed that the world can be peaceful. From the son of Heaven to the masses (i.e., from the highest to the humblest) all must consider the moral improvement of their own persons as the root (or starting point of all achievements). It is not in the nature of things that, when the source is in confusion, what has to be derived from it can be in good order. That one who cares little for what is the more important (to him) and (at the same time) cares much for what is less important (to him) is a case that has never existed.' [3]

Let us now come back to our main subject. The teachings of Confucius are not in the form of commands, but in that of observations, or of approbations or disapprobations of certain conduct or deeds, or of definitions of what is right and what is wrong, or of answers to questions on fundamental problems of life, leaving no doubt in the minds of those who either listened to him at the time, or might read his words afterwards, as to the path of duty that should be pursued. He never professed to teach anything new, not that he 'found that generally what was new was false', [4] but that he would

[1] The words 'made sincere' may well be rendered as 'steadied', that is, making the thoughts unswayed by false doctrines or ideas, or self-interest.

[2] See commentary for using the word 'can' in this paragraph.

[3] These passages are the teachings of Confucius, forming the commencing chapter of the work. As an instance of the meaning of the last sentence, it may be said that he who has little affection for those to whom he is bound by a natural tie and professes an excessive affection for others to whom he is not so bound, acts at best from caprice or selfish motives rather than from true benevolence.

[4] Saying of Goldsmith. Boswell's *Life of Johnson*; Ed. G. Birkbeck Hill, Vol. III, p. 376.

not claim any credit for himself, maintaining that he only 'transmitted the doctrines of the ancients'.[1] He declined to be ranked as a sage or even as a man of perfect virtue, saying: 'As to the sage or the man of perfect virtue,[2] how dare I consider myself to be one.'[3] Still less did he claim to have a divine mission. Voltaire said that he knew a philosopher who had in his study no other portrait than that of Confucius, at the bottom of which were written the following lines:

'Without assumption he explor'd the mind,
Unveil'd the light of reason to mankind,
Spoke as a *sage* and never as a *seer*,
Yet, strange to say, his country held him dear.'[4]

However, there are opinions that the following two passages consisting of words uttered by Confucius on two different occasions to allay the fear of his disciples, when he was in great danger, seem to indicate that he was conscious of a divine mission:

1. 'Heaven having endowed me with such virtue, what can Huan Hui[5] do to me (against the will of Heaven)?'[6]

2. 'Since the death of King Wen,[7] has not the cause of culture (i.e., truth)[8] been entrusted to me? If Heaven had allowed the cause of culture (i.e., truth) to perish, no one who died (i.e., lived) after him would possibly have been permitted to acquire a knowledge of that cause. If Heaven does not allow that cause to perish, what can the people of *Kang*[9] do to me (against the will of Heaven)?'[10]

---

[1] Confucius: *Lun Yu*, Pt. VII, Ch. 1.

[2] The Chinese word is *yun*, which sometimes, particularly when used with other terms of ethics, such as 'righteousness', for instance, means benevolence or perfect benevolence, that is, love of mankind accompanied with the desire to promote men's prosperity and happiness, but more often, as in the case here, means virtue or perfect virtue, that is, moral excellence of which benevolence forms part. Therefore the word has to be rendered sometimes in the one sense and sometimes in the other.

[3] Confucius: *Lun Yu*, Pt. VII, Ch. 33.

[4] *Dictionary of Philosophy*; English ed.

[5] A high officer of *Sung*, who threatened the life of Confucius.

[6] Confucius: *Lun Yu*, Pt. VII, Ch. 22.

[7] Virtual founder of the *Chow* dynasty (1122-255 B.C.) and one of the noblest and most venerated personages in Chinese history.

[8] 'It was out of modesty that Confucius used on this occasion the word *culture* instead of the word *truth*. By culture, which is the manifested part of truth, is meant the various noble institutions, such as moral rules of correct conduct (*Li*).'—Orthodox commentary.

[9] The people of *Kang* mistook Confucius for another person against whom they had a grievance.

[10] Confucius: *Lun Yu*, Pt. IX, Ch. 5.

To the above two passages may be added the following:

'The world has long been denuded of truth and righteousness. Heaven is about to use the Master as the clarion [1] (to proclaim them).' [2]

This passage indicates that, even when Confucius was living, there were people who believed that he had a divine mission. But whatever inference may be drawn from these passages, the Chinese people never thought of divinizing him—an act that would have been contrary to the teachings of Confucius, who never claimed to be superhuman. They have, however, followed his teachings for over 2,000 years and revere him as 'The Master for All Ages' (*Vann Si Schue Biew*). Speaking of the Confucian Analects (*Lun Yu*), the philosopher Ching Tze [3] said:

'There are people who, having read the Analects, feel nothing at all; there are others who, having read them, feel they have found one or two sentences to their delight; there are others who, having read them, begin (Lit. know) to love them, and there are others who, having read them, feel themselves in such an ecstasy ·that they dance with joy without realizing what they are doing.' [4]

To the above I may add that the teachings of Confucius are so true to Nature, so noble in diction, so lofty in conception, so full of wisdom, and so rich in good sense, that, in hours of joy, they give us moderation; in hours of trouble, they give us guidance; and, at all times, they serve to purify our hearts, strengthen our character, and pacify our souls. The fact that they are sporadic is itself an additional proof of their genuineness, and the fact that, when put together, they form a coherent and systematic whole, pointing to the same direction—from purification of the heart of the individual to the love of mankind—show convincingly that truth, as they reveal, is not obscure, transient, or accidental, but clear, permanent, and certain, and that the path of duty for man is one and the same.

Let me, for illustration, quote a simple passage from the Analects:

A disciple asked how parents should be served within the meaning of filial piety. The master replied: 'The difficulty lies in the countenance (i.e., the manner of service). When there is work to

---

[1] Lit., 'wooden bell', which was a bell with a wooden tongue, employed in ancient days to proclaim something important.
[2] Confucius: *Lun Yu*, Pt. III, Ch. 24.
[3] See *ante*, p. 58, *note* 2.
[4] See Preface to *Lun Yu*; Ed. *Sze Bu Bei Yao*, Chung Hua Publishing Co., Shanghai.

be done, the youths take the toil, and, when there are wine and food to be enjoyed, they offer them to the elders: can this (alone) be regarded as filial piety?'[1]

In other words, the service must be rendered in the proper manner; for if it is true that 'bounty always receives part of its value from the manner in which it is bestowed',[2] it must be more so in the case of service rendered in consequence of duty. However, what I intend to discuss here is not that passage itself but only the principle, 'when there is work to be done, the youths take the toil, and, when there are wine and food to be enjoyed, they offer them to the elders', which is regarded by the Chinese as a general rule of conduct for young men, and which well-behaved young men in China are often heard to quote politely in rendering service to elders, to whom they are under no obligation. Here the cynic may say that such a doctrine sounds like 'Heads I win, tails you lose for the elders'. But in the *Titanic* disaster did not men in conformity with the rule of the sea, even give up without a murmur their seats in the lifeboats to children and women, some of whom were very old, when the ship was sinking? The two cases are, indeed, different, but the spirit in them is the same, and I have cited the latter, merely because it is striking and familiar to my readers. The *Titanic* tragedy, on account of its magnitude, roused world-wide sympathy and raised a lively discussion in the press as to the economic wisdom of sacrificing men, in the prime of their lives and full of promises, in favour of old women whose days of existence might, perhaps, be numbered. But it was unanimously agreed that noble sacrifices were never made in vain, and, as a corner stone of civilization, would outweigh, in the long run, any economic advantages that might be apparent at the time. For what a world would it be, if things were otherwise? So we are taught by our Sages, the following rules:

1. 'The man of high aims or of perfect virtue will not seek life at the expense of virtue, and would even sacrifice his life for the attainment of virtue.'[3]

2. 'To do good is (a privilege) that one does not yield even to one's teacher.'[4]

3. 'I love life and I also love righteousness; but if I cannot have both, I will forgo life and choose righteousness.'[5]

[1] Confucius: *Lun Yu*, Pt. II, Ch. 8.
[2] Boswell's *Life of Johnson*; Ed. G. Birkbeck Hill, Vol. I, p. 376, 'Letter to Earl of Bute'.
[3] Confucius: *Lun Yu*, Pt. XV, Ch. 8.
[4] Confucius: *Lun Yu*, Pt. XV, Ch. 35.
[5] *Mencius*, Bk. VI, Pt. I, Ch. 10, Sec. 1.

4. 'In sight of profit, think of righteousness; in sight of danger, be prepared to give up (your) life.' [1]

5. 'In sight of wealth, it is not to be acquired contrary to righteousness; in face of danger, it is not to be avoided contrary to righteousness.' [2]

Now let me take another passage of a very different nature:

'The stable having been burnt down, the Master returning from Court asked: "Has any person been hurt?", without inquiring about the horses.' [3]

Here the cynic may say that the Master was unkind to animals; because, as a stable had been burnt down, it was more likely that horses than men had been killed or hurt, and he asked only about men and not horses. But are there not people who feel more pain at seeing a dog or an ass being kicked than at seeing a fellow creature being even worse treated, sneering, perhaps, that the latter is of an inferior race? And are there not people who would shed tears over the death of a pet and yet have no compassion for the sufferings of men? A man who loves his fellow beings is a kind-hearted man, and a kind-hearted man is likely to be kind to animals. But the reverse is not necessarily true; because a man who loves lower animals is not necessarily a kind-hearted man. In this light the anxiety felt by the Master about human lives at the time may be better comprehended.

The two passages just quoted have been selected not for their profundity in meaning, but rather for the simplicity of it, in order to show that, even in the most casual and simple remarks of the Sage, there is a grain of profound truth.

Foreigners who pay tributes to Confucius or Confucian teachings are many, e.g.:

1. 'Confucius', says Prof. Giles, 'taught man's duty to his neighbour; he taught virtue for virtue's sake, and not for the hope of reward or fear of punishment. . . . The Confucian teachings which are of the very highest order of morality, and which have moulded the Chinese people for so many centuries, helping perhaps to give them a cohesion and stability remarkable among the nations of the world, should not be lightly cast aside. A scientific training, enabling us to annihilate time and space, to extend indefinitely the uses and advantages of matter in all its forms, and to mitigate

---

[1] Confucius: *Lun Yu*, Pt. XIV, Ch. 13. This is only part of the chapter, but is always regarded as a maxim by itself.

[2] *Book of Li*, Bk. I; Ed. *Sze Bu Bei Yao*.

[3] Confucius: *Lun Yu*, Pt. X, Ch. 12.

the burden of suffering which is laid upon the greater portion of
the human race, still requires to be effectively supplemented by a
moral training, to teach man his duty towards his neighbour.'¹

2. 'It would be hard to overestimate', says Dr. Williams, 'the
influence of Confucius in his ideal princely scholar, and the power
for good over his race which this conception has ever since exerted.
The immeasurable influence in after-ages of the character thus
portrayed proves how lofty was his own standard, and the national
conscience has ever since assented to the justice of the portrait.'²
'No people', says Mr. Meadows, 'whether of ancient or modern
times, has possessed a sacred literature so completely exempt as the
Chinese from licentious descriptions, and from every offensive
expression. There is not a single sentence in the whole of the
sacred Books and their annotations that may not be read aloud in
any family circle in England.'³ 'Throughout the Confucian
Canon', says a third, 'there is not a single word which could give
offence, even to the most sensitive, on questions of delicacy and
decency.'⁴

3. 'Si l'on peut juger de la valeur d'un homme et de la puissance
de ses doctrines par l'influence qu'elles ont exercée sur les populations, on peut, avec les Chinois, appeler KHOUNG-TSEU (Confucius)
*le plus grand Instituteur du genre humain que les siècles aient jamais
produit!* En effet, il suffit de lire les ouvrages de ce philosophe,
composés par lui ou recueillis par ses disciples, pour être de l'avis
des Chinois. Jamais la raison humaine n'a été plus dignement
représentée. On est vraiment étonné de retrouver dans les écrits
de Khoung-Tseu l'expression d'une si haute et si vertueuse intelligence, en même temps que celle d'une civilisation aussi avancée.
C'est surtout dans *Lun Yu* ou les Entretiens philosophiques que
se manifeste la belle âme de Khoung-Tseu. . . . On peut dire que
c'est dans ces *Entretiens philosophiques* que se révèle à nous toute la
belle âme de KHOUNG-TSEU, sa passion pour la vertu, son ardent
amour de l'humanité et du bonheur des hommes. Aucun sentiment
de vanité ou d'orgueil, de menace ou de crainte, ne ternit la
pureté et l'autorité de ses paroles. "Je ne naquis point doué de la
science," dit-il; "je suis un homme qui a aimé les anciens et qui
a fait tous efforts pour acquérir leurs connaissances".'⁵

¹ *The Civilization of China*, pp. 70 and 116.
² Arthur Smith: *Chinese Characteristics*, p. 288.
³ Arthur Smith: *Chinese Characteristics*, p. 288.
⁴ H. Giles: *The Civilization of China*, pp. 128-9.
⁵ 'If one may judge of the value of a man and the sway of his doctrines by the
influence that they have exercised on populations, one may, with the Chinese,

There are of course others who think differently. Some of their criticisms, moreover, are such that it would be invidious to refer to them specifically. Suffice it to say that they fit in with the following lines:

'Should you do so in my country,
You'd be sued for blasphemy.
I may do so in your country,
Thanks to extraterritoriality!'

It is a sensible rule in trade that a man may sell his own goods without running down those of his neighbours. If this is practical in one sphere of life, there is no reason why it cannot be observed in others. Indeed, there is no reason why the Golden Rule, at least in its negative form, *What you do not wish to be done to yourself do not do to others*, should admit of any exception in its application, in regard to the religions of others or their revered Founders. Confucius teaches us 'He who respects his own parents dares not disrespect those of others'. [1] Therefore, by extension, we believe that he who respects his own religion should not disrespect those of others. 'The time has gone, if indeed it ever existed', says a contemporary sinologue, 'in which Western scholars had any ground for supposing that their pronouncements on Chinese culture were the only really significant ones.' [2] Happily, the beams of a new era of mutual respect and comprehension have appeared on the horizon, and the past is receding fast.

Now, let us resume. With deep humility and modesty, Confucius

call Confucius the greatest Teacher of the human race that the centuries have ever produced! Indeed, it suffices to read the works of this philosopher, composed by him or compiled by his disciples, in order to be of the opinion of the Chinese. Never has the human reason been more worthily represented. One is truly astonished to discover in these writings of Confucius the display of a mind so lofty and so virtuous as well as a civilization so advanced. It is especially in *Lun Yu* or the philosophical Analects that the beautiful soul of Confucius is manifested. . . . One may say that it is in these philosophical Analects that are revealed to us the beautiful soul of Confucius in its entirety, his passion for virtue, and his ardent love for mankind and the welfare of men. No sentiment of vanity or pride, or of threat or fear, tarnishes the purity and authority of his words. 'I am not born endowed with knowledge,' says he; 'I am a man who loves the ancients and has made every effort to acquire their learning.' G. Pauthier: *Livres Sacrés de l'Orient*; Introduction, pp. xi and xv.
The saying of Confucius therein referred to is found in *Lun Yu*, Pt. VII, Ch. 19. The English translation here follows the French, which is correct, though a strict translation of the text would be 'I am not one born endowed with knowledge; I am one who loves antiquity and has eagerly sought it (therefrom).'
[1] *Book of Filial Piety*, Ch. 2.
[2] E. R. Hughes: *Oxford and the Comparative Study of Chinese Philosophy and Religion*, p. 7.

not only declined, as already mentioned, to be ranked as a sage or even a man of perfect virtue, but also said:

1. 'If I could live a few years longer to make a (profound) study of the *Yi* (the sacred *Book of Change*) . . . I might be free from great faults.'[1]

Let us note here that the modesty of the Master was such that he would not say 'free from faults', but 'free from great faults'. His modesty, apparently misunderstood by Dr. Legge, has led him to comment: 'Confucius never claimed, what his followers do for him, to be a perfect man'[2]—a comment that will be discussed later.

2. 'The principal characteristics of the (perfect) *Jiun Tze* (i.e., Noble Man) are three, to which I am yet unable to attain: being perfectly virtuous, he has no anxiety; being wise, he has no doubt; being courageous, he has no apprehension.'[3] (But on this occasion his disciple Tze Kung interposed, saying: 'Master, this is only what you yourself say out of modesty.')[4]

These and similar sayings must not be taken to mean that the Master really had not yet been able to attain the 'three principal characteristics' of the (perfect) *Jiun Tze* (i.e., Noble Man) or really had faults, still less should they be regarded as 'admissions'[5] or 'confessions'.[6] In the one case, he was talking to, or in the presence of, a disciple (Tze Kung) who, though very ambitious in attempting to attain perfect virtue, was in his opinion, as we shall see later, apt to underrate the task; therefore, as an example of modesty, which is the basis of virtue, and as an indirect instruction, which is sometimes the more effective, he spoke with such humility. In the other case, he might indeed have felt, out of modesty and humility, that he had tried to reach, but had not yet reached, the peak of excellence that

[1] Confucius: *Lun Yu*, Pt. VII, Ch. 16.
[2] Legge: *The Chinese Classics*, Vol. I, *Confucian Analects*, Pt. VII, Ch. 16, *note*. A similar misunderstanding occurs in his comment on a passage of a similar spirit, where Confucius says: 'To serve my father, as I would require my son to serve me: to this I have not attained, etc.' (*Doctrine of the Consistent Mean*, Ch. 13, Sec. 4.) Commenting on this, despite that he said: 'The cases, as put by him (Confucius) are in a measure hypothetical, his father having died when he was a child', Dr. Legge called these 'admissions', and said: 'The admissions made by Confucius here are important to those who find it necessary, in their intercourse with the Chinese, to insist on his having been, like other men, compassed with infirmity.'—Legge: *The Chinese Classics*; Ed. London, Trubner & Co., 60 Paternoster Row, 1861, Vol. I, p. 258, *note*.
[3] Confucius: *Lun Yu*, Pt. XIV, Ch. 30, Secs. 1-2.
[4] Confucius: *Lun Yu*, Pt. XIV, Ch. 30, Secs. 1-2.
[5] See *note* 2, Dr. Legge's comment.
[6] See Legge: *The Chinese Classics*, Vol. II, p. 72; Ed. 1861.

he himself aimed at. On two occasions[1] he gently cautioned his disciples against taking an easy view of the task of fulfilling one's duties to mankind, observing that, in this, even Yao and Shun of the golden age were anxious, lest they might fall short of the standard to be attained. On one of these occasions, while he was enunciating the Golden Rule in its *positive* form, he explained, as we shall see, that there was a form of conduct even higher than this, and it was in reference to the latter that he made the observation. On the other, he made that remark in the following dialogue:

'Tze Loo asked what made (a man) the *Jiun Tze*. The Master said: "To cultivate himself in being reverentially careful (to his duties)." "Is that all?" observed (Tze Loo). "To cultivate himself (thus) in order to impart (virtue and) peace to others," answered (the Master). "And is that all?" observed (again the disciple). "To cultivate himself (thus) in order to impart (virtue and) peace to allpeople," said (the Master), "To cultivate oneself (thus) in order to impart (virtue and) peace to all people is what even Yao and Shun were anxious about (lest they might fall short of the standard to be attained)."'[2]

As to the comment that 'Confucius never claimed, what his followers do for him, to be a perfect man,'[3] is it not that the term 'perfect man' can be used only in the estimation of others? How can a man himself claim to be perfect? The very claim of perfection by oneself would itself be a mark of imperfection. Christ has even said: 'Why callest thou me good? *There is* none good but one, *that is*, God.'[4] Confucius would not have been Confucius, if he had himself claimed to be perfect. One of his principal teachings, which underlies the whole of Chinese culture, is that men should not be self-complacent either as to their knowledge or as to their virtue, but should constantly guard against making light of their duties or overestimating their own merits. He therefore untiringly urged men to march forward unceasingly on the path of virtue and not stop, thinking that they had arrived 'there'—the end of perfection. The path of virtue has no end. The farther one proceeds, the brighter it is; but self-complacency would soon cast a shadow on the pilgrimage. That is why, when the disciple, who had said that Confucius was modest in his self-estimation, was wont to compare others as to their merits, he reprovingly, though mildly, said: 'Chi (the disciple's name), you

[1] Confucius: *Lun Yu*, Pt. VI, Ch. 28, Sec. 1; Pt. XIV, Ch. 45.
[2] Confucius: *Lun Yu*, Pt. XIV, Ch. 45.
[3] See *ante*, p. 71.
[4] St. Matthew, Ch. XIX, 17.

must have reached a high stage of excellence! I would have no time (for such comparison).' [1] By this the Master meant that one should employ more time in judging oneself than in judging others; for the habit of constantly passing judgments on others argues a consciousness, voluntary or involuntary, of self-excellence, which may be only presumptuous.

Whatever might be Confucius's own estimation of himself, which was always in the most modest tone, posterity who, by comparing men of all ages, found that he stood high above all others, has spontaneously agreed that he did arrive at the highest peak of excellence. In the words of Mencius, 'since there were human beings, there has never been (one equal to) Confucius', and in the words of an ancient Worthy, 'the sages among men are the same in kind, but they stand out from their fellow men and rise prominently above them all, and (in this), since there were human beings, there has never been one so gloriously decisive as Confucius'. [2] It may be said that it is because he disclaimed to be ranked as a sage that subsequent generations have spontaneously acclaimed him to be a sage. It is because he would not claim to be perfect that people of after-ages have spontaneously acclaimed him to be perfect. And it is because he claimed no credit for himself, setting, throughout his life, the great and noble example of modesty and humility, that his countrymen have spontaneously acclaimed him as 'The Master for All Ages'. And there stands, too, a trait of Chinese characteristics.

The doctrines of Confucius were once summed up by his second most distinguished disciple Tseng Tze in two words:

'*Chung* (忠): to fulfil to the utmost one's duties as man; and *Shu* (恕): to act to others as one would act to oneself (or to love others like oneself).' [3]

In the opinion of Chu Tze, the acknowledged post-classical orthodox commentator of the Confucian classics, what is meant by *Shu* is

[1] Confucius: *Lun Yu*, Pt. XIV, Ch. 31.
[2] *Mencius*, Bk. II, Pt. I, Ch. 2, Secs. 23-8.
[3] Confucius: *Lun Yu*, Pt. IV, Ch. 15. See commentary and particularly commentary of the two words in Ch. XIII of the *Chung Yung* (*Doctrine of the Consistent Mean*):

盡己之心爲忠推己及人爲恕，張子所謂
以愛己之心愛人．'

The last seven words literally mean 'to love others with the heart with which one loves oneself'. See also commentary in *Lun Yu*, Pt. VI, Ch. 28:

以己所欲譬之他人，知其所欲亦猶是也：
然後推其所欲以及於人則欲之事而仁之
術也

really included in what is meant by *Chung*; because 'to fulfil to the utmost one's duties as man' leaves no room for extension, the fact that both terms have been used being merely for the sake of clearness and easy comprehension, as the one (*Shu*) explains how the other (*Chung*) may be performed. In the words of Ching Tze, [1] '*Chung* is the principle dictated by Heaven, while *Shu* is the way of carrying it out by men'. [2] Briefly, it may be said that the two terms taken together mean, so far as duties to one's neighbour are concerned, the complete observance of the Golden Rule in both its positive and its negative forms, as enunciated by Confucius. [3] It has been thought by certain critics that the Golden Rule formulated by Confucius is only negative. But in fact he has enunciated it in both the positive and the negative forms and, moreover, a principle even higher. This is found in the following dialogue:

'Tze Kung [4] asked: "If a man were to bestow benefits extensively on the people, and were able to succour all, what would you think of him? Might he be said to be perfectly virtuous?" [5] The Master replied: Must he not, in that case, be a sage? Even Yao and Shun [6] were still anxious, lest they might fall short of this. The man of perfect virtue, *wishing to have himself established, endeavours also to have others established*, and, *wishing to have himself enlightened or advanced, endeavours also to have others enlightened or advanced*. To be able *to judge of the wishes of others by one's own, and then act to them as one would act to oneself*, may be said to be the means of attaining perfect virtue".' [7]

The distinction therein drawn between the case of the man of perfect virtue, who spontaneously practises the Golden Rule in its positive form, and that of the sage, who bestows benefits extensively on mankind and is able to succour all, is that, in the one case, there is still the presence in mind of the *ego* and the doing good to others is capable of limitation, while, in the other, there is no presence in

[1] See *ante* p. 58, *note*.
[2] See *Complete Works of the Two Chings*, Vol. II, Bk. XI, p. 5. Incidentally, it may be mentioned that 'to teach good to others' is also called *Chung*. *Mencius*, Bk. III, Pt. I, Ch. 4, Sec. 10.
[3] See commentary in *Doctrine of the Consistent Mean*, Ch. XIII; and *Complete Works of the Two Chings*, Vol. III, Bk. XXI, Pt. II, p. 3.
[4] This disciple, it will be noted, often asked questions, giving the Master opportunities to pronounce great principles.
[5] The Chinese word is *Yun*, which may here be translated as 'perfectly benevolent'; but the words 'perfectly virtuous' bring out better the real sense of the term in accordance with the spirit of the whole chapter in question. See *ante*, p. 65, *note*.
[6] Sage Emperors of the Chinese Golden Age.
[7] Confucius: *Lun Yu*, Pt. VI, Ch. 28. See commentary.

mind of the *ego*, and the doing good to others is extensive and un-
limited. It is this distinction that throws an additional light on the
following passage:

> 'There were four things absolutely absent in the Master. He had
> no prejudice, no wilful [1] insistence, no obstinacy, and no presence
> in mind of the *ego*.' [2]

It is the absence in mind of the *ego* (i.e., selflessness) that characterizes the sage.

As to the Golden Rule in its negative form it was enunciated in
the following dialogue:

> 'Tze Kung asked: "Is there a maxim which one may observe as
> a rule of conduct for life?" The Master replied: "Is not this (to be
> found) in the word *Shu* (i.e., to act to others as one would act to
> oneself, or to love others like oneself?) [3] *What you do not wish to be
> done to yourself do not do to others".*' [4]

It is remarkable that the disciple who asked the question had once
said: 'What I do not wish others to do to me, I also do not wish to
do to others.' Thereupon the Master interposed, saying: 'Chi (the
disciple's name), you are not equal to it.' [5]

The principle which the disciple believed that he was already able
to follow differs little in substance from the maxim recommended
by the Master as a practical rule of conduct for life and a step to
something higher. But there is this distinction: in the case of the
maxim recommended by the Master, the 'not doing' is the result of
prohibition, though self-imposed, while, in the other case, the 'not
doing' is spontaneous and natural and, therefore, even nobler in
character and more difficult of attainment.

The recommendation of the Golden Rule in its negative form as
a maxim for the ordinary man shows that the sage's teachings are as
reasonable as they are lofty. 'As I know more of mankind,' says Dr.
Johnson, 'I expect less of them, and am ready to call a man *a good
man*, upon easier terms than I was formerly.' [6] Confucius might, like
Edmund Burke, have thought 'better of mankind'; [7] but, as a reason-

---

[1] 'Governed by will without yielding to reason.'—Webster's Dictionary.
[2] Confucius: *Lun Yu*, Pt. IX, Ch. 4.
[3] See *ante*, pp. 73-4.
[4] Confucius: *Lun Yu*, Pt. XV, Ch. 23. The same maxim in almost the same form
is given in *Chung Yung (Doctrine of the Consistent Mean*, Ch. 13): 'What you do not
like, if done to yourself, do not do to others.'
[5] Confucius: *Lun Yu*, Pt. V, Ch. 11.
[6] Boswell's *Life of Johnson*; Ed. G. Birkbeck Hill, Vol, IV, p. 239.
[7] Ibid., Vol. III, p. 236.

able man, he could not expect all men to act like saints, at least from the very beginning. Therefore, in order that the rule might not be 'more honour'd in the breach than the observance',[1] he, while expecting the man of perfect virtue at the outset, and all men in time, to conform to the Golden Rule in its positive form, as he had clearly and comprehensively enunciated, recommended it in its negative form for the average person, as the first step to the fulfilment of the duties of man. Another reason may be, to borrow the words of Prof. Westermarck, 'that negative commandments spring from the disapproval of acts, whereas positive commandments spring from the disapproval of forbearances or omissions, and that the indignation of men is much more easily aroused by action than by the absence of it'.[2] Anyhow, in the negative form, nobody could excuse himself for failing to observe it; for no person could very well say that he would insist on doing to others what he would not wish to be done to himself. Nevertheless, he felt that even this was not always easy of attainment, and this is only too true, as we know in life. 'I will dispute very calmly', says Dr. Johnson, if we may quote him again, 'upon the probability of another man's son being hanged.'[3] But when it comes to be a matter of one's own children, one's feelings will be very different. Therefore fearing that men might think lightly of the rule, as some people do, Confucius promptly and frankly corrected his disciple, as we have seen, in his over-confident, though sincere, self-estimation, with these words: 'You are not equal to it.' The Chinese have a saying: 'Since the *Three Generations*,[4] it is only to be feared that men would not covet honour.' For though in a saintly age it may be 'a sin *even* to covet honour',[5] the world, as it is, is only too glad to be filled with such 'offending souls'. However, Confucius expects every man to aim at the highest, and would not excuse him for not making the attempt. It was for this reason that, when one of his disciples said: 'Not that I do not rejoice in your doctrines, but that I am unequal to them,' he rebuked him, saying: 'A person who is unequal to something gives it up half-way, but now you preclude yourself from the very beginning.'[6]

In order to elucidate the meaning of certain important passages of the Confucian Analects to be introduced here, it will be necessary to discuss Dr. Legge's comments on those passages, particularly as

[1] Shakespeare: *Hamlet*, Act I, Sc. IV, L. 16.
[2] Edward Westermarck: *Ethical Relativity*, p. 171.
[3] Boswell's *Life of Johnson*; Ed. G. Birkbeck Hill, Vol. III, p. 11.
[4] *Hsia*, 1848-1783 B.C., *Shang*, 1783-1122 B.C., and *Chow*, 1122-255 B.C., Dynasties, in the hey-days of which, the standard of virtue was very high.
[5] Shakespeare: *Henry V*, Act IV, Sc. III, L. 28.
[6] Confucius: *Lun Yu*, Pt. VI, Ch. 10.

he is considered by many in the West as an authority on Confucian philosophy or doctrines. But first of all let the following words attributed to him be quoted:

'The teaching of Confucianism on human duty is wonderful and admirable. It is not perfect indeed. But on the last three of the four things which Confucius delighted to teach—letters, ethics, devotion of soul, and truthfulness—his utterances are in harmony both with the Law and the Gospel. A world ordered by them would be a beautiful world.' [1]

Now let us proceed:

1. Referring to the Golden Rule enunciated in the two negative forms (one by Confucius, the other by his disciple Tze Kung) as already quoted, Dr. Legge said: 'The Golden Rule of the Gospel is higher than both—"Do ye unto others as ye would that others should do unto you".' [2]

The fact that this comment has been made without mentioning that the Golden Rule in its positive form, together with a rule deemed by the Chinese to be even higher than it, has in fact been enunciated in another part of the Confucian Analects, as we have already seen, is apt to leave in the minds of the readers the erroneous impression that the Golden Rule is known to the Chinese at best only in the negative form—a question that the writer himself has been asked more than once. Such impression is further apt to be enhanced by Dr. Legge's using the word 'reciprocity' not only in translating the word 'Shu' which, as it has been explained, means 'to act to others as one would act to oneself (or to love others like oneself)', and from which the Golden Rule in its negative form is drawn, but also as a basis in commenting on the Rule itself and other passages where the word Shu occurs or is vital, though he says incidentally that 'Altruism may be substituted for reciprocity'. [3] But altruism and reciprocity are widely different things. What should be termed as altruism can-

---

[1] Arthur Smith: *Chinese Characteristics*, p. 288. I say 'attributed'; because no reference of the passage quoted is indicated, and the tribute therein contained, though made not without reserve, contrasts widely with the language used by its author in his Prolegomena to *The Chinese Classics*, Vol. I.

[2] Legge: *The Chinese Classics*, Vol. I, *Confucian Analects*, Pt. V, Ch. 11, *note*; Ed. Truber & Co., Lond., 1861. See also Prolegomena at page 110 for his remarks on Mr. Thorton's laudatory opinion of the Chinese rule.

[3] For translation of the word *Shu*, see Legge: *The Chinese Classics*, Vol. I, *Confucian Analects*, Pt. XV, Ch. 23; Pt. V, Ch. 11, *note*; and Vol. II, *Mencius*, Bk. VII, Pt. I, Ch. 4, Sec. 3, the text of which will be found at p. 151, *post*. For comment on the word *Shu*, see Vol. I, *Confucian Analects*, Pt. IV, Ch. 15, *note*, and Pt. V, Ch. 11, *note*.

not be represented as mere reciprocity, and what is mere reciprocity cannot be called altruism. Altruism is a principle of ethics which requires a man to regard the interests of others. Reciprocity, though a good principle in international practice, is hardly a rule of ethics, at least in the higher sense of the term. To reciprocate is 'to make a return for something given or done' or 'to give and return mutually'. [1] It is essentially 'give and take', or rather 'take and give', limiting itself to what others have done or will do to oneself. It is no more than the payment of a just debt. Poor indeed must be the ethical standard of a person, if he knows only reciprocity as the rule of conduct. If he were to observe it strictly, he would not even invite another to tea or dinner without being sure that the latter would 'reciprocate' his hospitality. *Shu*, which means 'to act to others as one would act to oneself (or love others like oneself)', and the rule 'what you do not wish to be done to yourself do not do to others' are, however, principles of benevolence of the highest order, the one (*Shu*) being in fact the Golden Rule in its positive form, while the other (the rule recommended for the average man) is the Golden Rule in its negative form. To call either of them, and *Shu* in particular, mere reciprocity is more than a misnomer. Moreover, the rule, though negative in form, is in substance and in practice no less benevolent or 'golden' than the rule in its positive form. For instance:

I do not wish others to invade my country; therefore I do not invade the countries of others. I do not wish others to harm my family; therefore I do not harm the families of others. I do not wish others to injure my person; therefore I do not injure the persons of others. I do not wish others to infringe my rights of any kind; therefore I do not infringe the rights of any kind of others. I do not wish others to speak disparagingly of my countrymen; therefore I do not speak disparagingly of the countrymen of others. I do not wish others to attack my religion; therefore I do not attack the religions of others. I do not wish others to speak irreverently of the Founder of my religion; therefore I do not speak irreverently of the Founders of the religions of others. I do not wish others to sin against me; therefore I do not sin against others. I do not wish others to tempt me to do evils; therefore I do not tempt others to do evils.

Thus the list may go on, until all evils of the world are uprooted and the world becomes so harmless that it is fit for the habitation

[1] Webster's Dictionary.

of angels. Moreover, the rule is not so negative in effect as it appears to be in form. For instance:

I do not wish others to be unkind to me; therefore I will not be unkind to others. I do not wish others to refuse me aid when I need it; therefore I will not refuse aid to others when they need it. I do not wish others to be indifferent to my sufferings; therefore I will not be indifferent to the sufferings of others. And so on.

To conclude these observations, it may be remarked that this rule is one of those Confucian doctrines that are most widely known and most often quoted by the Chinese in general, and must have exercised a great influence on Chinese thought. For the justification of this remark the readers are referred to the next chapter, where an incident is mentioned by a missionary, showing how a brother missionary was able to turn an unruly mob instantly into a civil assembly merely by quoting that rule. [1]

2. The next comment concerns the following passage:

'A certain person said: "What is your opinion as regards recompensing injury with kindness?" The Master said: "With what then would you recompense kindness? Recompense injury with justice, and recompense kindness with kindness." ' [2]

In other words, kindness and injury should not be treated in the same way. Kindness should always be recompensed with kindness, coupled with a feeling of gratitude and unforgetfulness; because, ethically, kindness creates, on the part of the person receiving it, a moral obligation to recompense with kindness. Injury, however, calls for no recompense; because, ethically, it neither creates, as it is obvious, any moral obligation to recompense with kindness, though, as we shall see later, to recompense injury with kindness is considered by Confucius as a virtue of magnanimity, nor admits of any 'recompense' in the sense of retaliation or revenge, for, apart from this being so in ethics, Confucius, as we shall see later, has expressly said: 'Not to retaliate or revenge wrongful acts is the way of the *Jiun Tze* (the gentleman).' [3] But if the injury is ever called in question, for instance, in unpardonable cases, one is, ethically, under a moral duty to the wrongdoer to be fair and just to him without any feeling of revenge or resentment—in other words, to recompense injury or injustice with justice.

[1] See *post*, p. 94.
[2] Confucius: *Lun Yu*, Pt. XIV, Ch. 36.
[3] Here the term may be rendered simply as 'gentleman', though generally it would be more correct to render it as 'Noble Man'.

Commenting on the passage quoted, Dr. Legge says: 'How far the ethics of Confucius fall below our Christian standard is evident from this chapter, and even below Lao Tze.' [1] He mentions Lao Tze, because this Chinese philosopher, who lived six centuries B.C., has, as we shall see in the next chapter, said: 'Recompense injury with kindness.' Now let the following observations be made:

First, as noted even by Dr. Legge himself in his comment, Confucius has, as recorded in the *Book of Li*, [2] once said:

'To recompense injury with kindness is a virtue of magnanimity.' [3]

It is true that there is a short editorial note of this passage, which says that the words translated here as 'magnanimity' (Lit. 'enlarging the body' 寬 身) are equivalent to 'loving the body' (愛 身), and that the word 'virtue' (仁) occurring in the text is believed to be a misprint for the word 'man' (人), the two words in Chinese having the same pronunciation (*yun*). But, in the literary as distinguished from the literal sense, 'enlarging the body' or 'loving the body', it is submitted, could only reasonably mean 'magnanimity'; and as the word 'virtue' harmonizes better with the text, and gives it a more reasonable meaning, than the word 'man', because it commences with an infinitive ('to recompense') or a gerund ('recompensing'), it is also submitted that there is no valid reason for modifying the text as it stands.

Secondly, Dr. Legge, apparently following, in this case, the editorial note rather than the text, [4] translated the passage in question as 'He who returns good for evil is a man who is careful of his person'. [5] But this translation is open at least to two observations:

1. To translate an infinitive, 'to recompense', or a gerund, 'recompensing', as 'He who returns etc.', is at least out of harmony with the text.

2. As Dr. Legge has already translated the material words 'to recompense injury with kindness' (以 德 報 怨), occurring in the passage commented upon by him, as 'The principle that injury should be recompensed with kindness', [6] to translate the said words in a second time as 'He who returns good for evil' is translating the

[1] Legge: *The Chinese Classics*, Vol. I, *Confucian Analects*, Pt. XIV, Ch. 36, *notes*.
[2] Bk. LIV, *Biew Chi*, 32.
[3] 以 德 報 怨 乃 寬 身 之 仁 也   Dr. Legge translated this passage as 'He who returns good for evil is a man who is careful of his person'. See observations that follow.
[4] 'The text, and not the commentary, has been his study.' *The Chinese Classics*, Vol. I, Preface, p. x.
[5] See Legge: *The Chinese Classics*, Vol. I, *Confucian Analects*, Pt. XIV, Ch. 36, *notes*.
[6] See Legge: *The Chinese Classics*, Vol. I, *Confucian Analects*, Pt. XIV, Ch. 36.

same words in different ways. This is an additional reason why the text, perfectly reasonable in sense as it is, should not be disturbed.

Thirdly, even when the text of the passage in question is modified by substituting the word 'man' for the word 'virtue', it still shows that Confucius in principle approved of such a course of conduct. Indeed, on one occasion he praised two worthy princes for 'not bearing in mind the past wicked acts of others (不念舊惡).'[1] On another occasion, reproving his disciples for being too severe in regard to one's past conduct, he said: 'If a person has his heart purified to come to see me, I receive him as purified, without answering for his past.'[2] On a third occasion, he would not consider even mere *suppression*, as distinguished from *absence*, of the feeling of resentment as enough, *inter alia* to constitute perfect virtue.[3] And on a fourth occasion, replying to a question about being strong, he said: 'To be forbearing[4] and unresentful as a means of correcting others (whose conduct is incorrect)[5] and not to retaliate or revenge wrongful acts: this is how the people of the Southern Regions are strong, and is the way of the *Jiun Tze* (the gentleman).'[6] For retaliation or revenge lowers oneself to the level of the wrongdoer, and resentment shows a lack of magnanimity; whereas forbearance raises oneself in the esteem of others, enhances one's own dignity, and elevates one's own soul. It is by forbearance, forgiveness, or forgetfulness, and not by revenge, retaliation, or resentment, that injuries can be radically expunged, just as evil can be intrinsically destroyed only by good. Forbearance or forgiveness, moreover, may make the wrongdoer repent; resentment seldom, if ever, does, while retaliation or revenge can only create a new injury or prolong an existing feud. This explains the words: 'To be forbearing and unresentful *as a means of correcting* others (whose conduct is incorrect),' and this, it must be said, is kindness for injury, in reality no less than in words. But in teaching men in individual cases a distinction between right and wrong should first be drawn, so that the person seeking instruction might first of all see the path of truth. This was the more necessary, as Confucius was living in an age in which the demarcation between right and wrong had been blurred and, according to the historian,

---

[1] Confucius: *Lun Yu*, Pt. V, Ch. 22.

[2] Confucius: *Lun Yu*, Pt. VII, Ch. 28, Sec. 2.

[3] Confucius: *Lun Yu*, Pt. XIV, Ch. 2.

[4] i.e., Indulgent towards offenders or enemies.—Webster's dictionary.

[5] The phrase 'as a means of correcting' has been rendered in certain translations as 'in teaching' or the like, which, it is submitted, cannot be the right meaning. See orthodox commentary.

[6] *Chung Yung*, Ch. 10, Sec. 3. Here the term *Jiun Tze* may be rendered simply as 'gentleman'.

'cases of treasonable murders of reigning rulers numbered thirty-six', [1] apart from cases of parricide and those of 'ingratitude more strong than traitors' arms'. [2] Has it not been said that 'when the history of the period, known as the *Spring and Autumn*, was completed by Confucius, traitorous ministers and treacherous sons were alarmed?' [3] Therefore, in reply to the question put to him, Confucius first drew the attention of the questioner to the fact that he must not treat kindness and injury in the same way, by asking back the question: 'With what then would you recompense kindness?' Much hinges on the word 'recompense', which implies purposely doing something in return for something done. As already explained, injuries call for no recompense. An injury not recompensed is forborne, forgiven, or forgotten, and according to Confucius, as already cited, the forbearance, forgiveness, or forgetfulness is a virtue, as in the case of 'not bearing in mind the past wicked acts of others', and is also a proof of moral strength, as in the case of 'not retaliating or revenging wrongful acts'. But kindness should always be recompensed. To ignore or forget it is ingratitude or lack of gratitude, either of which is a vice. Kindness, being always magnanimous, might not herself be offended, if she were forgotten or neglected, and, if Injury were also forgotten or forgiven, Kindness would even be pleased with your generosity, which, in her virtuous eyes, would go far to make up for your neglect of her. But she would feel hurt, if you put her and Injury in the same boat; not that she, being charitable, could, nevertheless, be jealous of your magnanimity towards Injury, but that you draw no distinction between Good and Evil by doing homage to both in the same manner. Confucius, knowing well of the evils of the age in which he was living, was not without fear that there were men who, fishing for popularity with an ulterior motive, [4] might be more minded to recompense injuries with kindness than to recompense kindness in any way—not to mention the case, which has happened in all lands and all ages, of recompensing kindness with injuries. Therefore, before giving his answer, he first asked the question: 'With what then would you recompense kindness?' and followed his own question up with the remark: 'Recompense injury with justice, and recompense kindness with kindness.' The emphasis is on the distinction between kindness and injury and on the obligation to recompense kindness, as already explained. This is clear from

---

[1] *History* by Sze Ma Chien (*Han* dynasty 206 B.C.–A.D. 220), Bk. CXXX, p. 8.
[2] Shakespeare: *Julius Caesar*, Act III, Sc. II, L. 190.
[3] See *ante*, p. 56.
[4] In the particular case under discussion, for instance, 'the question was asked evidently with a secret motive'.—Orthodox commentary.

the fact that it was Confucius who brought out the point of recompensing kindness, though it was not raised in the question put to him.

It is not without a feeling of incongruity that, when these lines are being penned, it curiously happens that the radio announces that a night ago over 1,000 aeroplanes of one belligerent were over the territory of another, and unloaded about ten tons of bombs a minute for ninety minutes, and that a great part of the world who remembers those cities and towns that have been ruthlessly destroyed by the latter is applauding this great feat of arms. Of course, this is war, which does not represent a permanent state of things. When the world is restored to its normal condition, all the painful memories of the war will be, it is piously hoped, buried for ever, so that the present discussion about recompensing injury with kindness may yet be found not unprofitable. However, living in an age distant by twenty-five centuries from the days, on which these questions under discussion were raised and answered, one may venture to observe that no rule of ethics can have very great meaning, if, in the last resort, indiscriminate adherence to it brings no unmixed benefit to society. To forgive, for instance, is a rule that can only do good. That is, perhaps, why when the parishioners of the Church of St. John, Massena, New York, wanted to perpetuate some words from the many admired speeches made by the First Lady of China, Madame Chiang Kai-Shek, in her mission to America, they unanimously chose the phrase, 'We must try to forgive.'[1] Suppose you say, 'If someone throws a stone at you, throw to him in return a bunch of roses,' that may be observed without any question. But suppose you say: 'If someone drops loads of bombs on your town in the night, drop sacks of coffee in return on his in the morning,' that would require reflection. There can be acts which, though noble in themselves, may produce results entirely contrary to the intention and expectation of the benevolent actor; largely, if not wholly, because they may blur the senses of the wrongdoer to the nature of his deeds, and prevent him from realizing that he is doing wrong. There must be good reasons that make modern criminal law regard every crime as an injury to the State and, as an offence, the compounding of a felony. In short, the line of demarcation between right and wrong should always be maintained. The principle of not putting Kindness and Injury in the same boat is essential to good navigation in the sea of morals.

After all, no less an authority on Christian ethics than Bishop Butler, in interpreting the precepts *'Love your enemies, etc.'*,[2] says:

[1] See Bulletin No. 12 (Série IX), Berne Scheuerrain, 7, Mar. 24, 1944.
[2] *St. Matthew*, Ch. V, 43, 44.

'But no man could be thought in earnest who should assert, that though indignation against injury, when others are the sufferers, is innocent and just, yet the same indignation against it, when we ourselves are the sufferers, becomes faulty and blamable. These precepts therefore cannot be understood to forbid this in the latter case, more than in the former. Nay, they cannot be understood to forbid this feeling in the latter case, though raised to a higher degree than in the former; because from the very constitution of our nature, we cannot but have a greater sensibility to what concerns ourselves. Therefore the precepts in the text, and others of the like import with them, must be understood to forbid only the excess and abuse of this natural feeling, in cases of personal and private injury. . . . We may therefore love our enemy, and yet have resentment against him for his injurious behaviour towards us. But when this resentment entirely destroys our benevolence towards him, it is excessive, and becomes malice or revenge. The command to prevent its having this effect, i.e. to forgive injuries, is the same as to love our enemies; because that love is always supposed, unless destroyed by resentment.'[1] In the light of this authority the critical remark passed on the Confucian precept needs no further observation. However, before leaving this subject it should be pointed out that it can never be too much emphasized that one must not consider every disagreeable act or behaviour on the part of others towards oneself as an injury. To do so only betrays one's own excessive sense of resentment or want of benevolence. Even in a true case of injury, one still has to examine oneself inwardly whether oneself has in any way caused, or contributed to, it.[2]

3. The third comment of Dr. Legge that calls for observation is in connection with the following passage:

'The Master said: "Great indeed was Yao as a sovereign. How sublime was he! It is only the sky that is immense and it is only (the virtue of) Yao that could be compared to (the immensity of) it.[3] How vast was his virtue! The people could find no word for expressing it. How sublimely stood he in his achievements! How illustriously stood he in his institutions!" '[4]

Commenting on this passage, Dr. Legge says: 'No doubt, Yao, as he appears in Chinese annals, is a fit object of admiration, but if

[1] Joseph Butler: *Fifteen Sermons*, Walker & Greig, 1816, IX, pp. 143, 149, and 155.
[2] See *Sayings of Mencius on Ethics*, No. 5, *post*, p. 150.
[3] Compare Milton's line: 'O Goodness infinite! Goodness immense!' *Paradise Lost*, Bk. XII, L. 469; 2nd ed.
[4] Confucius: *Lun Yu*, Pt. VIII, Ch. 19.

Confucius had had a right knowledge of, and reverence for, Heaven, he could not have spoken as he does here. Grant that it is only the visible heaven overspreading all, to which he compares Yao, even that is sufficiently absurd.' [1]

First of all let me say that, as already mentioned in my explanation of the Chinese word Heaven (*Tien*) for God, the same word also means the sky or physical heaven. Dr. Legge, however, translated the word *Tien* in that passage as Heaven with a capital letter, though in his comment he allowed the possibility of its meaning only the physical heaven. But as in that passage Confucius speaks of the immensity of *Tien* and the vastness of the virtue of Yao in metaphorical comparison, the word *Tien* therein used obviously means the sky or physical heaven, and this is in fact the meaning given to it in the orthodox commentary. Secondly, the Chinese are very fond of using metaphors and similes with the word sky (or heaven), like the expression 'sky-high', and are in the daily habit of using the phrase 'as high as the sky (or heaven) and as thick as the earth'. In scolding a person mildly for ignorance, for instance, the Chinese would say: 'He does not know the height of the sky (or heaven) or the thickness of the earth.' Once a Chinese student in America, who evidently knew more Chinese than English idioms, apologizing to his professor for ignorance, wrote: 'Pardon me, Sir, for not knowing the height of heaven or the thickness of the earth.' The professor, apparently well-humoured, replied, '*Moi non plus!*' [2]

To conclude these observations, let it be said that the Confucian Analects are to the Chinese their Bible, and that unless one studies them with a sense of awe or veneration due to all sacred books, one will, to say the least, miss their right meaning.

SELECTED DOCTRINES OF CONFUCIUS [3]

1. 'A youth, at home, should observe the doctrine of filial piety (i.e., fulfil his duties in the best manner to his parents) and, when away from home, should observe the doctrine of fraternal deference (i.e., fulfil his duties in the best manner to the elders). He should always be earnest (in his actions) and truthful (in his words). He should abound in love to all and attach himself to the virtuous. When he has leisure, he should employ it in cultural studies.' [4]

[1] Legge: *The Chinese Classics*, Vol. I, *Confucian Analects*, Pt. VIII, Ch. 19, *note*; Ed. 1861.
[2] Nor do I.
[3] These are quite apart from those quoted in other parts of this work, and should be read with the *Sayings of Mencius on Ethics* in the next chapter.
[4] Confucius: *Lun Yu*, Pt. I, Ch. 6.

2. 'Abide by faithfulness and truthfulness as the guiding principle. Have no (man as) friend who is not (morally) equal to yourself. If you have faults, do not fear to reform them.'[1]

'A fault unreformed is indeed a fault.'[2]

Compare the last sentence of the first saying to these words of Carlyle: 'Of all acts, is not, for a man, *repentance* the most divine?'[3]

3. 'As to the person without truthfulness, I do not know how he can get on.'[4]

'If you are faithful and sincere in your words, and honourable and careful in your actions, your conduct will avail you even in uncivilized countries. If you are unfaithful and insincere in your words, and dishonourable and careless in your actions, will such conduct of yours avail you in your own town?'[5]

4. 'Alas! I have not yet seen a person able to perceive his own faults and indict himself inwardly.'[6]

Compare: 'Conscience is a coward, and those faults it has not strength enough to prevent, it seldom has justice enough to accuse.'[7]

5. 'Do not be concerned for being not known, but endeavour to deserve to be known.'[8]

Compare: ' 'Tis not in mortals to command success,
           But we'll do more . . . we'll deserve it.'[9]

6. 'When you see a worthy man, try to be equal to his worthiness. When you see an unworthy man, examine yourself inwardly (to see if you have the same vices).'[10]
Such examination may be likened to a silent prayer.

7. 'Walking in three together I am certain to find my teacher (in my companions by comparison). I pick out their good points as something to follow, and their bad points as something to avoid.'[11]

---

[1] Confucius: *Lun Yu*, Pt. I, Ch. 8; Pt. IX, Ch. 24.
[2] Confucius: *Lun Yu*, Pt. XV, Ch. 29.
[3] *Heroes and Hero-Worship*; Lecture II.
[4] Confucius: *Lun Yu*, Pt. II, Ch. 22.
[5] Confucius: *Lun Yu*, Pt. XV, Ch. 5, Sec. I.
[6] Confucius: *Lun Yu*, Pt. V, Ch. 26.
[7] Goldsmith: *Vicar of Wakefield*, Ch. XIII.
[8] Confucius: Pt. IV, Ch. 14.
[9] Addison: *Cato*, Act I, Sc. I, Ls. 141-2.
[10] Confucius: *Lun Yu*, Pt. IV, Ch. 17.
[11] Confucius: *Lun Yu*, Pt. VII, Ch. 21.

8. 'Who can go out except by the door? Why (then) do not men (in their conduct) follow the right path?'[1]

'(He who) sees what is right and does not do it is lacking in courage.'[2]

'Men are born to be upright. He who is not upright and yet lives only narrowly escapes destruction.'[3]

9. 'When you perceive good, pursue it, as if you could not reach it; when you perceive evil, shun it, as if your hand had dipped into boiling water.'[4]

'Not to cultivate virtue (with constancy); not to try to be thoroughly instructed in what (should be and) has been learned; not to be able to adhere to what is righteous, when a knowledge of it is gained; not to be able to reform what are (known to be) faults—this is what gives me anxiety.'[5]

The last saying is one of the many instances of humility on the part of Confucius, who thus utters an indirect warning to others against taking a complacent view of things.

10. 'People depend on virtue even more than on water and fire. I have seen people die from treading on water or fire; but I have not yet seen a person die from treading on the path of virtue.'[6]

A person may lose his life for want of water or fire, but will lose his soul for want of virtue. However, Dr. Legge in his comment on this passage says: 'The case is easily conceivable of men's suffering from death on account of their virtue. There have been martyrs for their loyalty and other virtues, as well as for their religious faith.'[7] But, though men may die *for* virtue,[8] they are not killed *by* virtue as in the case of those who are killed by the water or fire trodden upon by them.

11. 'Set the mind to the path of duty, hold on to virtue, abide by benevolence, and seek relaxation in (liberal) arts.'[9]

12. 'If one bends one's mind on virtue, one will have no vicious practices.'[10]

At least there will be no conscious one.

---

[1] Confucius: *Lun Yu*, Pt. VI, Ch. 15.
[2] Confucius: *Lun Yu*, Pt. II, Ch. 24, Sec. 2.
[3] Confucius: *Lun Yu*, Pt. VI, Ch. 17.
[4] Confucius: *Lun Yu*, Pt. XVI, Ch. 11. This is only part of a saying, but has always been treated as a separate maxim.
[5] Confucius: *Lun Yu*, Pt. VII, Ch. 3.
[6] Confucius: *Lun Yu*, Pt. XV, Ch. 34.
[7] *The Chinese Classics*, Vol. I.
[8] See *ante*, p. 67.
[9] Confucius, *Lun Yu*, Pt. VII, Ch. 6.
[10] Confucius, *Lun Yu*, Pt. IV, Ch. 4.

13. 'Is there any person who would attempt one day to exert (all) his strength to be virtuous? (If there is such a one), I have not yet seen a case where his strength is unequal to the attempt. There might possibly be such a case, but I have not seen one.'[1]

The very exertion or attempt would put one on the path of virtue.

14. 'Is it that virtue lies afar? I desire virtue, and at once virtue is with me.'[2]

The man who is doing good, or performing his duty faithfully, or telling the truth, or having a charitable feeling for those who suffer, has certainly virtue with him; but even the would-be assassin who willingly withdraws his hand, or the would-be slanderer who voluntarily withholds his tongue, or the would-be wrongdoer who conscientiously desists from his act, or the vicious who resolutely abandons his vice or reforms his fault, has also, at once, virtue with him until it is forsaken.

15. 'Virtue never stands alone, but is bound to have neighbours.'[3]

'The spread of virtue is more rapid than the transmission of Government decrees by couriers on horseback or by post chaise.'[4]

16. 'The unvirtuous cannot live long in a state of poverty or want, or in a state of happiness (i.e. prosperity)[5] (without giving way to base desires). The virtuous find joy in virtue; the wise find advantages in virtue.'[6]

'The wise live happily; the virtuous live long.'[7]

'The virtuous man first tackles the difficulties of his task, and only afterwards thinks of success.'[8]

17. 'One who (only) knows (the truth) is not equal to one who loves it, and one who loves it is not equal to one who enjoys it.'[9]

18. 'If one has in the morning heard (i.e., gained knowledge of) the True Principle[10] (i.e., the principle which men should always follow and by which life should be permanently guided), one may

---

[1] Confucius: Lun Yu, Pt. IV, Ch. 6.

[2] Confucius: Lun Yu, Pt. VII, Ch. 29.

[3] Confucius: Lun Yu, Pt. IV, Ch. 25.

[4] Quoted in Mencius, Bk. II, Pt. I, Ch. 1, Sec. 12.

[5] See Webster's Dictionary, Definition 1.

[6] Confucius: Lun Yu, Pt. IV, Ch. 2. As to the latter part of the last sentence, compare the English saying: 'Honesty is the best policy.'

[7] Confucius: Lun Yu, Pt. VI, Ch. 21.

[8] Confucius: Lun Yu, Pt. VI, Ch. 20.

[9] Confucius: Lun Yu, Pt. VI, Ch. 18.

[10] The Chinese word is Tao, literally meaning 'way', and is the same word used by the Taoists for their religion. It may, indeed, be translated by the term 'the Way', to be understood in the same sense as the Christians would use it in their religion. See Webster's Dictionary. But I prefer the translation as rendered above.

TEMPLE OF CONFUCIUS

die in the evening without regret.' [1] (Because the world is flooded with so many doctrines that are either entirely false or only apparently or partially true.)

19. 'To provide the aged with comfort; to treat friends with sincerity; to endear the young with tenderness.' [2]

20. 'When the *Great Principle* (i.e. the ideal social order that Confucius had in his mind) prevails, the world is like one home common to all; men of virtue and merit are to be elected to be rulers; sincerity and amity pervade all dealings between man and man; people shall love not only their own parents and own children, but also those of others; the aged, the young, the helpless widows and widowers, the orphans, the destitute, the incapacitated, and the sick shall be well provided for and well looked after, while the able-bodied shall exert themselves in their aid; men shall be appropriately employed and women suitably married; one detests that things are abandoned or wasted on earth, but, when gathered or stored up, they are not to be retained exclusively for oneself; one detests that exertion does not proceed from oneself, but its fruits are not to be regarded exclusively as one's own. Thus, there will be no, and no cause for, conspiracy, robbery, theft, or rebellion, and no need to bolt one's outside door. This is a True Commonwealth.' [3]

SELECTED PASSAGES FROM THE BOOK OF HISTORY

1. 'Forsake (what is wrong in) yourself and follow (what is right in) others; ill-treat not the helpless and abandon not the needy.' [4]

2. 'The doctrine of love was originally instituted for one's own parents, and the doctrine of respect was originally instituted for one's own elders. Begin these with the family and the State, and extend them to the four seas (i.e., the whole of mankind).' [5]

3. 'The benediction or condemnation of *Shang Ti* (God) is not constant (on any one). Those who do good will be blessed with a hundred forms of happiness; those who do evil will be afflicted with a hundred forms of disasters.' [6]

4. 'Virtue has no constant teacher. To abide by good as the guiding principle is the teacher.' [7]

[1] Confucius: *Lun Yu*, Pt. IV, Ch. 8.
[2] Confucius: *Lun Yu*, Pt. V, Ch. 25, Sec. 4.
[3] *Book of Li*, Bk. XXI, Title *Li Yun*, Ch. 9.
[4] Bk. IV, Title *Da Yu Mu*, No. 3. *Da Yu Mu* means the tombstone of the Great Yu (2205 B.C.), on which the words quoted were found.
[5] Bk. VIII, Title *E Yun*, No. 4.
[6] Bk. VIII, Title *E Yun*, No. 4.
[7] Bk. VIII, Title *Han Yau Yee Tak*, No. 8.

5. 'The practice of virtue eases the heart and makes the day happy; the practice of hypocrisy weighs on the heart and makes the day miserable.' [1]

To conclude this chapter, it may be observed that, though there are men who fear that the progress of science may in time undermine the belief in religion, I do not share the apprehension, without, however, committing myself to the proposition that the methods of teaching it, or at least some of them, may not in time become out of date. In my opinion, the more science is developed, the more will a large part of mankind see the gulf between the spiritual and material worlds—a gulf that can be bridged only by religion, using the word, of course, in its liberal and enlightened sense. For, however much science may accomplish, it cannot supply those rules of conduct that are indispensable to men in a civilized world and, what is more, those that ennoble the soul. It is for this reason that Confucian teachings, which are precisely a body of such rules and, moreover, have weathered more than twenty centuries by the sheer force of their own, appealing to man's conscience and reason rather than invoking supernatural power, are in still less danger of being supplanted by science. As long as human conscience and reason remain, faith in Confucian teachings is bound to remain, and so far as the Chinese are concerned, they are simply bound up with them. A Chinese who is proud of his own country is in fact proud of its civilization and culture that are permeated with the teachings of Confucius.

[1] Bk. XVIII, Title *Chow Kwan*, No. 22.

CHAPTER 4

PHILOSOPHY

THE Chinese have been called a nation of philosophers. What this really means is another matter. But it is certainly true that the Chinese people, whatever may be their stations in life, are in a high degree amenable to the influence of philosophy. That they have a large amount of patience and perseverance, a great capacity for endur- ance, and a remarkable sense of contentment, is well known and often noticed by foreigners. These qualities are not necessarily born in them, but are more often the result of a philosophic culture. To witness this, one has only to watch, in a summer evening, the Chinese peasants who, after their day of toil, wash their feet in a running stream in front of a setting crimson sun, singing folksongs, as if all their earthly cares of the day were flowing away with the dirt. There is also a touch of philosophy, not without a sense of humour, in the monotonous cries, used to be heard in the once-narrow streets of Canton from load-bearers who, trying to ease their fatigue, uttered, as they went along with their loads: 'Who the devil asks you to be poor! Who the devil asks you to be poor!' By this they meant that the proper way to get over poverty was to work and not to grumble. And so, they found the key of life.

Chinese philosophy, though often pessimistic in form, is optimistic in substance. This is quite consistent with the view, stated in the preceding chapter, that God is the supreme embodiment of love and justice. In a practical world sorrows and calamities are inevitable, but very often they are only blessings in disguise or the turning point for the better. To murmur against one's lot, without exerting oneself in the right way to overcome it, not only sows the seed of envy and hatred, but is in reality a subdued allegation of divine injustice. Men therefore should be taught not to lose hope, but to rise above their material conditions to attain true happiness, which is within the reach of everyone who seeks it in the right way. To recall the words of the English poet already quoted:

' 'Tis not in mortals to command success,
But we'll do more . . . we'll deserve it.' [1]

Hence we have, *inter alia*, the following teachings:

1. 'With only coarse rice as meal, only plain water as drink, and

[1] Addison: *Cato*, Act I, Sc. I, Ls. 141-2.

only my arm as pillow, I still find joy in the midst of these conditions. Wealth and honour acquired contrary to righteousness are to me like the passing cloud.'[1]

2. 'When Heaven is going to entrust a person with a great task, it is certain first to accustom his heart to affliction, his sinews and bones to fatigue, his body to hunger, and his person to poverty and wants, as well as to bewilder him in all his undertakings. Thus it stirs his heart, reinforces his nature with patience, and augments his capacities.'[2]

3. 'Life is bred in sorrow and adversity, death in ease and comfort.'[3]

4. 'To have nothing to be ashamed of either before Heaven, on looking up, or before men, on looking down, is a form of happiness . . . to which even the glory of ruling an empire is unequal.'[4]

There may be people who think that these are mere high-sounding words but would not make an empty bag stand. Here is a point on which I would like to say something before I pass on. First, I do not mean that the mere citation of a doctrine or a legend would be evidence of a general practice or would establish a fact. What is cited here or elsewhere is meant only to show the existence of certain ideas that throw light on certain habits and thoughts of a people, some of which are noticed even by foreigners, as may be seen from passages quoted here and there from their works. As the existence of a custom house, though it may not prevent smuggling, does show that duties are paid, so the existence of certain moral principles and legends, taught and repeated from generation to generation, though it cannot thus ensure their observance, does show that they are commonly accepted as the right standard of conduct—an acceptance which, through its cumulative influence, cannot fail to have a profound effect on the second nature and the general outlook of life of the people. For instance, no one in China would dare look down on another, merely because he is dressed shabbily. Nay, no one who is dressed shabbily would himself feel humiliated in the company of others who are better dressed. This habit is due largely to the fact that Confucius once spoke approvingly of a disciple who, though

[1] Confucius: *Lun Yu*, Pt. VIII, Ch. 15.

[2] *Mencius*, Bk. VI, Pt. II, Ch. 15, Sec. 2. See commentary in *Correct Interpretation of Mencius* (Vol. VII, Bk. XXV, p. 18) for the words 'reinforces his nature with patience'.

[3] *Mencius*, Bk. VI, Pt. II, Ch. 15, Sec. 5.

[4] *Mencius*, Bk. VII, Pt. I, Ch. 20. In order to bring out the right sense of the text, the latter part of the sentence has been slightly paraphrased.

dressed in a shabby robe, felt no shame in standing by the side of a
person dressed in rich furs. [1] When, in reading the life Johnson, I
came to the passage that he had once to eat behind a screen as a guest,
because he was poorly attired, [2] I could not help feeling that had he
been a Chinese, he would have unquestionably been accorded by his
countrymen the seat of honour, and, on account of his poverty, the
respect paid to him, for his learning and moral character, would have
been all the greater, approaching to awe.

Secondly, nobody would deny that philosophy can make a vast
difference in the contemplation of things. The English proverb that
'good company upon the road is the shortest cut' is nothing but
philosophy. No less so, I believe, is, as recounted in Lord Haldane's
Autobiography, [3] that King Edward VII found admirable the coffee at
a little wayside inn on the Austrian frontier. Why? because he was
able on such occasions to 'stand treat' to his minister and, in order
to preserve his *incognito*, 'to give only a small tip'—a thing which
Crowned Heads rarely have the privilege to do, and the doing of
which, like the forbidden fruit, must have afforded rare pleasure and,
consequently, enhance the taste of the coffee.

Thirdly, the doctrines of Confucius are not something to be taught
only from the pulpit. For centuries they have formed the main curriculum of schools and colleges; they have supplied the main subjects
in competitive examinations for public service; they have been
quoted in official documents, cited in tribunals, overheard in discussion in the tavern or the tea-room, and taught by parents to their
children as well as by the old to the young. As the English would
say that their Constitution is merely part of the law of the land, the
Chinese may well say that the teachings of Confucius are merely
part of the rules of conduct of the people. No Chinese would think it
strange of you if, in attempting to conciliate him or settle his dispute,
you should, for instance, quote the Confucian canon: 'What you do
not wish to be done to yourself do not do to others,' or other similar
appropriate sayings. It does not follow that you will thus succeed in
your attempt. What I mean is—and this is what matters—that the
man whom you thus talk to would not feel that you are merely
quoting some pious doctrines from a sacred book and smile at you,
but would feel that you are using some familiar and sensible arguments,
though in that particular case he may not be convinced by them. An
instance of this is furnished by the author of *John Chinaman at Home*. [4]

---

[1] See Confucius: *Lun Yu*, Pt. IX, Ch. 26.
[2] See Boswell's *Life of Johnson*; Ed. G. Routledge and Sons, Vol. I, p. 86, *note*.
[3] Page 208.
[4] By the Rev. E. J. Hardy, p. 213.

'A missionary who asked his way was answered only by the jeers and hooting of a crowd. Turning to them he asked in excellent Chinese: "Do you thus observe the injunction of your ancient writers, to treat kindly the stranger from afar? Are you ignorant that Confucius said that what we would not have done to ourselves we should not do to others?" In an instant the mood of the crowd changed, the old men bowed approvingly, and a number of young ones jumped forward to show the way. Would the Sermon on the Mount, if quoted in English by a Chinese in a London or New York street, have the same effect upon an excited mob?'

Dr. Johnson once said: 'Go into the street and give one man a lecture on morality and another a shilling and see which will respect you most.'[1] In the light of the passage just quoted, if the lecture is given in China and on Confucian morality, the answer is obvious. The explanation of all this is simple. If we see a man in Buddhist robe in London or New York, we think that he looks queer among the crowd. But if we live in Tibet, we will soon realize that it is the man who is not in such a religious garment that looks strange. Similarly, the Chinese, who until recent years had for generations been wont to learn and be taught, both in the school and in the college, almost nothing but the doctrines of Confucius and the philosophy developed from them, not only would feel at home, when you talk to him in that philosophic language, but would rather feel odd, if you do otherwise.

This cumulative philosophization of the Chinese mind does not of course abolish poverty or other hardships of life, but it can dull the edge of affliction. 'Honest poverty', says Prof. Giles, 'is no crime in China. Nor is it in any way regarded as a cause for shame. It is even more amply redeemed by scholarship than is the case in Western countries.'[2] 'It seemed to me', says Bertrand Russell, 'that the average Chinaman, even if he is miserably poor, is happier . . . because the nation is built upon a more humane and civilized outlook than our own.'[3]

However, this does not mean that the Chinese are philosophic fanatics, who hate to be rich and love to be poor. 'Wealth and honour are things that men desire,' says Confucius; 'but if such desire cannot be given effect to (i.e., if wealth and honour cannot be obtained) in the proper way, they should not be obtained. Poverty and humble conditions are things that men dislike; but when such dislike cannot

[1] Boswell's *Life of Johnson*; Ed. G. Routledge and Sons, Vol. I, p. 254.
[2] *The Civilization of China*, p. 228.
[3] *The Problem of China*, p. 197.

be given effect to (i.e., if poverty and humble condition cannot be avoided) in the proper way, they should not be avoided.'¹ The Chinaman is therefore only human, but he is taught to follow the proper way. To desire, moreover, is not the same thing as to esteem, nor is to dislike the same thing as to despise. In the words of Grotius, *'En Chine personne n'est estimée ou honorée à cause de son origine ou naissance ou de ses richesses, mais seulement à cause de son érudition et ses connaissances.'*² 'A Chinaman', says the author of *John Chinaman at Home*, 'is fond of money, but he respects learning and literature far more. . . . The most notable men in a neighbourhood are not the wealthy, but the learned.'³

The Chinese certainly respect learning; but they respect virtue even more, and this may be seen from the following two passages:

1. 'The wealth of (the rulers of) *Tsin* and *Cho* [two richest States], says Tseng Tze (is indeed so great as) cannot be equalled. They may abide by their wealth; I abide by my virtue. They may abide by their ranks; I abide by my righteousness. What do I lack (in respect and honour) in comparison with them?'⁴

These are not empty words. The simple case of the man or woman, who would not go wrong even in defiance of rank or wealth, suffices to demonstrate the truth of them. Indeed, even savages have often been known to show a high sense of honour; because they have no passion for worldly distinctions and still less for gold, *'worst* poison to men's souls'.⁵ It is in this light that we can best understand those words under comment and the meaning of the saying already quoted, that 'the *Jiun Tze* (i.e., the man of principles) can unswervingly endure want'.⁶ For how often does it not happen that 'my poverty, but not my will, consents', and that the world accordingly 'pays thy poverty, and not thy will?'⁷

2. 'There are three things that are universally honoured: rank, age, and virtue. In court, rank comes first; in the village, age comes first; in aiding one's generation and leading the people, these two are not equal to virtue.'⁸

¹ Confucius: *Lun Yu*, Pt. IV, Ch. 5.
² 'In China a person is not esteemed or honoured on account of his origin or birth or riches, but solely on account of his knowledge and learning.' *Grotiana*, VIII, p. 27; *Vereenigin Voor de Uitgave Van Grotius*.
³ By the Rev. E. J. Hardy, p. 207.
⁴ *Mencius*, Bk. II, Pt. II, Ch. 2, Sec. 6.
⁵ Shakespeare, *Romeo and Juliet*, Act V, Sc. I, L. 79.
⁶ See Chapter II, General Survey, 'Contrast between *Jiun Tze* and *Siao Yun*', No. 8.
⁷ Shakespeare, *Romeo and Juliet*, Act V, Sc. I, Ls. 75-6.
⁸ *Mencius*, Bk. II, Pt. II, Ch. 2, Sec. 6.

A well-known essay of comparatively modern time, winning the blue ribbon in an official competitive examination, contains a passage, celebrated for its beauty both in style and in thoughts, reads:

'As to those who have position but no merit, the scholars of future generations in the study of history will not have time even to remember their names, though they may have been Prime Ministers.'

My translation of this passage must, I am afraid, have done injustice to its literary beauty. Some kinds of Chinese prose, of which this is one, though they are not in rhyme, have nevertheless a fixed form with a graceful rhythm which, if clothed with beautiful ideas, appeals to the ear like the best of music, and the charm of which is impossible to be brought out fully in translation. However, this is only by the way. The philosophy that makes virtue, learning, and achievement the foremost objects of esteem is essentially democratic. It not only enhances the dignity of man, but also puts within the reach of every individual, whatever may be his station, what makes life pleasant, namely veneration by his fellow beings. The Chinese historical conception of this philosophy may be traced to the fact that Yao, sage Emperor of the Golden Age, gave his Empire, in preference to his son, to Shun, then the most virtuous man of the country, and Shun likewise gave his Empire, in preference to his son, to Yu, the most meritorious man of the time. The practice of giving empires away cannot of course be expected to continue in every generation. But the two incidents sanctified the conception that virtue and merit are the highest objects of admiration.[1] This conception fits in well with the sentiment of the people, as testified by the various monuments erected in all ages in honour of the 'Village Hampdens'—persons, without rank or wealth are celebrated only for their virtue. It has been said by Carlyle that reverence for Excellence in others is an ever noteworthy quality in man.[2] The fact that the Chinese have a profound veneration for others' virtue reflects, therefore, no little credit on their social system and their assessment of the ultimate value of things.

Veneration is not idolization, which has no place in Chinese philosophy. Yao and Shun are, as my readers must know by this time, among the most venerated figures in Chinese history; yet Mencius would say: 'Yao and Shun were men just as others,'[3] and,

---

[1] In the works of the ancient philosopher Moh Tze (see *post*) there is a chapter entitled 'Honour the Virtuous and Meritorious', in which the reasons for honouring virtue and merit are discussed.

[2] See *Heroes and Hero-Worship*; Lecture V.

[3] *Mencius*, Bk. IV, Pt. II, Ch. 32.

'The Sages among men are the same in kind.'[1] The most distinguished disciple of Confucius, Yen Yuen, whom the Master frequently and highly commended for his virtue, also said: 'What sort of man was Shun, and what sort of man am I? He who exerts himself worthily like him will likewise become one like him.'[2] All this incidentally furnishes an additional explanation as to why the Chinese never thought of deifying Confucius. The fact of regarding him as one of us indeed conforms to his teachings, but it also elevates mankind; because his example shows what men can attain, being thus to them a source of inspiration. And the fact that he had men like Yen Yuen as his devoted disciples and men like Mencius as devoted expounders of his doctrines throws an additional light on his greatness.

As Yen Yuen and Mencius are the most revered personages of the Confucian School after Confucius, an account of them should be given. That of the latter will be found at the end of the chapter; that of the former may be gathered from the following anecdotes:

1. 'One day Confucius in his Northern trip was on the top of a mountain with his disciples Tze Loo, Tze Kung, and Yen Yuen[3] standing by. Looking around, Confucius contemplatively observed with a sigh: "Here we may express our thoughts without reserve! Now, my lads, tell me individually your ambitions and I will express my opinions by way of selection." Thereupon Tze Loo (who was celebrated for generosity and bravery) stepped forward and said: "I would like, in the midst of noise of gongs and drums vibrating up to heaven and in the midst of military banners waving over the earth, to lead an army against the enemy, repulsing him back for a thousand miles,[4] seizing his banners, and pulling him by the ear. (I think) I can do this."

'Confucius said: "Brave indeed!"

'Tze Kung (the disciple who, as seen in the preceding chapter, was wont to ask questions, giving the Master opportunities to pronounce great principles) then stepped forward and said: "I would like, if *Chi* and *Cho* (then two largest States) are engaged in a mortal struggle in the wild plain with storm of dust raging everywhere, while arms and armours are locked in fatal clash, to dress myself in mourning and intervene between them, removing their misunderstanding and settling their disputes, by expounding

[1] *Mencius*, Bk. II, Pt. I, Ch. 2, Sec. 28.

[2] *Mencius*, Bk. III, Pt. I, Ch. 1, Sec. 4.

[3] All the three were among the seventy-two Worthies of the 3,000 disciples of Confucius. They must then be still of tender age; because Yen Yuen, the most distinguished of all, died young.

[4] Lit., *Le*, which means mile, but is equivalent to only one-third of an English mile.

to them the advantages (of peace) and the disadvantages (of war). (I think) I can do that."

'Confucius said: "Eloquent indeed!"'

'Yen Yuen, however, withdrew and said nothing. (Seeing this) Confucius said: "Come, Hui (Yen Yuen's name). How is it that you alone have no ambition to express?"

'To this Yen Yuen replied: "As my fellow disciples have already spoken on both the civil and the military aspects of things, what else have I to say?"

' "Nevertheless," said Confucius, "everybody has his own ambition. Tell me, my lad, what yours is."

' "I have heard", replied Yen Yuen, "that what is fragrant and what stinks are not kept in the same vessel, and that Yao (benevolent ruler) and Chieh (villainous ruler) do not rule together; because they are not of the same class. I would like (therefore) to aid an enlightened King or a sage Master to spread the five fundamental doctrines (i.e., paternal righteousness, maternal tenderness, elder brother's affection, younger brother's respectfulness, and filial piety) among the people, and guide them with Li (propriety) and (cultural) music,[1] so that they will not have to repair their city walls (as protection against invasion); they will not trespass on the domains of others (Lit., jump over ditches); they may beat their swords into ploughshares; they may let loose their cattle on the wild plains; families will be spared the pain of separation or abandonment; and there will be no calamity of war for a thousand years. In that case Yau (Tze Loo's name) will have no occasion to display his bravery and Chi (Tze Kung's name) will have no occasion to employ his eloquence."

'(When Yen Yuen had terminated his speech), the Master solemnly observed: "Admirable indeed is Virtue!"'

'Tze Loo then respectfully asked the Master of whose ambition he would approve. Confucius replied: "To waste no money, to injure nobody, and to need no eloquence—it is the son of Yen who is up to it." '[2]

2. '(The ruler of) Cho, hearing that Confucius was staying in a region between Chen and Tsai, sent a special envoy to welcome him.[3] As he was about to leave, the ministers of Chen and Tsai conferred in secret, saying: "Confucius is a worthy. All his criticisms concerning the vices of the rulers of the day are to the point. He has stayed long between our two States, whose ministers' policy and

[1] For the importance of Music in ancient days, see chapter on Art.
[2] *Family Sayings of Confucius*, Bk. II, p. 1.
[3] This happened when Confucius was sixty-one years of age.

conduct are all at variance with his principles. Now, *Cho*, a great Power, has sent a special envoy to welcome him. If he is given office by *Cho*, we shall be in danger." They then conspired to have his departure impeded. As a result, he could not leave, provisions were exhausted, and some of his followers were so ill that they could not rise. . . . Seeing that some of his disciples were impatient, he sent for Tze Loo and put him the question: "Are my principles wrong? If not, why are we in such a pitch?"

'Tze Loo replied: "Is it possible that people think that we are not virtuous enough and so they do not trust us, or that people think that we are not wise enough and so they do not follow our principles?"

'Confucius said: "Is this possible? Yau (disciple's name), if the virtuous were always trusted, there would have been no Pao E and Shoo Chi.[1] If the wise were always followed, there would have been no Prince Bei Gan."[2]

'Tze Loo went out and Tze Kung came in. Confucius put him the same question. Tze Kung replied: "My Master's principles are so lofty that the world is unable to listen to you. Why do not you, Master, modify them a little?"

'Confucius said: "Chi (disciple's name), the good farmer can grow things well, but he cannot ensure the crops. The good artisan can be skilful in his work, but he cannot ensure that it will meet the taste of others. The *Jiun Tze* (i.e. the man of principles) can cultivate his principles, formulate them definitely, and co-ordinate them properly, but he cannot ensure that he will be listened to. Now, you aim not at the cultivation of principles but at being listened to by others. Chi, your aim is not high."

'Tze Kung went out and Yen Yuen came in. Confucius put him the same question. Yen Yuen replied: "My Master's principles are so lofty that the world is unable to listen to you. But let you, Master, (continue to) push them forward and put them into practice. What harm is there, if the world does not listen to us? . . . If principles are not cultivated, it is our fault (Lit. shame). If they are well cultivated but not adopted, it is the fault of those who possess States. It is indeed when not listened to that the *Jiun Tze* (the man of principles) is revealed (because it is only the *Jiun Tze* who would not in such circumstances deviate from his principles)."

'Confucius, delighted with this reply, smilingly said: "Is that

---

[1] Two brother princes who voluntarily died of hunger for righteousness.
[2] A wise statesman cruelly put to death by a tyrant for criticizing his ill conduct boldly though loyally.

so? Son of Yen, if you are rich, I will be your treasurer (i.e., our interests are identical)".' [1]

3. 'One day Confucius asked Yen Yuen and another disciple to express their respective cherished wishes. Yen Yuen said: "I should like not to vaunt any merit (that I may possess) nor to parade any service (that I may have rendered)".' [2]

4. 'Worthy indeed is Hui!' [3] says Confucius. 'With only a bowl of rice and a dish of soup (as his food), and living in a dilapidated lane—a misery which others would not be able to endure—he does not allow to be affected his joy (in the virtuous path he has been pursuing).' [4]

5. 'Yen Yuen asked about perfect virtue. The Master replied: "To subdue (selfishness in) [5] oneself and regain completely (the sense of) propriety (derived from Nature) is perfect virtue. . . . To be perfectly virtuous depends (entirely) on oneself, and not on others." [6] Yen Yuen said: "I respectfully ask for a formulation of the rules (for the practice of perfect virtue)." The Master replied: "Cast no eye on (Lit., see not) what is contrary to propriety (i.e., what is selfish); [7] lend no ear to (Lit., hear not) what is contrary to propriety (i.e., what is selfish); give no tongue to (Lit., speak not) what is contrary to propriety (i.e., what is selfish); have no hand in (Lit., touch not) what is contrary to propriety (i.e., what is selfish)." Yen Yuen said: "Though I am dull, I will make it my duty to conform to these rules".' [8]

Having given my readers a glimpse of the character of Yen Yuen, who is considered by the Chinese as the best model for man aspiring to be worthy and is ranked only after a sage, [9] I may now resume my theme. The elevation of man, as distinguished from idolization, has its background in the conception of human equality and fraternity. 'All things of the same kind resemble one another,' says Mencius. 'Why then particularly in the case of human beings should we sus-

---

[1] *History* by Sze Ma Chien, Bk. XLVII, pp. 15-16. The explanatory words, 'our interests are identical', are from the commentary.

[2] Confucius: *Lun Yu*, Pt. V, Ch. 25, Sec. 3.

[3] Yen Yuen's name.

[4] Confucius: *Lun Yu*, Pt. VI, Ch. 9. It is obvious that Yen Yuen's joy was not in his material condition but in something spiritual, which could only be the virtuous path he had been pursuing.

[5] See commentary.

[6] The latter part of this sentence is in the form of a question; but it is not really a question, and to translate it so would weaken its true meaning. See commentary.

[7] This is the meaning given in the orthodox commentary.

[8] Confucius: *Lun Yu*, Pt. XII, Ch. 1.

[9] See *Complete Works of Two Chings*, Vol. I, Bk. II, p. 5; Bk. V, p. 1.

pect that they might be an exception? The sage and we are the same in kind. That is why the philosopher Lung observed: "Should any person make shoes for others, not knowing (the size of) their feet, I know he would not make them into baskets." Shoes resemble one another; because the feet of men of the whole universe resemble one another.'[1] Though this passage refers only to the semblance of human nature, the idea therein contained has its root in the conception of human equality. This conception crystallized in that of human fraternity, as embodied in the principle, 'Within the four seas all are brethren',[2] is the seed of the custom that in China men address one another as brothers, women address one another as sisters, and children address the friends of their parents as uncles or aunts. In recent years the term *sen sung* (first born) is generally used as a term of address instead of the word 'brother', which is reserved for friends, as distinguished from casual acquaintances. Formerly, the term *sen sung* was used almost exclusively in the sense of 'master', a term of respect. It is still so used, for instance, when pupils address their teachers; but in general it is now employed simply as a term of politeness. As it literally means 'first born', its use as a term of respect or politeness has a poetic echo in Shakespeare in the line:

'The courtesy of nations allows you my better, in that you are the *first born*."[3]

The democratic nature of Chinese philosophy acts on the taste of the people. Generally speaking, the Chinese do not like things that display the 'air of riches and high life', even though they may in their way be artistic. What they like is something that is simple but means much, or something that has a scholarly appearance or, as they say, the 'book spirit'. The Temple of Heaven in the old capital of China, which is a most solemn piece of architecture and one that most impresses the tourists, is a triumph of simplicity. In the way of furniture, the following passage from De Quincey would certainly appeal to the Chinese taste: 'Books are the only article of property in which I am richer than my neighbours.'[4] What has been said is true not only in architecture, but also in other spheres of life. For example, in painting, the steamship or the motor-car would be ill at ease in a Chinese picture; not because they are modern, for they have existed long enough to lose their modernity, but because there is something in them that approaches to the 'air

[1] *Mencius*, Bk. VI, Pt. I, Ch. 7, Sec. 3.
[2] See Confucius: *Lun Yu*, Pt. XII, Ch. V, Sec. 3.
[3] *As You Like It*, Act I, Sc. I, Ls. 50-1.
[4] *Confessions of an English Opium-Eater*, Pt. II.

of riches and high life'. In enjoyment, the same rule prevails. The Chinese have, of course, their feasts, and they do take pleasure in them. But in general, the average Chinese would prefer, by far, a meal with a few intimate friends to a banquet. He would enjoy much more a homely but specially cooked repast at a cosy little restaurant than a costly but indifferently prepared dinner at a luxurious hotel. Nothing, for that matter, would please him more than the accidental discovery of an unlooked for eating house where some new palatable dishes are offered: the relish of the unknown being added with the pleasure of revelation. The honour that King Edward VII did to the wayside inn on the Austrian frontier [1] for its coffee can, as a matter of taste, be well appreciated by a Chinese connoisseur. It is a sensible surmise, not without a grain of Chinese philosophy, that Emperor Chien Lung of the *Ching* dynasty, well-known for his patronage of art and literature, repeated his pleasure trips to the provinces, south of the River Yangtze, no less for his appreciation of rustic food than for his admiration of country scenery.

Even in the admiration of feminine beauty, it is not the pearl and diamond, but the 'wooden hairpin and the cloth skirt' as the Chinese say (i.e., beauty derived from Nature and not from Art), that have captured their poets' hearts. The Chinese traditional queen of beauty, Hsee Shee, who lived in the fifth century B.C., was found washing by the side of a river called *Yueh Chi*. In a poem, with her as the theme, written by the *Tang* poet, Wang Wei, a name familiar to all Western lovers of Chinese art, there appear these two lines:

> 'At dawn a simple *Yueh Chi* girl she was.
> At dusk a queen of State *Wu* she became.' [2]

Here I may be treading on delicate soil. Perhaps, it will be my own countrymen who will be the foremost to say, not without a sense of gallantry, that the belief in Hsee Shee being the Venus of the Middle Kingdom is not merely a matter of taste, even if it may be philosophic, but in fact a homage to truth. Be sure, though it has become proverbial that 'Hsee Shee creeps out of the lover's eyes', I have not the least intention to dispute, after more than two thousand years, her title to the throne of beauty or, if I may recall, with a little variation, a phrase once used by Balfour in defence of an eminent English statesman against press criticism, 'to snatch *her* from the *queenly* niche' in which she is firmly lodged. Indeed, it is my sincere conviction that her title, as Queen of Beauty, is as safe as the death of Queen Anne is sure. The point that I try to make out is simply

---

[1] See *ante*, p. 93.
[2] *Tang Poems*; Standard ed., Bk. I, p. 5.

that, from 'wooden hairpin and cloth skirt' by the riverside in the
morning to enthronement in the palace in the evening, she owed, in
no small measure, her 'crown' to a democratic philosophy.

Chinese philosophy, by the way, has also its lively side. It must
not be thought that the Chinese are taught simply to feed on virtue.
The lines:

> 'Say, then, physicians of each kind,
> Who cure the body or the mind.
> What harm in drinking can there be,
> Since punch and life so well agree?' [1]

have their echo—pardon an anachronism—in a poem of the *Tang*
dynasty (A.D. 618-906):

> 'Be gay when thou art in a happy tone.
> Let not an empty bottle face the moon. [2]
> God gave us the talents not in vain.
> A thousand ducats spent shall come again.
> From ancient times all sages have been dry.
> But drinkers leave their names that never die.' [3]

Similarly, Goldsmith's felicitous phrase, 'I was tired of being
always wise', [4] has its earlier counterpart in the following lines:

> 'Seeing that all men are drunk, [5]
> How can I bear remaining sober?'

With this diversion, 'let us come back to our sheep' (*revenons à
nos moutons*), as the French say. In the field of philosophy Chinese
original thinkers have been numerous. But it is generally classified
into four main schools, headed by Kung Tze (Confucius), Lao Tze,
Moh Tze, and Han Fei Tze respectively, and it is this classification
that is to be followed here. Though this work is principally concerned
with the Confucian School of philosophy, which, it may be mentioned, will, for the sake of convenience, be treated at the end of the
chapter, Chinese civilization cannot be adequately represented
without presenting, at least in outline, the others, which complete
the whole. Moreover, by comparison with the latter, the former may
also be better comprehended. First of all, it may be helpful to give
a short explanation of the word *Tze*. My readers must have been

[1] Boswell's *Life of Johnson*; Ed. G. Routledge & Sons, Vol. I, p. 189.
[2] Lit., 'Let not the Golden Bottle emptily face the moon.'
[3] By Li Tai-Po. See *Tang* Poems; Standard edition.
[4] *Vicar of Wakefield*, Ch. X.
[5] Morally, of course. It was a satire of the poet on the men of his days.

struck by the fact that all the names just mentioned end with that word. *Tze* is a term of veneration applied in ancient times to men of profound learning or high positions. It is also an elliptical form for *Fu Tze*, meaning 'Master'. This explains the *Fu* in the word *Confucius*, Latinized by Western scholars for *Kung Fu Tze*, by which or, shortly, *Kung Tze* (The Master Kung), one calls Confucius in Chinese. Another name, similarly Latinized but without the *Fu*, is Mencius, who in Chinese is called *Meng Fu Tze* or, shortly, *Meng Tze* (The Master Meng). All the great philosophers of the classical period are honoured by the term *Tze*. Besides them three philosophers of the *Sung* Dynasty (A.D. 960-1127), the two Ching Brothers and Chu Hsi, as mentioned before, [1] are also accorded the same honour.

With these preliminary explanations an outline of the different schools of philosophy mentioned may be set out in the following pages.

PHILOSOPHY OF LAO TZE

Lao Tze is now the acknowledged founder of Taoism. *Lao* is not the surname of the philosopher, but means 'old'. Therefore Lao Tze means the 'Old Master'. The exact date of his birth is not known; but as it is traditionally believed that he was once consulted by Confucius on matters of *Li* (moral rules of correct conduct), they must have been contemporaries. History records little about his life. What is best known of him is a work of his on philosophy, entitled *Tao Tek Jing*, consisting of eighty-one chapters. It deals with fundamental questions, and the philosophy it teaches is very original, though often clothed in paradoxes and sometimes a little mystic, forming thus a fruitful source of philosophic speculation even beyond the national boundary. His philosophy has been characterized by some as that of 'doing nothing'. This is misleading. There are, it is true, a few passages in his essay that seem to indicate a tendency in favour of something like the doctrine of *laissez-faire*, e.g.:

'If you do the *not doing*, nothing will not be in order.' (Ch. 3.)

According to one interpretation [2] 'not doing' means tranquillity, and 'nothing will not be in order' means that everything will flourish. In other words, tranquillity breeds prosperity. This is understandable. If, however, we take the words literally, they may seem to be somewhat mystic; yet from the words '*do the not doing*', it is tolerably clear that the philosopher does not mean to teach a doctrine of simply 'doing nothing'. A reasonable interpretation would be that nature

[1] See *ante*, p. 58.
[2] *History* by Sze Ma Chien, Bk. CXXX, p. 4, commentary.

should be allowed to take its own course as far as possible, and that unnecessary interference, though well intended, might often have the opposite effect. Whatever may be the applicability or inapplicability of such a doctrine as a general rule, particularly in the complications of modern life, anyone who has any experience in affairs must have sometimes found that the adoption of a passive attitude within certain limits amounts almost to prudence. The Chinese *sometimes* say: 'The best solution of the unsolvable is not to attempt to solve it.' This is the paraphrase of a philosophic pun (*E buoo liou liou tsee*, literally meaning 'by not solving solve it'), which plays upon the word 'solve', meaning also 'to end', and displays an attitude that lies between, on the one hand, 'To take arms against a sea of troubles, And by opposing end them?' and, on the other, 'To die: to sleep; and, by a sleep to say we end the heart-ache and the thousand natural shocks that flesh is heir to.' [1] For the pun means solving (i.e., ending) the unsolvable (or 'a sea of troubles') not by 'opposing', but by doing nothing, and yet not by 'sleeping', or forgetting it, but by leaving it to be solved by time and changed circumstances—a natural *ending* of an 'outrageous fortune'.

This is, of course, not meant to be the meaning of the doctrine under discussion, but only something by the way. However, it is noteworthy that in recent years there are medical authorities, who, as a result of research and experience, are, in certain treatments, in favour of leaving nature undisturbed. The following passages furnish also a vivid illustration:

1. 'When you are ill, take no medicine, but take care, and you will be a doctor of medium ability to yourself.' [2]

2. 'The child of an eminent doctor dies in most cases through illness; that of an eminent sorcerer dies in most cases through spiritual influence.' [3] For in both cases there is the risk of overdoing; because the parent is eminent in the art of cure.

SELECTED SAYINGS OF LAO TZE [4]

1. 'Namelessness is the origin of the universe; naming is the mother of all things.' (Ch. 1.)

[1] Shakespeare: *Hamlet*, Act. III, Sc. I, Ls. 59-61.
[2] A saying.
[3] *Collected Ancient Essays:* 'Essay On Deep Thought', by Fong Hsiao Yu.
[4] These are taken from the *Tao Tek Jing*, but form only a part of the different chapters referred to. There is no orthodox commentary of the text, and, in consequence, some parts of it have been interpreted in different ways by different commentators, forming a fruitful source of philosophical speculations.

At the beginning of the universe things had only a physical existence, which becomes a certain thing through naming. Hence, it is
naming that gives birth to things.

2. 'If things that are difficult to obtain are not prized, people
will not steal; if what is desirable is not seen, the mind will not
be disturbed.' (Ch. 3.)

These propositions should, of course, be understood largely in the
relative rather than the absolute sense, which may seem too sweeping.
However, their truth is seldom evident until one is confronted with it.

3. 'Heaven and Earth are not benevolent: they treat all things
like *grass dogs*' (objects used on sacrificial occasions and abandoned
after they have served the purpose). (Ch. 5.)

That is to say, Heaven and Earth are neutral, representing a
natural law, operating without mercy or malice towards all.

4. 'When there are knowledge and intelligence, there will be
great deceit and hypocrisy. When the Six Relations (i.e., parents
and children, elder and younger brothers, husband and wife) are
in discord, there will be (revealed the truly) filial son. When the
country is in calamity, there will be (revealed the truly) loyal
minister.' (Ch. 18.)

Paradoxes, real or apparent, such as these, are very characteristic
of the philosophy of Lao Tze. However, that knowledge, and not
merely 'a little knowledge', may be dangerous recalls not the words of
Pope, 'A little learning is a dangerous thing', [1] but the Biblical story
of the forbidden fruit.

Adversity, while it is always a test of virtue, often also brings forth
its very existence. [2] Moreover, if harmony always prevails in the
family and peace perpetually reigns in the country, people will hardly
realize in full the meaning and sweetness of love and loyalty, like
those who, 'being frugal by habit, scarcely knew that temperance
was a virtue'. [3]

5. 'It is when you do not dispute that nobody in the world can
dispute with you.' (Ch. 22.)

In the words of the philosopher himself, 'Nature does not dispute
(but takes its normal course) and succeeds well.' (Ch. 73.) Cases are

[1] *Essay on Criticism.*
[2] See *post*, p. 167, for the story of Min Tze Hen, who in his tender age owed the
revelation of his great filial piety to the unkindness of his stepmother.
[3] Oliver Goldsmith: *Vicar of Wakefield*, Ch. IV.

also not wanting, where one who does not assert his own merits receives the highest recognition.

6. 'Soldiers (i.e. war) are instruments of evil, to be used only in case of absolute necessity.' (Ch. 31.) 'A great war is bound to be followed by years of affliction.' (Ch. 30.)

The wisdom of the first *dictum*, which practically condemns what is now called 'the recourse to war as an instrument of national policy', is amply demonstrated in the two World Wars; the truth of the second was fully shown in the lean years that followed after the first World War.

7. 'He who knows others is wise; he who knows himself is luminous. He who conquers others has strength; he who conquers himself is vigorous.' (Ch. 33.)

In other words, self-knowledge of one's own shortcomings and self-control are the 'better halves' of wisdom and valour.

8. 'All things of the universe grow out of something, which itself grew out of nothing.' (Ch. 40.)

In other words, existence presupposes non-existence, which, if it 'existed', must have preceded existence.

9. 'Greatness materializes at a late hour.' (Ch. 41.)

These words must afford no little encouragement to those who fail in their first attempts at anything that is worth attainment, or who have worthy ambitions that are yet to be attained. English history, for instance, has so far produced only one Younger Pitt, most other statesmen whose achievements shine in its pages being or approaching to be 'Grand Old Men'.

10. 'What is the softest of the universe can go against what is the hardest of the universe.' (Ch. 43.)
'The meek prevails over the strong (i.e., what is harsh or violent).' (Ch. 78.)

These propositions, being somewhat the opposite of the saying, 'Diamond cut diamond', recall rather the words of the Bible, 'Blessed are the meek: for they shall inherit the earth,' [1] and may be best explained in the philosopher's own language. 'Nothing of the world', says he, 'is softer and milder than water; yet it can go against what is the hardest and, physically, the strongest, and never fails to vanquish it (in the long run).' (Ch. 78.) 'When a man is alive,

[1] St. Matthew, Ch. V, 5.

his body is soft and supple; but death makes it hard and rigid. All things of the botanic world are soft and pliable when they are alive, but become dry and hard when they are dead. Therefore hardness and rigidity are the signs of death, while softness and mildness are the signs of life.' (Ch. 76.) As an illustration, there is a story that a man, who was asked whether hardness or softness was intrinsically the stronger, gave his answer for the latter, saying: 'I am now eighty years of age. Though my teeth (which are hard) have fallen one after another, my tongue (which is soft) still remains.'

11. 'He who covets fame will exhaust himself; he who accumulates much runs the risk of losing all; he who knows when to be content will not be disgraced; he who knows when to stop will not be in danger.' (Ch. 44.)

12. 'The most innocent has the semblance of being guilty; the most clever has the semblance of being dull; the most eloquent has the semblance of speaking with difficulty.' (Ch. 45.)

The first proposition finds its expression in the triumph of justice in acquitting the innocent in complicated cases; the second recalls the saying, 'All that glitters is not gold'; the third reminds me of the impression, in my first reading of *Julius Caesar* in Shakespeare, that Antony seems to speak with hesitation.

13. 'No (cause of) crime is greater than being desirable; no (cause of) calamity is greater than being in lack of contentment; no fault (as a cause of calamity) is greater than being passionate for possession.' (Ch. 46.)

The last two propositions need no comment. The first must be evident to those who remember the story of the *Rajah's Diamond* in Robert Louis Stevenson's *New Arabian Nights* or the Chinese saying: 'The man has committed no crime, but the gem he carries makes him guilty (i.e., the object of crime).' [1]

14. 'To those who are good, I would be good; to those who are not good, I would also be good.' (Ch. 49.)

This, it may be observed, is not quite the same as 'recompensing injury with kindness'. In the one case, like the Confucian teaching, 'abound in love to all', [2] the act of being good to those who are not good has no relation to any specific wrong on the part of the 'not good'; it is simply a benevolent attitude adopted towards mankind generally. In the other, however, there seems to be an implication

[1] *Jaw Chuan*, Bk. I, Title 'Duke Yu coveted the Jade Sword'.
[2] See *ante*, p. 85.

that the kindness proceeds in direct response to some wrongful act on the part of others. The distinction may not always be obvious, but exists. For instance, there may be little or no distinction between the case:

'To those who are polite I would be polite, and to those who are impolite I would also be polite,'

and the case:

'A man has been impolite to me (injury); but I will be polite to him (kindness).'

Indeed this would always be the course of conduct that a gentleman would adopt and, in so doing, he, like the King of England, 'can do no wrong'. Let us, however, vary a little the illustration as follows:

'To those who are good, I would send them each a cake on their birthdays; to those who are not good, I would also send them each a cake on their birthdays.'

This may be capricious, but nobody could see anything amiss in it. There are persons who do send Christmas presents to convicted criminals. But the case will not be quite the same, if you say:

'A person has deliberately knocked me down on my birthday (injury). I must send him a cake on his birthday (kindness).'

One may, perhaps, argue that if you should send a cake to every person on his birthday, whether he is good or bad, the person who has deliberately knocked you down on your birthday would necessarily be one of the recipients of your bounties. The answer to this is that I do not send him the cake for having deliberately knocked me down.

15. 'More laws there are, more thefts (i.e. crimes) there will be.' (Ch. 57.)

Compare Milton's line:

'So many laws argue so many sins.' [1]

16. 'Govern a great country as you would cook a small fish.' (Ch. 60.)

In other words, do it with care, and do not overdo it.

17. 'The female always conquers (the male) by being passive.' (Ch. 61.)

[1] *Paradise Lost*, Bk. XII, L. 283; 2nd ed.

The Chinese in their philosophy use the term *Yin* (passive) for expressing the female sex, and the term *Yang* (active) for expressing the male sex. In the expression *Yin Yang* (female and male) it is the *Yin* that is given precedence. Possibly, the traditional view that women are of the weaker sex may one day have to be revised.

18. 'Recompense injury with kindness.' (Ch. 63.) This has been discussed in the preceding chapter.

19. 'Promises lightly made must often lack fulfilment; easy successes must often be fraught with difficulties. The sage never takes things easy; therefore he never encounters difficulties.' (Ch. 63.)

'Sincere words are not pleasing; pleasing words are not sincere. The good are not disputatious; the disputatious are not good. He who knows (profoundly) does not (profess to) know many things; he who (professes to) know many things does not know (profoundly). The sage does not accumulate (things for himself). The more he gives to others, the more (he feels) he possesses.' (Ch. 81.)

20. 'The net of Heaven is vast. Its meshes may be large, but nothing will escape from it. (Ch. 73.) The way of Heaven admits of no favouritism. It is always with the good.' (Ch. 79.)

PHILOSOPHY OF MOH TZE

The second school of philosophy is headed by Moh Tze, who lived in the period of the *Warring States* (481-205 B.C.) but before Mencius (372 B.C.), and is now known generally by his work, consisting of fifteen books. He was no 'armchair' theorist, but a very energetic man of action. Not contented with the mere enunciation of political doctrines, he would have society reconstructed. He preached the doctrine of 'equal' or 'universal' love [1] and certain others so similar in some respects to Buddhism that there were people in the *Tang* Dynasty who called Buddhism Mohism. With the spirit of the Puritans, he would ban most, if not all, forms of amusements, [2] and believing that economy is the most fruitful source of wealth and social happiness, he would insist on a minimum of expenditure and the interdiction of all things that are not strictly necessary or may be classed as luxury. [3] Above all, he vehemently condemned war as a policy of State. [4] It is remarkable that at a time distant from the

[1] *Moh Tze*, Bk. IV.
[2] *Moh Tze*, Bk. IX.
[3] *Moh Tze*, Bk. VI.
[4] *Moh Tze*, Bk. V. Title *Anti-Aggression*.

present by nearly twenty-five centuries, he should have forestalled
the Kellogg Pact. Reading his work, in connection with his missions
of peace, one cannot help feeling that, if he were a man of the present
century and provided, I suppose, he spoke at least one of the principal European languages, he might have saved mankind from the
misery of two world wars. A vivid story, apparently recorded by his
disciples, who were many, and some of whom held high offices in
different States, was told in his work that when he had heard that
a large and powerful State, *Cho*, was about to invade a small and weak
State, *Sung*, he made a special journey, lasting ten days and nights,
to *Cho* in order to persuade her to abandon the plan of invasion. On
arrival in *Cho*, he first sought an interview with her Prime Minister,
Kung Shu Pan. As he was a well-known philosopher, his request for
an interview was readily granted. At the interview he was asked by
the Prime Minister Kung what he (Kung) could do for him. He
replied that there was a certain disreputable man in the North, whom
he wanted to kill and desired that Kung would help him. Kung was
displeased. He then offered Kung a thousand ducats for his help, but
Kung said: 'It is a question of principle that I would not kill anyone.'
Thereupon he rose from his seat, bowed twice to Kung, and said:

'I have heard that you, Sir, have invented a military ladder (an
engine of siege) with which you are going to invade *Sung*. What
wrong has *Sung* committed to justify the invasion? *Cho* possesses a
territory that exceeds the needs of her people, while *Sung* has not
enough for the needs of hers. If you destroy a State that "has not"
for the aggrandizement of a State that "has", this cannot be called
wisdom. Since *Sung* has committed no wrong, and you attack it,
this cannot be called benevolence (i.e., justice). If you know an act
to be wrong and yet do not prevent it, this cannot be called loyalty
to duty. If you try to prevent it and do not succeed, this cannot be
called competence. If you would not as a matter of principle take
a single life and yet would not mind killing many, this cannot be
called consistency.'

Kung admitted that his arguments were reasonable; but said that
it was too late to alter the decision, because the plan of invasion had
been submitted to the King. Thereupon he requested an audience, at
which the following dialogue took place:

'Suppose', said Moh Tze, 'there is a man who, in spite of the
possession of a fine carriage, would desire to steal the dilapidated
chariot of his neighbour; in spite of the possession of fine garments,
would desire to steal the rags of his neighbour; in spite of the

possession of wheat and meat in abundance, would desire to steal the draff and chaff of his neighbour; what would Your Majesty think of him?'

'He must be a victim of kleptomania,' replied the King.

'Now', said Moh Tze, 'the territory of *Cho* is ten times that of *Sung*. The comparison is just like that of the fine carriage with the dilapidated chariot. The natural resources of *Cho* are immense, whereas those of *Sung* are almost *nil*. The comparison is just like that of the fine garments with the rags and of the wheat and meat with the draff and chaff. Pardon me, Your Majesty, for saying that your contemplated invasion of *Sung* puts you and the man just described in the same boat.'

The King, moved by this appeal, was willing to reconsider his decision. Then, as the story went, Moh Tze played, in the presence of the King, a game of strategy with the Prime Minister, who used a broken stick as his new weapon, while the philosopher used a girdle as the city wall. In nine games successively, the attacks were repulsed. Then the following conversation ensued:

'I know how to defeat you, but I do not want to say it,' said the Prime Minister.

'I know, too, what you mean,' replied the philosopher, 'but I do not want to say it.'

'What is it?' interposed the King.

'What your Prime Minister meant is', said the philosopher, 'that, by killing me, *Sung* will be deprived of the benefit of my strategy, and can then be successfully invaded. But three hundred of my pupils have already been taught the strategy, and are waiting on the city wall of *Sung* for the impending attack.'

The King then stopped the invasion. [1]

This may sound to the modern ear like a fairytale, but is genuine history all the same. If my readers have not found it wearisome, let me give one more; not that they may be amused, but that they may have an intimate idea of the man whose philosophy is being related here.

The King of State *Lu* was about to invade State *Cheng*. Moh Tze, having heard of this, sought an audience of the King of *Lu*, at which the dialogue was as follows:

'If in *Lu*', asked Moh Tze, 'big towns attack small towns, and big families attack small families, for the purpose of plunder, what will Your Majesty think of that?'

[1] *Moh Tze*, Bk. XIII, Title, *Kung Shu*, No. 50.

'All those who are within my territory', replied the King, 'are my subjects. If big towns attack small towns, and big families attack small families, for the purpose of plunder, I will have them severely punished.'

'The Empire in relation to Heaven', said Moh Tze, 'is just like the territory of *Lu* in relation to you. If you invade *Cheng*, Heaven will punish you.'

'Why, Master,' replied the King, 'do you want to dissuade me from invading *Cheng*? My policy would be only in accord with the wish of Heaven; for, as the rulers of *Cheng* have for three generations been guilty of parricide, it must be the wish of Heaven that they should be chastised.'

'Suppose the case of an unruly son', said Moh Tze, 'where, while the father is beating him for unruly conduct, a neighbour should come along with a pole and hit him hard, saying that he does so only in accord with the wish of the father, is not this absurd?'

'In the light of what you have said,' replied the King, 'then what the world says to be right is not necessarily right?'

'The world', rejoined Moh Tze, 'generally knows small things, but not great things. When a man has stolen a dog or a pig, he is called wicked; but if he has stolen a kingdom or city, nobody thinks he is wrong.'[1]

The concluding part of the dialogue recalls the saying already quoted of the philosopher Chwang Tze, viz.:

'He who steals a coin is hanged;
He who steals a State is crowned.'[2]

SELECTED SAYINGS OF MOH TZE

1. 'In very ancient times, when men were still primitive and no such thing as government or punishment existed, there was no standard of righteousness. One man had one standard, another had another, and the more men there were, the more standards there were also. Therefore every man thought that he himself alone was right, and that every other was wrong; complaints and ill-feelings arose even between parent and child[3] and among brothers, ending in separation; and the people among themselves were like water and fire, hating one another like poison, so that no person would help others, though he was well able to do so, or would

[1] *Moh Tze*, Bk. XIII, Title, *Lu Yun*, No. 49.
[2] See *ante*, p. 34.
[3] Lit., father and child.

share his superfluous property with others, though it was left to
rot and perish, or would teach others the right way (though he
knew it). Thus the world was in a state of complete chaos, and
men were just like beasts. It was at last realized that this was due
to the absence of a ruler. Therefore, a man of virtue and merit was
elected to be Emperor. After the Emperor had been elected, it was
felt that he alone could not rule. . . . In consequence, other men
of virtue and merit were selected to assist him. But on account of
the vastness of the Empire and the difference of the people in
various parts of it, together with their conflicts of interests, all of
which could not be settled directly (by the Central Government),
the Empire was divided into States to be governed directly by their
own rulers assisted by men of virtue and merit selected from the
country. When all these were done, the Emperor issued decrees
to the people, providing that all acts found to be good or bad should
henceforth be reported to those who governed, and that whatever
those who governed might consider to be right must be regarded
as right by all and whatever they might consider to be wrong must
be regarded as wrong by all.' [1]

This may be regarded as the historical basis of a *Social Contract*,
and one wonders whether Rousseau ever had knowledge of the
writings of this Chinese philosopher.

2. 'If one has the same regard for the house of another as he has
for his own, who will commit theft? If one has the same regard
for the person of another as he has for his own, who will inflict
injuries on others? If one has the same regard for the family of
another as he has for his own, who will cause disturbance? If one
has the same regard for the country of another as he has for his
own, who will make war?' [2]

This is the gist of what is known as Moh Tze's doctrine of 'Equal
Love', which not only regards selfishness in any form as the root of
all evils and, consequently, altruism as the panacea, but also insists
that one's love for others should be the same for all without distinction or discrimination, based on any consideration. The said
doctrine is often spoken of, or translated, as 'the Doctrine of Universal Love'; but as it goes beyond mere universality and dwells on
equality or non-discrimination as well, the term 'Equal Love' is more
appropriate. Moreover, the doctrine of universal love is, properly
speaking, a doctrine of the Confucian School, which preaches *Yun*

[1] *Moh Tze*, Bk. III, *Shang Tung*, No. 11.
[2] *Moh Tze*, Bk. IV, *Jen Aou*, No. 14.

(perfect benevolence), *Shu* (to act to others as one would act to oneself), and the precept that men should from their days of youth learn to 'abound in love to all'. [1] It is on the idea of being 'equal', as distinguished from being 'universal', that Mencius criticized Moh Tze's doctrine; for it would be against man's nature that one should love another man's father exactly like one's own. [2] Indeed, Moh Tze himself says, as shown in the next paragraph, 'A bondman who serves his parents does not merely serve men', thus impliedly making a distinction, as it is rightly so; for, in serving one's parents, the service is rendered in consequence of a natural duty and not from a contract or a status imposed.

3. 'A thing may seem to be so and is so, or may seem to be so but is not so. A white horse is a horse. To ride on a white horse is simply horse-riding. A bondman is a man. To love a bondman is simply to love man. A bondman serves men; but a bondman who serves his parents does not merely serve men, nor does the fact that a man, who loves his younger sister [3] having a handsome face, mean that he loves a handsome woman. A thief is a man. But when we say that there are many thieves, this does not mean many men, just as "no thief" does not mean no man. Consequently, to love thieves does not mean to love men, and not to love thieves does not mean not to love men.' [4]

This is an illustration of Moh Tze's doctrine concerning the proper way of looking at things and discerning between right and wrong.

4. 'If a man, who is asked to lead a pig and is incompetent, would decline, is it not absurd that a man, who is asked to be the Prime Minister of a State and is incompetent, should consent?' [5]

This remark is certainly a very poignant one.

5. 'Tze Chin asked: "Is it profitable to talk much?"'
'Moh Tze replied: "Some creatures like the frogs and certain insects croak and cry day and night until their mouths get dry, and yet nobody listens to them. The cocks crow only at a certain hour in the morning, and the whole world is awakened by them. What is, therefore, the good of talking much? What matters is to talk at the right moment." ' [6]

[1] See *ante*, p. 85, 'Doctrine of Confucius', No. 1.
[2] See *Mencius*, Bk. III, Pt. II, Ch. 8, Sec. 9.
[3] Lit., 'brother'; but as the word was sometimes used in ancient days also to mean sister (see *post*, p. 176), the translation is believed to be correct.
[4] *Moh Tze*, Bk. XI, *Siou Chu*, No. 45.
[5] *Moh Tze*, Bk. XII, *Kwei Yi*, No. 47.
[6] *Moh Tze*, Bk. XV, Title, *Yat Vun*.

It was Burke who said: 'It generally argues some degree of natural impotence of mind, or some want of knowledge of the world, to hazard plans of government, except from a seat of authority.'[1]

Compare also: 'A man who does not talk (too much and thoughtlessly) is sure to hit the mark when he speaks.'[2]

PHILOSOPHY OF HAN FEI TZE

The third school of philosophy is the *Fa Chia* (Juridical School) headed by Han Fei Tze (or Han Fei), who lived in the third century before the Christian era. A prince of State *Han* by birth, he learned what may now be called political science from the great philosopher Hsun Tze, and had, as his fellow student, Li Se, future Prime Minister of the First Emperor of the *Chin* Dynasty. This school of philosophy regards, as futile and out of date, the time-honoured doctrine of benevolent rule, preached by the Confucian School, and insists on government by law, particularly in the form of rewards and punishments faithfully and sternly enforced, as the only political wisdom.[3] The point is pushed so far that no relaxation of the law is allowed even on moral ground, for fear of weakening the force or authority of law and sowing the seed of confusion.[4] When a later exponent of the Juridical School was asked what would happen if the law was bad, his answer was: 'Bad law is better than no law, because it establishes uniformity. If you divide money or·cattle by drawing lots, it does not follow that such drawing makes a fair division, but disputes will thus be avoided.'[5] This ancient view is rather interesting in the light of the modern view of Bentham, who thinks that 'every law is an evil, for every law is an infraction of liberty, and that government has but the choice of evils'.[6]

But the doctrines of the Juridical School consist not so much in the advocation of the supremacy of law—a principle which nobody would contest, and which is in fact also the teaching of the Confucian School, as Mencius has vividly illustrated in the supposed case of homicide committed by the father of Emperor Shun[7]—as in the supreme

---

[1] Speech on the *Conciliation with America*.

[2] Confucius: *Lun Yu*, Pt. XI, Ch. 13. This saying was probably not intended to be of a general application; because it was spoken specifically in approval of a remark made by the disciple Min Tze Hen, well known for filial piety, (see *post*, p. 167, for a story about him). But it gives much food for thought all the same.

[3] See *Han Fei Tze*, especially Chs. 48-51 (Bks. XVIII-XX); Ed. *Sze Bu Bei Yao*.

[4] See Ch. 49 (Bk. XIX).

[5] *Seun Tze*, Ch. 1.

[6] *Theory of Legislation*, p. 48; Ed. C. K. Ogden.

[7] See *ante*, p. 44.

belief that law alone is the panacea, almost to the entire exclusion of the human factor. Such a view, treating law as if it were almost an automatic machine, rather assumes that those who administer the law are necessarily good, and ignores the fact that law is after all made and administered by men. Curiously enough, it was his master Hsun Tze, who said: 'It is men, not laws, that govern.' [1]—a dictum having its echo in the following words of William Penn (1682):

'Wherefore governments rather depend upon men, than men upon governments. Let men be good, and the government cannot be bad. If it be ill they will cure it. But if men be bad, let the government be never so good, they will endeavour to warp and spoil it to their turn. I know some say, let us have good laws, and no matter for the men that execute them. But let them consider, that though good laws do well, good men do better.' [2]

As the undoubted most brilliant exponent of the Juridical School, Han Fei is generally spoken of as the greatest jurist in Chinese history. But he must not be understood, as he often is, in the same sense as Gaius or Justinian. What he taught were not things like *vinculum juris* [3] or *nemo debet bis vexari* [4] or *vigilantibus non dormientibus equitas subvenit*, [5] but methods of government, based, *inter alia*, on safeguard of power, maintenance of vigilance, and reliance on the efficacy of law or, rather, rewards and punishments. A great part of his work was primarily intended for the instruction of kings, princes, and those destined to be rulers, particularly 'to put them on their guard', in the light of striking historical precedents, recalling, in many instances, [6] Shakespeare's words in *Julius Caesar*, such as, 'Security gives way to conspiracy' and 'None that I know will be, much that I fear may chance'. [7] In this respect, and in this only, there is a certain resemblance between his work and Machiavel's *Prince*. But the essential difference between the two is that there is in the work of Han Fei not a word that may be said to be 'Machiavellian'. Two instances will suffice:

1. While Machiavel cynically teaches: 'A Prince . . . who is

[1] *Hsun Tze*, Ch. 12; Ed. *Sze Bu Bei Yao*, Bk. VIII.
[2] See Arnold J. Lien and Merle Fainsod: *The American People and their Government*, p. xi; Appleton-Century Co., 1934.
[3] Bond of law.
[4] A man must not be put twice in peril for the same offence. Kenny: *Outlines of Criminal Law*, p. 475 (1929).
[5] A maxim of Equity in Anglo-Saxon jurisprudence, meaning that Equity gives relief only to those who apply for it in due time.
[6] See Chs. 30-5 (Bks. IX-XIV).
[7] Act II, Sc. III, Ls. 8 and 32.

wise and prudent cannot or ought not to keep his parole, when the keeping of it is to his prejudice. . . . Nevertheless, it is of great consequence to play the hypocrite well'; [1] Han Fei, as we shall see, insists on the importance of keeping faith, though the matter concerned may itself be of no importance, saying that 'if one makes it a habit of keeping promises even in small things, one will not fail to keep promises in great things'. [2]

2. While Machiavel counsels that a prince is to have no other design, nor thought, nor study, but war; [3] Han Fei, like Lao Tze, instructs that 'soldiers (i.e., war) being an instrument of evil should not be employed without careful consideration'. [4]

Han Fei was no less renowned by his work as a philosopher than by his birth as a prince, possessing, even in his lifetime, a fame surpassing that of Voltaire at the time when his company was solicited by Frederick the Great and other Crowned Heads of Europe; for when a copy of his work first fell into the hands of the King of *Chin*, then the most powerful kingdom of the *Warring States* period, the latter was so impressed by its contents that he said that if he could meet the author and have him as his adviser, he (the King) might die without regret. It is, however, remarkable that, in spite of Han Fei's own philosophy that a ruler should always be 'on his guard', he himself should be 'off his guard' and die in the prison of *Chin*, thanks to the intrigue of his former fellow student, Li Se. [5] Taking his work as a whole, it may be said that his doctrines consist in conclusions drawn from concrete cases rather than in *a priori* principles, that his opinions were not a little influenced by the time in which he lived, when political morality, measured by the traditional standard, was at the lowest ebb, and that his preference for the efficacy of law to benevolent rule and personal virtue was possibly the result of a feeling of despair, without realizing, apparently, that, as Mencius says, 'law cannot prevail by itself'. [6] His argument against benevolent government, it should be mentioned, is not that it is fundamentally unsound, but that it was unsuitable to his time, because circumstances had then materially changed. [7] However, his conception of benevolent government is, at least in some instances,

[1] *Prince*, Ch. XVIII; Ed. G. Routledge & Sons.
[2] See *post*, p. 127.
[3] *Prince*, Ch. XIV.
[4] *Han Fei Tze*, Ch. 2 (Bk. I).
[5] See Preface to *Han Fei Tze*; Ed. *Sze Bu Bei Yao*.
[6] See *post*, p. 146.
[7] Ch. 49 (Bk. XIX).

not free from confusion with the notion of sentimentality, or mere
tenderness of heart, in government, e.g.:

> 'It is said', says he, 'that the ancient sage kings, on hearing that
> a person was punished with death, would shed tears. . . . If a ruler
> should shed tears when a person is punished according to law,
> this may be the way of being benevolent but is not the way to
> govern.'[1]

Similarly, his view regarding the doctrine of the Confucian School
that rulers should consider themselves to be *in loco parentis*[2] to the
people, that is, should take such an interest in the welfare of
the people as parents would in that of their children, is open to the
observation that he seems to have confounded parental interest with
parental indulgence. For instance, he says:

> 'People are spoilt by affection but submit to authority.'[3]

But it is obvious, as we shall see in the doctrines of Confucius and
Mencius on politics, that neither mere tenderness of heart towards
the people is what is meant by benevolent government, nor to be
'parental' in government is simply to spoil the people with affection.
It may be that the Confucian School, in preaching the gospel of
benevolent or 'parental', as distinguished from 'paternal', government, rather aims at perfection, as distinguished from idealism. But
this is no fault; for one must aim at the top in order to be sure to
reach a point above the middle, just as one must aim at being a
gentleman in order to be sure not to become a rascal, and this is true
no less in public, than in private, life.

With these observations it may be summed up that Han Fei's
philosophy is original and practical, his reasonings are sharp and
shrewd, and his illustrations are full of human interest and rich in
historical precedents, some of which are saturated with a high sense
of humour, e.g.:

> 'The Duke of *Chi*, who had lost his hat one day as a result of
> drunkenness, felt shameful and, in consequence, held no court for
> three days. His Prime Minister Kwan Chung said to him that this
> would not do, and suggested that he might redeem his shame by
> some benevolent act. Pleased with this advice, the Duke ordered
> a distribution of food among the poor and the release of prisoners
> detained for minor offences. Three days after, the people (looking

[1] Ch. 49 (Bk. XIX).
[2] See *post*, p. 138.
[3] Ch. 49 (Bk. XIX).

for more favours) sang in the street: "Why the Duke has not lost his hat again!" '[1]

Han Fei saw in this ridiculous incident the result of the violation of two political maxims:

1. To give rewards only where reward is due.
2. To inflict punishments always where punishment is deserved.

A violation of either of these maxims is, according to him, to sow the seed of unruliness; for, in the first, people are encouraged to indulge in expectations of unmerited favour and, in the second, they are encouraged to commit unlawful acts with the hope of immunity.

SELECTED SAYINGS OF HAN FEI TZE

1. 'If promises of reward and threats of punishment are not faithfully kept and strictly carried out, men will not (be prepared to) give their lives (in the performance of duties).'[2]
2. 'An enlightened ruler does not give secret rewards, or (take upon himself to) remit punishments (or pardon crimes).'[3]
Still worse would it be therefore for rulers, like James II, to claim *Dispensing* and *Suspending* powers.
3. 'No State can be always strong or always weak. Those which are strong in the enforcement of law will be strong; those which are weak in the enforcement of law will be weak.'[4]
4. 'Order and strength (of a State) spring from the observance of law; disorder and weakness (of a State) spring from the disregard of it.'[5]
5. 'Rewards that are excessive spoil the people; punishments that are excessive cease to be deterrent.'[6]

These words are those of a statesman no less than those of a jurist. The reduction of capital punishments and the abolition of the cruel forms of penalty, in modern time, are therefore not only humane but also politic.

6. 'The King of *Yueh* said to his minister Vun Chung: "I wish to invade *Wu*. Do you think I can succeed?" The latter replied: "Yes, but rewards (for merits) must be substantial and prompt,

[1] Ch. 37 (Bk. XV).
[2] Ch. 1 (Bk. I).
[3] Ch. 5 (Bk. I).
[4] Ch. 6 (Bk. II).
[5] Ch. 35 (Bk. XIV).
[6] Ch. 19 (Bk. V).

while punishments (for demerits) must be severe and sure. If you are in earnest, why not set the palace on fire to have a test?" The King followed the advice and accordingly had the palace set on fire. But nobody tried to put the fire out. Thereupon it was decreed that those who should die in trying to put the fire out would be rewarded, as if they had died in battle; those who should survive in doing so would be rewarded, as if they had been victorious in battle; and those who should make no attempt to do so would be punished, as if they had surrendered to the enemy in battle. Immediately, thousands of men ran right and left to put the fire out. This was the sure sign of victory.'[1]

It is a common saying of the Chinese that 'if you offer a handsome reward, you may be sure to find a brave man'.

7. 'The King of *Yueh*, wanting to encourage bravery before his intended invasion of *Wu*, saw an angry toad in the street, and bowed to it deeply. His carriage driver (being astonished by this strange behaviour) asked him why he did that. The King replied: "As the toad has courage like this, is it not worthy of my respect?" As soon as the people heard of this, they said: "When a toad has courage the King would show it such respect. What would he not do to a man who has courage?" In the same year in which this incident happened, there were men who, in order to show their scorn for death, offered their heads to the King.'[2]

The incident of the toad recalls a story current at the beginning of the present century that one day when an English newspaper magnate entered the lift with a friend, the latter raised his hat and bowed deeply to the lift boy. After they had come out of the lift, the newspaper magnate remonstrated with his friend for his unbecoming behaviour, saying: 'You would make discipline difficult.' In reply, his friend said: 'How do I know that one day you will not make him (the lift boy) an editor?' referring to the fact that the newspaper magnate had not long ago raised a person from a very insignificant position to the editorial chair.

8. 'A shaking mirror produces no clear image, nor does a moving measure serve as a standard. This is (a physical) law. Therefore the ancient sage kings used law as the basis of judgment. If a fixed standard is dispensed with in favour of personal skill, or law is discarded in favour of individual wisdom, it will lead to confusion.'[3]

[1] Ch. 30 (Bk. IX).
[2] Ch. 30, No. 7 (Bk. IX).
[3] Ch. 19 (Bk. V).

9. 'A man of *Cheng*, wishing to buy a pair of shoes, first took the measurement of his feet, but, through inadvertence, left it on his seat without taking it with him. When he arrived in the market and was given a pair of shoes to try on, he said: "I have forgotten to bring my measurement." Thereupon he went home to fetch it; but when he was back in the market, the shoes were already sold. Someone then asked him why he had not tried the shoes on his feet (instead of going home to fetch the measurement, which was really superfluous), he answered that he would rather trust to the measurement than to himself.' [1]

In other words, law is more reliable even than one's own judgment.

10. 'The ancients, because their eyes could not enable them to see their own faces, invented the mirror and, because their intelligence could not enable them to know themselves, adopted certain principles to go by. One never accuses the mirror of showing one's facial defects, nor does one complain of the principles to go by for revealing one's faults. If the eyes were not assisted by the mirror, one could not even adjust one's moustache or eyebrows, and if conduct were not guided by certain principles, one could not know when oneself was wrong. Se Mund Pow, realizing his own impulsive nature, wore a soft pad as a "brake", while Tung On Ue, realizing his own inertness, wore a bow as a "spur". Therefore a ruler who knows how to adjust what is deficient with what is excessive and the short with the long is enlightened.' [2]

Personally I know a man who, when still in his teens, invented a game of patience by putting on his desk a dozen or more matchboxes, only one of which contained matches, so that, every time he wanted matches, he had to go through a number of these boxes. After practising this for a few days he felt he was much better equipped for meeting disappointments, and never lost hope; because, remembering his own game of patience, he was confident that he would 'find the matches', if he had enough patience. One may say: 'For a Chinaman to cultivate patience, it might be just as well to carry coal to Newcastle!' Well, since genius has been defined as 'transcendent capacity of taking trouble', [3] let wisdom be defined as 'transcendent capacity of storing patience', which can never be too much even for a Chinaman.

---

[1] Ch. 32 (Bk. XI).
[2] Ch. 24 (Bk. VIII).
[3] Carlyle: *Frederick The Great*, Bk. IV, Ch. 3; Ed. Bedford, Clarke & Co., Vol. I, p. 331.

11. 'There is an ancient saying: "To govern is like having a shampoo." Although some hairs may have to be sacrificed, one must have it. To grudge the sacrifice of a few hairs, forgetting the advantage that may be done to the hair as a whole, is to ignore the relative importance of things.'[1]

In other words, in order to procure 'the greatest happiness to the greatest number', some sacrifice has to be made sometimes.

12. 'Confucius says: "A ruler is like a vessel, while the people are like water. If the vessel is square, the water is square; if the vessel is round, the water is round." '[2]

Those who govern should themselves behave well in order that those who are governed may well behave.

13. 'You cannot make noise with one hand, however hard you may strike (in the air); nor can you succeed, if you try to draw a circle with the right hand and a square with the left at the same time.'[3]

This is an illustration of the doctrine that no one can rule successfully without the hearty support of the people, nor can one serve two masters properly at the same time.

14. 'The maker of palanquins, when they are completed, is interested in men becoming rich and ennobled, whereas the maker of coffins, when they are completed, is interested in men dying early. This does not mean that palanquin makers are kind, and that coffin-makers are wicked. It is simply that, if men do not become rich or ennobled, the palanquins will not sell, and if there is no death, none will buy coffins. All this is simply natural (on account of their trade) without any question of wickedness.'[4]

This is an illustration of his counsels to rulers for vigilance against any secret formation of cliques or under currents that may, as a natural sequence of things and a consequence of self-interest, without being necessarily treacherous, desire and bring about their downfall.

15. 'A man of *Sung*, having found a stone containing jade, presented it to Tze Han, who refused to accept it. Then the man said: "This is a precious stone. It should be possessed by you, a gentle-

---

[1] Ch. 46 (Bk. XVIII).
[2] Ch. 32, No. 5 (Bk. XI).
[3] Ch. 28 (Bk. VIII).
[4] Ch. 17 (Bk. V). Compare this saying to the modern allegation that armament firms desire war.

man, not by me, a common person." In reply Tze Han said: "You consider the jade to be precious; but I consider the refusal to accept it as being (more) precious." ' [1]

'A person presented a rich fox fur to the King of *Tsin*, who, receiving it, exclaimed: "Alas! this poor animal had its beautiful fur as its crime!" ' [2]

Compare Lao Tze's saying: 'No (cause of) crime is greater than being desirable,' and the saying: 'The man has committed no crime, but the gem he carries makes him guilty (i.e. object of crime).' [3]

16. 'Tze Hsia (disciple of Confucius) saw Tseng Tze (another disciple of Confucius), who asked the former: "Why are you (lately) so fat?" The former replied: "I have conquered myself and am therefore fat." "What do you mean by this?" asked Tseng Tze again. "Well," said Tze Hsia, "when I was indoors, I used to think of the righteousness of the doctrines of the ancient sage kings and was influenced by it. When I was outdoors, I used to think of the pleasure that might be derived from wealth and honour and was also influenced by it. The two (thoughts) battled inside me without a decision; therefore I became thin. Now, the (thought for the) righteousness of the doctrines of the ancient sage kings has triumphed; therefore I am fat".' [4]

Personally, I know a case where a man could not sleep for days; because someone had been ungrateful to him. Ultimately, he decided to forgive and did the latter a good turn. From that moment, he felt as if a great load had been off his mind, and consequently slept well.

17. 'Kwan Chung and Chup Ming were with the Duke of *Chi* in an expedition against *Koo Jook*. As they started in Spring and returned in Winter, they lost their way on their homeward journey. Confronted with this difficulty, Kwan Chung said: "The sagacity of an old horse will assist us." Order was accordingly given that an old horse should be put to lead the way, and the way was found. In the midst of the journey across a mountain another difficulty was encountered, and this time it was that the water supply was running short. Thereupon Chup Ming said: "The ants live, in Winter, on the side of the hill that faces the sun and, in Summer, on the side of the hill that is shaded. Dig deep where the ants are, and you will find water." This was accordingly done and

[1] Ch. 21 (Bk. VII).
[2] Ch. 21 (Bk. VII).
[3] See *ante*, p. 108.
[4] Ch. 21 (Bk. VII).

water was found. If even Kwan Chung, with his wisdom, and Chup Ming, with his knowledge, would not disdain, when they were in difficulties, to seek guidance from an old horse and the ants, is it not wrong that in these days a man, not realizing his own ignorance, should belittle the wisdom of the sages?' [1]

18. 'A man was going to present to the King of Jink a certain medicine which, once taken, would, according to him, make death impossible. While he was on his way to the palace with the medicine, a sentinel asked him whether he (the sentinel) might take it, and, on receiving an affirmative reply, snatched it from the carrier's hand and swallowed it. The King, on learning this, being very indignant, ordered the sentinel to be executed. Thereupon the latter pleaded with the King, saying: "I asked the carrier whether I might take the medicine, and he answered affirmatively. It was only after this that I took it. Therefore not I but he is guilty. Moreover, as he said that the medicine would make death impossible and I have taken it, if you were to have me executed, the medicine would in fact be a 'death medicine' and he guilty of deceiving Your Majesty. Instead of killing an innocent person and exposing the fact that Your Majesty has been the victim of deception, Your Majesty had better release me." The King (being wise) pardoned him accordingly.' [2]

'A man offered to teach the King of Yen the means of becoming immortal. Order was given by His Majesty to some person to learn it; but before the latter was able to do so the man making the offer died. The King, on hearing this, was so furious that he had the person executed. Here the King failed to realize that he himself had been deceived and killed an innocent person; for nothing is of greater interest to a man than his own life, and, if he is unable to prevent his own death, he is certainly unable to teach others to live for ever.' [3]

19. 'A man of Cho sold lances and shields. In regard to the lances, he said that they would pierce through anything and, in regard to the shields, he said that nothing would pierce them through. Someone then said to him: "I will use your lances to attack your shields," and he had nothing to say.' [4]

One cannot have things both ways.

20. 'A man was employed to draw pictures for the King of Chi.

1 Ch. 22 (Bk. VII).
2 Ch. 22 (Bk. VII).
3 Ch. 32 (Bk. XI).
4 Ch. 36 (Bk. XV).

who asked him what was the most difficult thing to draw. In reply he said that dogs and horses were the most difficult. Then he was asked what was the easiest thing to draw, and he replied that ghosts were the easiest. "For", he added, "dogs and horses are known to everybody, while ghosts have no definite shape; therefore the former are difficult, and the latter are easy, to draw." ' [1]

21. 'Tsang Choong Tze was a sword expert. The ruler of *Wei* was on bad terms with the King of *Wu.* Tsang said: "The King of *Wu* loves swords, and I am a sword expert. I can offer to examine swords for him and, in trying them in his presence, kill him for you." The ruler of *Wei* replied: "You offer to do this for gain and not for righteousness. Now, *Wu* is strong and wealthy, while *Wei* is poor and weak. If you do go, I fear that you will allow yourself to be employed by the King of *Wu* against me." The man was then shown the door.' [2]

22. 'Yang Bu, younger brother of the well-known philosopher Yang Chu (who taught the philosophy of individualism), had one day gone out in a plain coat. As it rained afterwards, he took off his plain coat and came back in a pink one. His dog, not recognizing him, barked at him. This made him angry, and he wanted to hit the dog. Thereupon his brother said to him: "Don't do that. You would have done the same in such circumstances as the dog. If it had been white when it went out, and became black when it came home, would not you be surprised?" ' [3]

23. 'Yao offered his Empire to Hsu Yau. The latter refused to accept it and ran away, taking shelter at the house of his servant, who took great care of his fur hat. Where a man had refused an empire and his servant took great care of his hat, as if it would matter to him, it is obvious that the servant had no idea of what sort of man he was.' [4]

24. 'There were a man and a woman of *Wei* who were husband and wife. One day the wife prayed:

"May I acquire without whatever cost
A hundred rolls of new (and handsome) cloth!"

The husband, astonished by the moderation of her expectation, asked why she did not pray for more. "Well," replied she, "if I get more, you may keep another woman!" ' [5]

[1] Ch. 32, No. 2 (Bk. XI).
[2] Ch. 22 (Bk. VII).
[3] Ch. 23 (Bk. VIII).
[4] Ch. 23 (Bk. VIII).
[5] Ch. 31, No. 6 (Bk. X).

What the philosopher intended to mean was that fortune easily acquired was often the cloak of disaster. But the story chosen shows that although law is said to be a dry subject, lawyers are not without a rich sense of humour.

25. 'The wife of Tseng Tze was going to the market with her infant son, who cried on the way. Hoping to stop him crying, she told him that on reaching home she would kill a pig for dinner. When they reached home, Tseng Tze, who heard of this, proceeded to seize the pig. The wife stopped him, saying that she had only joked with the child. To this he replied: "You cannot joke with a child in this way. A child has no knowledge of his own, but depends for it on his parents and follows their instructions. If you deceive him, you will be teaching him to practise deceptions. This will not do." Accordingly they had the pig killed for dinner.'[1]

In the words of Han Fei himself, 'If one makes it a habit to keep promises even in small things, one will not fail to keep promises in great things.'[2]

26. 'The Duke of *Tsin* (a most powerful feudal prince living in about 650 B.C.) invaded *Yuen* (a small State), but had provisions with his army enough to last only about ten days. He therefore agreed with his ministers and high officers that the campaign should terminate in ten days. At the end of this period, however, *Yuen* did not capitulate, and accordingly he gave order for a general withdrawal of his troops. It happened at that moment that a man who had just come out from *Yuen* gave the information that *Yuen* was so exhausted in food and means of defence that it would be forced to capitulate in three days. In consequence, the Duke's advisers counselled against the withdrawal; but the Duke said: "I have agreed with my officers and men that the campaign should last only ten days. If I do not now order a retreat, it means that I have to break my promise. To take *Yuen* by breaking my promise is a thing that I would not do. He therefore ordered a retreat at once. When these words reached the ears of the people of *Yuen*, they said: "To a ruler so faithful to his words as he, should we not declare our allegiance?" They therefore capitulated. The people of *Wei*, having heard this, also capitulated, saying: "To a ruler so faithful to his words as he, should we not submit?" Confucius learning these incidents recorded them with the remark: "The (unexpected

[1] Ch. 32, Pt. II, No. 6 (Bk. XI).
[2] Ch. 32, Pt. I, No. 6 (Bk. XI).

and additional) acquisition of *Wei* in the invasion of *Yuen* is due
to being faithful to one's words." '[1]

27. 'Duke Huan (of *Chi*) had married the daughter of the Ruler
of *Chai*. One day the Duke and the Duchess were taking a pleasure
trip on a yacht. Suddenly, she caused the yacht to rock so violently
that the Duke was terrified. He stopped her doing this, but she
persisted. He was so angry that he afterwards divorced her, and
wanted to declare war on *Chai*. His Prime Minister Kwan Chung,
being consulted, advised against the expedition, saying: "You cannot make a *casus belli* out of an incident arising from flirtation." '[2]

People were more scrupulous about the ethics of war in ancient
days than some have been in modern time.

28. 'Good medicine is bitter to the mouth, but a wise man,
when advised, takes it; faithful words are unpleasant to the ear,
but an enlightened ruler listens to them.'[3]

29. 'The Duke of *Chi*, who visited *incognito* some families and
found an old man by himself, asked why he was alone. In reply,
the old man said that he had three sons, who owing to poverty
were still unmarried, and, as they were out for work, he was left
alone. Being back in the palace, the Duke told this to his Prime
Minister Kwan Chung, who said: "When there is food accumulated in store and allowed to perish, there will surely be hunger
among the people, and, when there are murmuring women in the
palace, there will surely be men without wives." The Duke exclaimed: "Good!" and ordered all the unmarried women of the
palace to get married, decreeing at the same time that in the whole
country all men, on reaching the age of twenty, and all women, on
reaching the age of fifteen, [4] should be married, so that *there should
be no murmuring woman within nor lonely man without.*'[5]

The last sentence may be said to have always been a guiding principle in Chinese sociology, constituting one of the main reasons for
which Chinese parents have been wont to arrange marriages for their
children, and contributing largely to the good morals for which
China is well known, as we shall see in the chapters on family and
marriage.

[1] Ch. 32 (Bk. XI).
[2] Ch. 32, No. 3 (Bk. XI).
[3] Ch. 32 (Bk. XI).
[4] According to *Book of Li*, the proper marriageable age for men is thirty and for
women twenty. See Bk. LXI, Title *Marriage 44, note.*
[5] Ch. 35, *Yau Jing*, No. 5 (Bk. XIV).

30. 'In ancient times, people competed in virtue; in the Middle Ages, people rivalled in intelligence; at the present day, people struggle in strength.' [1]

Han Fei, though he used the term 'Middle Ages' was speaking before the Christian era. Hence the Chinese Middle Ages were in advance of the Middle Ages of the West by more than a thousand years. His reference to the ancients, 'competing in virtue', shows that Chinese reverence for the past is not due to any inherent conservatism, but has good reasons. In speaking admiringly of a man for his virtuous act rare in these days, the Chinese would say: 'He has the ancient mood.' Similarly, the phrase 'Your ancient way shines on the people' is an idiomatic expression for conveying one's admiration or gratitude for some highly appreciative act, such as exceptional generosity or magnanimity, on the part of others. Reverence for the past, however, is not the same thing as 'looking backward' or despair in the future. The Chinese, as taught by Confucius, always place high hope in the younger generation. It was Confucius who said: 'The younger generation should be regarded with awe; for who knows that those who come after will not be equal to (or even surpass) [2] those who live at present?' [3]

PHILOSOPHY OF THE CONFUCIAN SCHOOL

I now come to the Confucian School. Logically, historically, and in order of importance, it should have been treated first. But, as I have said, it is for the sake of convenience that it has been reserved to the last. One may also ask why, as Confucian teachings have already been dealt with in the preceding chapter, they should again find a place here. The answer to this question will incidentally also supply the reason why this school of philosophy is treated at the end of this chapter. Confucius is the acknowledged Founder of the Yu Religion. Therefore his selected fundamental doctrines are treated under that heading. But it must be remembered that Confucius was once the Prime Minister of his native State—'a prophet not without honour even in his own country'—and was, though not in office, often consulted by reigning rulers and eminent men of his days both on politics and on various problems of life. He has thus left many sayings that are essentially of a philosophic nature. Besides, in treating of his philosophy, one cannot omit that of Mencius, whose doctrines form

---

[1] Ch. 49 (Bk. XIX).

[2] See orthodox commentary, which says: 'Who knows that they will not attain the peak of excellence?'

[3] Confucius: Lun Yu, Pt. IX, Ch. 22.

such an integral part of those of Confucius that the Chinese people use the expression, 'The doctrines of Confucius and Mencius' (*Kung Meng Tsee Tao*) almost as an inseparable term. And as the two may with advantage be treated together, that is why it is considered convenient to have this school of philosophy treated after the others.

SELECTED SAYINGS OF CONFUCIUS ON POLITICS

1. 'To govern a State (even) of a thousand chariots (i.e., a principality) demands devotion to duty, sincerity (deserving of the confidence of the people), economy in expenditure, love for (i.e., deep interest in the welfare of) the people, and employment of the people at the proper time (i.e., without interfering with their seasonal occupations).' [1]

'He who governs with virtue (as the basic principle) is like the North Polar Star, which remains at its place, while all the other stars turn towards it (for guidance and enlightenment).' [2]

Compare the following saying of Burke:

'There is no qualification for government but virtue and wisdom, actual or presumptive.' [3]

2. 'If the people are guided by laws, and order (i.e., conformity to law or decorum) among them is enforced by punishments, they will try to avoid the punishments, but have no sense of shame. If they are guided by virtue (in the form of good examples), and order among them is enforced by *Li* (i.e., propriety or moral rules of correct conduct), [4] they will have the sense of shame and be also reformed (i.e., become good citizens).' [5]

This does not mean that laws and punishments can ever be dispensed with in government. Indeed, when Confucius himself became Prime Minister, he had a well-known treacherous and dangerous man, named Siao Jeng Mow, executed. That is why the word 'guided' and not the word 'governed' is used. What is meant is that laws and punishments alone are insufficient for good government—a doctrine which, it will be noted, differs from the philosophy of the *Juridical*

---

[1] Confucius: *Lun Yu*, Pt. I, Ch. 5.
[2] Confucius: *Lun Yu*, Pt. II, Ch. I.
[3] Burke: *Reflections on the French Revolution*; Ed. E. J. Payne, Vol. II, p. 58.
[4] See Chapter I for a fuller meaning of the word.
[5] Confucius: *Lun Yu*, Pt. II, Ch. 3. This passage throws further light on the true meaning of the word *Li*.

School, already dealt with. In order to have good government, the State must have good rulers and good citizens, and, in order to attain this, those who govern must set good examples (i.e., Virtue) and those who are governed must be taught to cultivate in themselves a sense of moral duties and personal honour, independent of legal obligations or sanctions (i.e., *Li*). In other words, just as mere legal justice is not regarded as the ideal form of justice, so government only by laws and punishments is not considered to be the ideal form of government. The very fact that a people need constantly be threatened with the prison or the concentration camp speaks ill of the government, if not also of the people. It has been sagaciously remarked by a modern political writer that a people has only the government that it deserves. In the country where I am penning these pages, I have seen, in some parks, notices, requesting the public not to do injury to certain places, worded simply as *'cette promenade est placée sous la sauvegarde des citoyens'* [1] instead of the usual formula *'sous peine d'amende etc.'.* [2] Within the meaning of the saying under discussion, it may be said that the latter appeals to punishment, while the former appeals to *Li*, that is, the good sense of the people. The fact that the government can rely on the good sense of the people reflects no little credit on both the government and the citizens. This does not mean that the mere putting up of such notices is sufficient or will ensure their observance. What is meant is that the object of government should be directed to that end, that is, to bring the people up to that standard. In this light the passage quoted expresses almost a political truism. The doctrine therein formulated has always been accepted, if not always been observed, by the Chinese as the guiding political maxim.

3. 'Raise the upright and discard the perverse, the people will be heartily submissive. Raise the perverse and discard the upright, the people will not be heartily submissive.' [3]

4. 'It is possible to make the masses follow what should be followed, but it is not possible to make them comprehend why it should be followed.' [4]

5. 'Disciple Tze Kung asked about government. The Master said: "Have sufficient food, sufficient military preparedness, and the confidence of the people." Tze Kung asked again: "If it is imperative that one of these must go, which of the three should

[1] This public walk is placed under the care of the citizens.
[2] Under the penalty of a fine, etc.
[3] Confucius: *Lun Yu*, Pt. II, Ch. 19.
[4] Confucius: *Lun Yu*, Pt. VIII, Ch. 9.

go first?" The Master said: "Let military preparedness go." Tze Kung asked once more: "If it is imperative that one of the remaining two must go, which of them should go first?" The Master said: "Let the food go. (Without food one may die; but) from time immemorial death has been inevitable to men. Without confidence of the people government does not stand (i.e., ceases to exist)." '[1]

This is remarkable both for its wisdom and for the fact that the essentials of government are so comprehensively summed up in one sentence.

'To employ in war people not instructed (in the defence of their country) is to abandon them.'[2]

The ideal social order aimed at by Confucius is, as has been dealt with in one of his doctrines set out in the preceding chapter, a true Commonwealth for all nations, in which a common brotherhood prevails and there will be no war. But as long as the world is not yet ripe for such an ideal order, the defence of the State cannot be neglected. It would not do, therefore, to provide no adequate defence for the State, in spite of ample means at one's disposal, and to hurl an untrained people at the eleventh hour against an enemy well trained and well armed.

6. 'Chi Kang Tze (a powerful minister of *Lu*) asked Confucius about government, saying: "What is your opinion as regards killing the bad for the sake of the good (as a rule of government)?" Confucius (respectfully) replied: "Sir, in government, why need you resort to killing? If you are earnestly for good, the people will be good. The conduct of those who govern is like the wind, and that of the governed is like the grass. When the grass is blown by the wind, it must bend." '[3]

---

[1] Confucius: *Lun Yu*, Pt. XII, Ch. 7. A well-known ancient writer, Wang Chung (see *Lun Heng*, Bk. IX, p. 11) commenting on this passage, has interpreted the word 'confidence' in the last sentence as meaning 'trustworthiness' rather than 'trust' and treated the word 'stand' as the predicate of the word 'people' rather than of the word 'government' understood. But having regard to the word 'confidence' in the first sentence, which can reasonably mean only 'trust' and not 'trustworthiness', and to the fact that the question asked was about government, it is submitted that the translation rendered above, which accords with orthodox commentary, is correct.

[2] Confucius: *Lun Yu*, Pt. XIII, Ch. 30. See commentary of Chapter 29 for the words inserted in brackets, explaining the word 'instructed'.

[3] Confucius: *Lun Yu*, Pt. XII, Ch. 19.

'To govern (a people) is to make them right. If you lead them by (setting the example of) being right, who will dare to be not right?' [1]

7. 'If the personal conduct of those who govern is just and irreproachable, their commands, though unexpressed, will be observed. If their personal conduct is unjust and reproachable, their commands, though expressed, may not be obeyed.' [2]

8. 'Should good men govern a State for a century without interruption, they could have (even) the worst criminals reformed, and the death penalties abolished.' [3]

9. 'Duke Ting asked if there was a maxim (the observance of) which would bring prosperity to a country. Confucius (respectfully) replied: "So much cannot be expected from one maxim. There is, however, a popular saying: 'To be (i.e., to fill [4] the office of) ruler is difficult; to be (i.e. to fill the office of) minister is not easy.' If a ruler realizes the difficulties of being ruler (and adjusts his conduct accordingly) may it not be expected that (the observance of) this one maxim will bring prosperity to the country?" The Duke then asked: "Is there a (bad) principle (the practice of) which will bring ruin to a country?" Confucius (respectfully) replied: "So much cannot be expected from one principle. There is, however, a popular saying: 'I have no joy in being ruler save in that my words are not to be contradicted (by anyone).' If the ruler's words are right and nobody contradicts them, does not this fare well? But if they are wrong and nobody contradicts them, may it not be expected that (the practice of) this one principle will bring ruin to the country?" ' [5]

Bonar Law, who once said: 'The position of the Prime Minister is not a bed of roses,' must have felt something like the latter part of the first saying. King Canute, who, preferring helpful counsel to pleasing flattery, told his courtiers: 'The power of Kings is but vanity. He only is King who can say to the ocean: "Thus far shalt thou go and no further," ' [6] would have appreciated the second saying and all that it implies.

[1] Confucius: *Lun Yu*, Pt. XII, Ch. 17. It may be noted that the Chinese word 'government' (政) has the same pronunciation (*jeng*) as the word 'right' (正) and, as can be seen, is partly composed of the word 'right'.
[2] Confucius: *Lun Yu*, Pt. XIII, Ch. 6.
[3] Confucius: *Lun Yu*, Pt. XIII, Ch. 11. This is an old saying quoted by Confucius with approval.
[4] 'To possess and perform the duties of'—Webster's Dictionary.
[5] Confucius: *Lun Yu*, Pt. XIII. Ch. 15.
[6] *History of England*, by David Hume, p. 60,

10. 'In serving a ruler one should devote his attention to the service and consider the emolument as a matter of secondary importance.'[1]

In other words, the motto for public service is: 'Service above reward.'

'Disciple Tze Loo asked about the way in which a ruler should be served. The Master said: "Deceive him not, and correct him boldly (when he has faults)."'[2]

This sums up neatly the proper attitude of a minister towards the ruler, and explains the words of Voltaire in his homage to Confucius: '*Il ne flatte point l'empereur sous lequel il vivait.*'[3] The 'yes man' and those whom King Canute justly rebuked cannot be said to be faithful in their duties towards their political superiors, who may well profit by this and the two sayings quoted in the preceding paragraph. Chinese doctrines, which all aim at righteousness and the elevation of mankind, never teach blind obedience, and Chinese history is rich in instances where men risked not merely their careers but, like Prince Bei Gan,[4] even their lives for correcting boldly but loyally their rulers.

SELECTED SAYINGS OF CONFUCIUS OF A GENERAL PHILOSOPHICAL NATURE

1. 'Learning without thinking is empty; thinking without learning is dangerous.'[5]

Compare: 'He thinks too much: such men are dangerous.'[6]

2. '(One should) pursue learning, as if it could not be reached, and (even if it has been reached, should constantly) fear lest it may be lost.'[7]

In the words of the philosopher Ching Tze, 'in the pursuit of learning, never put off until to-morrow what you can do to-day.'[8]

3. 'In days of old men learned for self-cultivation; in these days men learn for gaining the notice of others.'[9]

[1] Confucius: *Lun Yu*, Pt. XV, Ch. 37.
[2] Confucius: *Lun Yu*, Pt. XIV, Ch. 23.
[3] Voltaire, *Dict. phil.*, éd. Kehl, *De la Chine*, section première.
[4] See *ante*, p. 99, *note*.
[5] Confucius: *Lun Yu*, Pt. II, Ch. 15.
[6] Shakespeare: *Julius Caesar*, Act I, Sc. II, L. 194.
[7] Confucius: *Lun Yu*, Pt. VIII, Ch. 17.
[8] See commentary.
[9] Confucius: *Lun Yu*, Pt. XIV, Ch. 25.

These words, spoken more than twenty-five centuries ago and not without some bitterness, tell us the original and true object of learning, which, in the language of a later sage, Mencius, is 'to recover the lost heart'. [1]

4. 'When you know a thing, avow that you know it, and, when you do not know a thing, admit that you do not know it: this is knowledge.' [2]

5. 'Every man's faults (if any) indicate the class of men to which he belongs. (Even) by observing his faults it is possible to know whether he is virtuous.' [3]

In other words, in the case of the man of virtue, 'ev'n his failings lean'd to Virtue's side'. [4]

6. 'It is possible to carry off the Commander-in-Chief of three army corps; but it is impossible to take away the will from even a simple individual.' [5]

The Second World War has shown in many instances that, though a country may be conquered, the will of its people to resist cannot be destroyed.

7. 'It is only when the time of the year becomes cold that one knows that the pine and cypress are the last to wilt.' [6]

Adversity is the test of character and loyalty.

8. 'He whose words lack modesty and moderation will find them difficult of fulfilment.' [7]

'He who is severe to himself and indulgent to others will keep resentment at a distance.' [8]

'Specious words confuse virtue (with vice); lack of tolerance in small matters spoils great plans.' [9]

'A person who gives no earnest thought to what lies afar will find anxiety that is near.' [10]

---

[1] See post, p. 149.
[2] Confucius: Lun Yu, Pt. II, Ch. 17.
[3] Confucius: Lun Yu, Pt. IV, Ch. 7. See commentary.
[4] Goldsmith: Deserted Village, L. 164.
[5] Confucius: Lun Yu, Pt. IX, Ch. 25.
[6] Confucius: Lun Yu, Pt. IX, Ch. 27.
[7] Confucius: Lun Yu, Pt. XIV, Ch. 21.
[8] Confucius: Lun Yu, Pt. XV, Ch. 14.
[9] Confucius: Lun Yu, Pt. XV, Ch. 26.
[10] Confucius: Lun Yu, Pt. XV, Ch. 11.

Compare Goethe's saying: 'The greatest difficulties often lie where we do not look for them.' [1]

9. 'By nature men resemble one another; through habit they differ widely.' [2]

10. 'Instruction admits of no distinction (even based on moral considerations).' [3]

According to Chinese accepted philosophy, as we shall see, man's nature is good. It is only through habit that some men become bad or 'differ widely'. It is, however, believed that by proper instruction or education they may be made good again or at least improved. In the notable British trial, known as the 'Brides in the Bath Murder Case', the learned judge in sentencing the prisoner to death said: 'Exhortation to repentance would be wasted on you.' [4] But such cases are, after all, rare. That is why in moral instruction there should be no discrimination; because, though the man may be bad at the time, he may be reformed as a result of instruction. The truth of this is well illustrated in Goldsmith's *Vicar of Wakefield*, where Dr. Primrose, when in prison as a victim of persecution, preached to the convicted criminals, as he would do, as his wont, to his congregation, hoping thus to reclaim them. Though he was at first made the object of ridicule by his prison flock, he succeeded in the end. To use his own words, 'in less than six days some were penitent, and all attentive'. [5] It is true that this is only a fiction; nevertheless, the philosophy therein contained is sound all the same. But in order to attain such result the instructor must, of course, be absolutely sincere and earnest in his instruction, and must not simply discharge his duties as a matter of routine. In the words of Mencius, 'absolute sincerity has never failed to have a moving effect; insincerity can never produce a moving effect'. [6]

As already mentioned, this chapter would be incomplete without the inclusion, in a special section, of the philosophy of Mencius, though his teachings have been referred to on numerous occasions, and will have to be referred to again and again. His importance in the domain of Chinese philosophy lies not merely in the fact that he was the foremost exponent of Confucian doctrines and the last

[1] *Criticisms, Reflections, and Maxims*, p. 220. Trans. by W. B. Rönnfeldt; Lond., Walter Scott.
[2] Confucius: *Lun Yu*, Pt. XVII, Ch. 2.
[3] Confucius: *Lun Yu*, Pt. XV, Ch. 38.
[4] Eric R. Watson: *Trial of George Joseph Smith*, p. 310.
[5] *Vicar of Wakefield*, Ch. XXVII.
[6] *Mencius*, Bk. IV, Pt. I, Ch. 12, Sec. 3. For the use of the word 'effect', see commentary.

MENCIUS AND HIS MOTHER SEEKING A NEW ABODE
Painting of Ching Dynasty (A.D. 1644-1912)
Old Palace Museum Collection

of the few men in Chinese history to be ranked as a sage. In expounding the doctrines of Confucius and the ancients, he himself contributed much, particularly in connection with the doctrine that man's nature is good and the doctrine of righteousness, as distinguished from benevolence or perfect virtue, and thus enlarged to mankind[1] the light revealed by former sages. The fact that his opinions were partly recorded by himself made it possible that his views were presented comprehensively, and the fact that the age in which he lived was rich in doctrinal controversies was at least one of the reasons why his views were expressed with so much vigour, particularly in the matter of politics. It was once observed by an eminent scholar that one could rule an empire successfully with the principles set out in only half the work of Mencius, which consists of seven books, containing 261 chapters and 34,585 words. [2] How far this observation is justified may be difficult to say; but in reading his work one cannot help feeling that had a few of his main doctrines been followed by some rulers, who paid heavily for their misrule, the history of the world might be very different. Personally, I know a man who, having completed ten years' studies in a great Occidental university, where he achieved no mean academic success, one day picked up a dusty copy of Mencius, which he had, of course, like many of my countrymen of his days, learned by heart in school. As it roused his curiosity, he read it once more with the view not, indeed, of refreshing his memory of it, but rather of seeing, in the light of his new 'knowledge', how much the philosophy expounded therein could still hold water, as it were. But he confessed that he was overwhelmed by it with ecstasy from the start, experiencing a thrill of joy to the end.

SELECTED SAYINGS OF MENCIUS ON POLITICS

1. 'King Hui of *Liang* said (to Mencius): "I wish earnestly to be enlightened by you (on the subject of government)."

' "Is there any difference between killing a person with a stick and doing so with a sword?" asked Mencius (respectfully).

' "There is no difference," answered the King.

' "Is there any difference between killing a person with a sword and doing so through the administration of government?" asked Mencius again.

' "There is no difference," answered the King.

' "Now", said Mencius, "there is fat meat in your kitchen and

[1] The use of this word has its justification in the fact that the Chinese nation constitutes a quarter of the human race.
[2] See preface to *Correct Interpretation of Mencius*; Ed. *Sze Bu Bei Yao.*

there are fat horses in your stables; but your people have famine in their cheeks,[1] and on the wild plains there lie corpses of men who died of starvation. This (as a result of your heavy taxation levied on the people in order to enable you to give luxury to your beasts) is (like) leading beasts to devour men. When beasts devour one another, men yet hate (the sight of) it. If a ruler, who is *in loco parentis* to his people, so neglects their welfare in his administration as (exposes him to the reproach of) leading beasts to devour men, where, then, does that parental relation still subsist between him and his people?" '[2]

The French Revolution, at the beginning of which people cried for bread in their march on Versailles,[3] is a good illustration.

2. 'King Suen of *Chi* asked Mencius: "As regards the achievements of (the former Dukes) Huan of *Chi* and Wen of *Tsin*, may I hear them from You?"

'Mencius (respectfully) replied: "None of the disciples of Chung Nei [name of Confucius] ever mentioned the deeds of Huan and Wen; (because, though they were great in the form of military conquests and territorial aggrandisements, they were so tainted with vices that they were not considered worthy of being transmitted to posterity). Therefore subsequent generations have no record of them. I, your humble servant, have not heard any of them. If you insist (on talking on a subject of this nature), may I talk about the right way[4] of attaining the rule of the whole empire (which would be a worthier theme)?"

' "What virtue must (a ruler) possess in order that he may be able to attain the rule of the whole empire?" asked the King.

'Mencius replied: "To love and take care of the people (i.e., to assume an ardent responsibility for their safety, prosperity, and welfare)[5]. (If he does this), nothing can hinder him from attaining the rule of the whole empire."

' "Is a person like me capable of loving and taking care of the people?" asked the King again.

'Mencius replied: "Yes."

'The King said: "How do you know that I am capable of that?"

---

[1] Compare: 'Famine is in thy cheeks,
              Need and oppression starveth in thine eyes.'
Shakespeare: *Romeo and Juliet*, Act. V, Sc. I, Ls. 69–70.
[2] *Mencius*, Bk. I, Pt. I, Ch. 4, Secs. 1-5.
[3] François Mignet: *Histoire de la Révolution française*, p. 66 (Macmillan & Co.).
[4] See commentary.
[5] See, in Webster's Dictionary, 4th. definition of 'care'.

' "I have", said Mencius, "heard this incident (about you) from (a man named) Hoo Hut, who said: 'The King was sitting in the upper part of the hall, when a man was conducting an ox across the lower part of it. The King, seeing this, asked (the man): "Where is the ox going?" The man replied: "I am going to (have it killed and) use its blood for consecrating a (new) bell." The King said: "Set it free. I cannot bear the sight of its terrified appearance like that of an innocent person being led to the place of execution." "Shall then the consecration of the bell be dispensed with?" asked the man. "How can this be dispensed with?" said the King. "Substitute a sheep for it."

' "I do not know", continued Mencius, "whether this incident did in fact happen."

'The King answered: "It did."

'Mencius then said: "The heart revealed in this incident suffices to enable you to attain the rule of the whole empire. The people all thought that Your Majesty was parsimonious, but I well know that Your Majesty was (simply) compassionate."

' "Right," said the King, "there was, indeed, some semblance of what the people thought to be. But though (my) kingdom Chi is limited (in space) and small (in resources), yet why should I be parsimonious over an ox? It was merely because I could not bear the sight of its terrified appearance like that of an innocent person being led to the place of execution that I ordered the substitution of a sheep for it."

' "Do not consider it strange, Your Majesty," said Mencius, "that the people should have thought that Your Majesty was parsimonious. When you ordered the substitution of a small animal for a large one, how could they know your true motive? For if you had been distressed simply by the sight of an innocent victim being led to the place of execution, what choice would there have been between an ox and a sheep?"

'The King, laughing, said: "What really was the state of my mind then? I was (truly) not parsimonious over the cost of an ox, and yet I ordered the substitution of it by a sheep. It was only natural that the people should have said that I was parsimonious."

' "There is no harm in that," said Mencius, "What you did was a means of (practising) benevolence. You saw the ox, but did not see the sheep. The *Jiun Tze* (i.e., the gentleman)[1] in regard to animals, having seen them alive, cannot bear seeing them die, and, having heard them cry (at their death) cannot bear eating their

[1] Here the term may be rendered simply as 'gentleman'.

flesh. Therefore the *Jiun Tze* keeps away from the kitchen." [1] (As you could not dispense with the sacrifice that must be made, though your heart was touched, the fact that you substituted an animal that you had not seen for one that you had seen was nevertheless a response to a benevolent cord of the heart under the circumstances.)

'The King, being pleased, said: "An ancient Ode says:

> 'Other men have (motives in their) minds,
> While I discover them by guessing fine.' [2]

This is the case with you, Master. I was the person who acted, but when I searched inwardly for the motive of my action, I could not discover it in my heart. When you, Master, mentioned it, my heart was still quite affected. But what has such a heart to do with the attainment of the rule of the whole empire?"

'Mencius replied: "If someone said to Your Majesty: 'My strength is great enough for lifting three thousand catties (i.e., 4,000 lbs.) but not great enough for lifting a feather; my sight is clear enough for examining a tip of the autumn down (of a bird) but not clear enough for seeing a wagon-load of wood,' would Your Majesty admit that?"

' "No," replied the King.

' "Now," (said Mencius, "you have) kindness enough to be extended to animals, and yet no benefit of it reaches the people. Why is this singularly so? (Is it not that men should come first?) The fact is that (as in the cases instanced) the feather is not lifted, simply because the strength is not exerted; the wagon-load of wood is not seen, simply because the vision is not exercised; the people receive no love or care, simply because kindness is not bestowed. Therefore the fact that Your Majesty has not attained the rule of the whole empire is due to *not doing*, and not to *being incapable of doing*."

' "How would you depict the difference between *not doing* and *being incapable of doing?*" asked the King.

'Mencius replied: "Take the case of carrying the Tai mountain [3] and leaping with it over the North Sea, for instance, if you say to others, 'I am incapable of doing it,' that is really *being incapable of*

---

[1] The Chinese kitchen is also the place where small domestic animals, such as poultry, are killed.

[2] *Book of Odes (Mow Sche)* Title *Siao Yah;* Ed. *Sze Bu Bei Yao,* Bk. XI. Fine in the sense of 'well'—Webster's Dictionary.

[3] The highest mountain in China. Paraphrased, the sentence may be rendered as 'carrying the Himalaya and leaping with it over the Atlantic'.

doing. Take the case of breaking a branch off a tree for an elder, for instance, if you say to others 'I am incapable of doing it', that is only *not doing*, and not *being incapable of doing.* Therefore, the fact that Your Majesty has not attained the rule of the whole empire is not a case like that of carrying the Tai mountain and leaping with it over the North Sea. The fact that Your Majesty has not attained the rule of the whole empire is (only) a case like that of breaking a branch off a tree. (Here is a principle:) *I treat my own elders with kindness due to age, and extend it to the elders of others; I treat my own youths with tenderness due to youth and extend it to the youths of others.* [1] Observe this, and the (rule of the whole) empire may be (attained as easily as a thing) made to circulate in the palm. In the *Book of Odes* it is said (in praise of the sage King Wen):

'He treated well his rarely model [2] wife.
His kindness was extended to his brothers.
In this way [3] he shaped the family life,
And ruled all those within the country borders.' [4]

These words mean that King Wen, after all (observed the principle just stated and) extended the (kindness of his) heart to others (from the near to the distant). Therefore, by extending his kindness, a ruler is able to love and take care of his entire people within the Empire, and by not extending it, he will not be able to love or take care of even his own wife and children. What made the ancients greatly surpass men (of these days) was merely this: they knew well how to extend (their kindness in) what they did. (They were affectionate to those closely related to them; then, by extending these sentiments, they loved all men generally; and, by further extending these sentiments, they were kind to animals

---

[1] It is the kindness, and not the practice of the principle, as some have interpreted, that is extended to others, though the extension of the practice may also be a natural consequence through following good examples. This may be gathered from the orthodox commentary and the context of the discourse of Mencius, and is also the meaning given in *Correct Interpretation of Mencius* (Vol. I, Bk. III, p. 10).

[2] The Chinese word is 'rare', i.e. having rare qualities or being unusually excellent. See commentary of the Ode given in *Mow Sche*.

[3] i.e., extending his kindness to others from the near to the distant. See commentary in *Mencius*.

[4] This Ode appears in *Mow Sche*, Title *Da Yah, King Wen*; Ed. *Sze Bu Bei Yao*, Bk. XVI, No. 3. Some opinions collected in the *Book of Odes* regard the Ode as meaning that King Wen by his good example was able to make others follow his principles. But having regard to the context of the discourse of Mencius e.g., 'by extending his kindness, etc.', the meaning given in the translation rendered above is in my opinion correct. Besides, the translation is almost literal.

and things as well.)[1] Now, you have kindness enough to be extended to animals, and yet no benefit of it reaches the people. Why is this singularly so? By weighing, one knows what is heavy and what is light and, by measuring, one knows what is long and what is short. This is so with everything, and especially so with (the sentiments of) the heart. Your Majesty, please think (whether it is right for you to love and take care of your animals more than your people). Is it, by making wars, by endangering the lives of your warriors, and by incurring the enmity of the rulers of other States, that your heart will be pleased?"

' "No," replied the King, "how can I take pleasure in this? I use this only to achieve what I greatly desire."

' "As to what Your Majesty greatly desires," asked Mencius, "may I hear it?"

'The King laughed and remained silent. Mencius then continued: "(As to what you greatly desire) is it that you have not enough rich and delicious meat for your mouth, and not enough light and warm (garments) for your body, or is it that you have not enough beautiful objects for your eyes, or not enough delightful musics for your ears, or not enough favourites to flaunt about you? Any of your numerous ministers is capable of procuring you all these things. Could any of these be what Your Majesty is after?"

' "No," replied the King, "I am not after any of these."

' "Then", said Mencius, "what Your Majesty greatly desires can be known. You desire to enlarge your territory, to make States *Chin* and *Cho* do homage to you at your Court, to rule the Middle Kingdom (i.e., the Empire), and to enlist the sympathy of the surrounding tribes. But, by what you are doing in order to achieve what you desire, it is like climbing up a tree to look for a fish."

' "Is it so bad as that?" said the King.

' "It is worse than that," replied Mencius. "In climbing up a tree to look for a fish, though you do not find the fish, no disaster will ensue. But by what you are doing in order to achieve what you desire, and by so doing wholeheartedly, disasters are bound to follow."

' "May I hear what these disasters are?" asked the King.

' "Suppose the people of *Chou* (a small State) were at war with the people of *Cho* (a large State), which of the two, in your opinion, would win?"

' "The people of *Cho* would win," replied the King.

' "Thus it follows", said Mencius, "that a small State cannot fight against a large State, the few cannot fight against the many,

[1] Orthodox commentary.

and the weak cannot fight against the strong. There are in the Empire nine States, each of which has a territory of a thousand *li* [1] square. The whole of *Chi* forms only one of them. If you, with the possession of only one of them, try to subdue the other eight, what is the difference between this and the case where *Chou* fights against *Cho*? Turn (your mind) to the root of the matter. Now, if Your Majesty institutes good laws and practises benevolence in your government, making all those who hold office in the Empire desire to serve in your Court, all those who cultivate the land desire to cultivate your plains, all those who trade desire to place their goods in your markets, all those who travel desire to pass by your roads, and all those who have grievances against their rulers desire to bring their complaints before you, then, as they so desire, who can prevent them from so doing?"

' "I am dull", said the King, "and have been unable to come up to this. I wish you, Master, would aid my intentions and instruct me in clear terms. Though I am ignorant, I will try to put into practice your instructions."

' *"Without any settled means of livelihood and yet maintaining a settled state of mind,"* said Mencius, *"this is what only a highly educated man can do. In the case of the people generally, if they have no settled means of livelihood, they will in consequence have no settled state of mind. When they have no settled state of mind, there is nothing that they will not do in the way of self-abandonment, vicious addiction, moral debasement, and unrestrained dissipation. To allow them thus to become entangled in crimes and then to follow them up with punishments would be to ensnare the people.* How is it possible that, when a benevolent man is on the throne, the people should be ensnared? *Therefore an enlightened ruler, in regulating the means of livelihood of the people, ensures that they all will get enough, upwardly, to support their parents and, downwardly, to maintain their wives and children, that in years of prosperity they will have food in abundance for all time and in years of affliction they will escape death (from hunger).* Then he directs and leads them to the path of good, and they will follow his direction and example with ease. . . . See that, in (the land appurtenant to) dwellings of five *mows* (acres), [2] mulberry trees are planted, and persons of the age of fifty will be able to wear silk; see that those who rear cattle [3] observe the proper time of breeding, and persons of the age of seventy will be able to eat meat; encroach not upon the time of those who cultivate a hundred *mows*, and families of eight dependants will be able to

[1] One third of a mile.
[2] One *mow* is 6,000 sq. ft. Chinese.
[3] Lit., fowls, small pigs, dogs, and pigs.

escape hunger; supervise carefully the instructions given in the schools, making sure that filial and fraternal duties are taught, and aged persons with grey hair will not be seen on the road carrying loads on their shoulders or heads. *When the aged (are able to) wear silk and those whose hair is not yet grey suffer neither from hunger nor from cold, it has never happened that a ruler (responsible for this) would not attain the rule of the whole empire." *[1]

The concluding part may sound primitive to the modern ear; but, with a little reflection, one will realize that it covers industry, agriculture, education, and ethics of government, and it is in this spirit that it should be understood.

3. 'King Suen of *Chi* asked (Mencius): "Toung[2] exiled Chieh[3] (after having dethroned him). Emperor Wu[4] (before he became Emperor) waged war on Tsou[5] (and put him to death). Was this true?"

' "History has this on record", answered Mencius (respectfully).

' "Is it permissible (then) for a subject to kill his sovereign?" asked the King.

' "One who violates all rules of benevolence", replied Mencius, "is called a public danger; one who violates all rules of righteousness is called a public evil. One who violates all rules of righteousness and benevolence is called an outlaw. I have heard of the killing of an outlaw Tsou. I have not heard of the killing of a sovereign by a subject." '[6]

It is often said that this passage indirectly recognizes the implicit right of revolt against a tyrant, who is considered to have forfeited his right through gross misrule. There is therefore an essential difference between the limited divine right claimed by the Chinese monarchs of old and that claimed by those of certain countries; for the Chinese people always asserted that the monarch ruled also by a divine duty, the violation of which by misrule would nullify his right to rule. Hence this following passage in the *Book of History*: 'The crimes of (the ruler of) *Shang* being up to the limit, Heaven decreed that he should be slain.'[7] Commenting on this book,

---

[1] *Mencius*, Bk. I, Pt. I, Ch. 7.
[2] Founder of the *Shang* Dynasty (1783 B.C.).
[3] Last Emperor of the *Hsia* Dynasty, a tyrant.
[4] Founder of the *Chow* Dynasty (1122 B.C.).
[5] Last Emperor of the *Shang* Dynasty, a tyrant.
[6] *Mencius*, Bk. I, Pt. II, Ch. 8, Secs. 1-2.
[7] Bk. XI, Records of *Chow*, Title *Tai Si*, No. 1. It is remarkable that no ruler ever dared question this passage.

Pauthier said, *inter alia*: 'The exercise of sovereignty, which in our modern societies is very often only the exploitation of the greatest number for the benefit of a few, is according to the *Book of History* the religious fulfilment of a Heavenly mandate for the benefit of all, a noble and great mission entrusted to the most devoted and worthiest, which mandate is withdrawn the moment the agent fails to discharge his duties. Nowhere, perhaps, have the respective duties between kings and peoples or between the governors and the governed been taught in a manner so lofty, so worthy, and so conformable to reason. It is there that the great maxim of modern democracy is constantly put in practice: *Vox populi, vox Dei*, "the voice of the people is the voice of God". This maxim is manifested in every part of this Book; but one finds it thus formulated at the end of the chapter entitled "Kao-yao-mo", Sec. 7: "What Heaven sees and hears is only what the people sees and hears. What the people judges to be worthy of recompense or deserving of punishment is what Heaven wishes to recompense or punish." One finds it formulated also in this manner in the *Great Learning*, Ch. 10, Sec. 5:

> "If you gain the affection of the people, you will gain the country. If you lose the affection of the people, you will lose the country." ' [1]

4. '(Advantages of) time afforded by Heaven are not equal to advantages derived from the Earth, and advantages derived from the Earth are not equal to (the advantages of co-operation due to) the harmony of men. (Take the case of) a city which has an interior wall of only three *li* (Chinese mile) in circumference and an exterior wall of only seven, and (which the invader) has invested and stormed, but fails to conquer. Here he must have availed himself of the (advantages of) time afforded by Heaven, and his failure to conquer it shows that the (advantages of) time afforded by Heaven are not equal to the advantages derived from the Earth. (Take now the case of) a city which has ramparts that are high, ditches that are deep, arms and armaments that are strong and sharp, and stores of food (Lit., rice and other grains) that are ample, and which is undefended and abandoned by the defenders, this shows that advatages derived from the Earth are not equal to (the advantages of co-operation due to) the harmony of Men (i.e., the people). Therefore it is said: "the demarcation between nations is not (necessarily) sustained by territorial boundaries; the security of a State is not (necessarily) sustained by strategic mountains or rivers; the might of an empire is not (necessarily) sustained by the strength and force of arms". Those who are in the right have

---

[1] G. Pauthier: *Livres Sacrés de L'Orient*, p. x.

many on their sides; those who are in the wrong have few on theirs.'[1]

5. 'Good intentions alone are not enough in government, nor can law prevail by itself.'[2]

6. '(A ruler who) oppresses his people in the extreme will lose his life and State. If he oppresses his people, though not in the extreme, his life will, nevertheless, be in danger and his State undermined.'[3]

Compare: 'If a sovereign oppresses his people to a great degree, they will rise and cut off his head.'[4]

'The (tyrants) Chieh and Tsou lost the Empire; because they lost (the loyalty of) the people. They lost (the loyalty of) the people; because they lost (the attachment of) their hearts. There is a way of gaining the Empire. If you win the people, you will gain the Empire. There is a way of winning the people. If their hearts are won, they will be won. There is a way of winning their hearts. Give and assure them what they desire (such as security, peace, liberty, wealth, comfort, and the like)[5] and do to them nothing that they dislike (such as the opposite of what they desire).'[6]

7. 'Mencius said to King Suen of *Chi*: "When a sovereign treats his subjects[7] like his own hands or feet, they will treat him like their own bellies or hearts; if he treats them like dogs or horses, they will treat him like the man in the street; if he treats them like earth or grass, they will treat him like a robber or an enemy."'[8]

8. 'Not to instruct the people (in their duties) but to employ them (in war) is to ruin them.'[9]

9. 'Good government (in the form of laws and prohibitions) is less effective in gaining (the hearts of) the people than good instructions. Good government (in the form of laws and prohibitions) inspires the people with fear; good instructions inspire them with love.'[10]

---

[1] *Mencius*, Bk. II, Pt. II, Ch. 1, Secs. 1-3.
[2] *Mencius*, Bk. IV, Pt. I, Ch. 1, Sec. 3.
[3] *Mencius*, Bk. IV, Pt. I, Ch. 2, Sec. 4.
[4] Boswell's *Life of Johnson*; Ed. Everyman's Library, Vol. I, p. 424.
[5] Orthodox commentary.
[6] *Mencius*, Bk. IV, Pt. I, Ch. 9.
[7] The term is to be understood in its wider sense and so includes ministers.
[8] *Mencius*, Bk. IV, Pt. II, Ch. 3.
[9] *Mencius*, Bk. VI, Pt. II, Ch. 8, Sec. 2.
[10] *Mencius*, Bk. VII, Pt. I, Ch. 14, Sec. 3. Compare No. 2 saying of Confucius on politics; *ante*, p. 130.

10. '(As regards a nation) the people is the first in importance, statehood[1] the next, and the ruler the last.'[2]

The last saying expresses a profound truth, as demonstrated in the case where States have been able to revive after extinction because their peoples remain. This, together with sayings Nos. 3, 6, and 7 and that 'without the confidence of the people government ceases to exist',[3] shows that the basic conception of Chinese political philosophy has always been democratic, and that, according to it, government is of the people, for the people, and with the confidence of the people—a doctrine that, as a result of political evolution and thanks to 'The Three Principles of the People' of Dr. Sun Yat Sun, Father of the Republic, has taken the definite form of 'government of the people, by the people, and for the people'. It is, therefore, difficult to see the grounds of observation of a critic of the Chinese Classics, living in the nineteenth century, who said: 'His (Mencius's) faults as a political teacher are substantially the same as those of Confucius. More than was the case with his sayings of a political character; the utterances of Mencius have references to the condition and needs of his own age. They were for the time being, and not for all time.'[4] One fails, however, to see any limitation of this nature in any of the fundamental political utterances either of Confucius or of Mencius, which throughout emphasize the paramount importance of the people and the imperative necessity of devotion to duty on the part of the rulers. It is no more obsolete to say to-day, as Mencius said twenty-four centuries ago, that, if you win the people, you will gain the Empire[5] than to say, as a political doctrine, that England lost her American possessions by a policy of force and held her Empire together by a policy of Imperial fraternity. Nor is it less true to-day, than it was in the days of old, that the essentials of government are 'sufficient food, sufficient military preparedness, and confidence of the people',[6] or that 'good intentions alone are not enough in government nor can law prevail by itself'.[7] It would not do, in opening a book of the ancients of any land in search of wisdom, to expect that it should read like a modern textbook with phraseology that fits in with every aspect of modern life

[1] Lit., the National Altar established on the foundation of a State for seasonal sacrifices—emblem of a State.
[2] *Mencius*, Bk. VII, Pt. II, Ch. 14.
[3] See *ante*, p. 132.
[4] Legge: *The Chinese Classics*, Vol. II, Prolegomena, pp. 78-9; Ed. 1861.
[5] See *ante*, p. 146.
[6] See *ante*, p. 131.
[7] See *ante*, p. 146.

and society. But one with a receptive mind, coming across, in an ancient text, an expression like 'a State of a thousand chariots' or 'sufficient food', can easily, in the one case, assimilate it to a State possessing a thousand tanks or the like, and, in the other, see in it the injunction for a sound economic system. The ancients could not have used expressions like 'châteaubriand' or 'cocktail', for they were not yet invented; but they spoke of eating and drinking, which are common to all and invariable. We look to the ancients or the wise always for their teachings on fundamentals and never for their teachings on details. Burke, whose works are still read with admiration by the present generation and, I am sure, will be by many to come, merely says: 'There is no qualification for government but virtue and wisdom, actual or presumptive'; [1] yet many a student of politics must have found that this single sentence teaches him more on essentials than, perhaps, volumes he may have read. It is true that Mencius spoke against war. [2] But was he not right in the light of recent world events? In other words; there is nothing faulty in the political doctrines of either Confucius or Mencius. It was only the age in which the critic of these doctrines lived made him think they were faulty. The nineteenth century had its glory as well as its dark side. It was an age in which imperialism paid a handsome dividend; but the iniquity of the father is apt to be visited in his children, and the present generation has paid heavily in the double World Wars. Anyone who thinks lightly of the wisdom of the ancients may well note that it is fatal to world statesmanship to know the history of the nineteenth century too well and that of other periods too badly. Moreover, it is no more correct to say that the fundamental teachings of either Confucius or Mencius were only 'for the time being and not for all time' than it would be to affirm that the Sermon on the Mount was only for those who listened to it at the time.

SELECTED SAYINGS OF MENCIUS ON ETHICS

1. 'Benevolence is the peaceful dwelling of man, righteousness his right path. Woe unto him who quits the peaceful dwelling uninhabited, and abandons the right path unpursued!' [3]

'Benevolence to a person is (like) his heart, righteousness to a person is (like) his (unalterable) path. Woe unto him, who abandons his (unalterable) path unpursued and loses his heart without feeling the need of recovering it! When a person has lost a fowl or a dog,

[1] *Reflections on the French Revolution.*
[2] See *ante*, p. 33.
[3] *Mencius*, Bk. IV, Pt. I, Ch. 10, Sec. 2.

he feels the need of recovering it; but when he has lost his heart he does not feel the need of its recovery. The great object of learning is nothing but to recover the lost heart.'[1]

2. 'To dwell in the spacious habitation of the Universe (i.e., to practise benevolence); to stand in the right place of the Universe (i.e., to conform to propriety or moral rules of correct conduct); to walk on the grand path of the Universe (i.e., to observe righteousness); in office,[2] to practise these principles with (and for the benefit of) the people; not in office, to practise them alone (for self-elevation); to be incapable of being either corrupted by wealth or honour, or demoralized by poverty or humble condition, or bent by might or force: these are what one calls (the characteristics of) a great man.'[3]

3. 'The woe of men lies in being fond of being others' teachers.'[4]

'The (common) malady of man is that they neglect their own fields but weed those of others, and that they expect much from others while they themselves undertake little.'[5]

These two passages teach almost the same lesson, namely, men should not too often consider themselves wiser than others, and should always be more critical of themselves than others.

4. 'A man must have (made it a principle that there are certain) things which he would not do, before he can act worthily (in what he would do).'[6]

Men of principles would in no circumstance act against their principles, and it is only from such men that great things can be expected. Indeed, what would be the man, if there were nothing that he would not do?

'The *Jiun Tze* (i.e., Noble Man) is ashamed of a reputation that exceeds his merits.'[7]

---

[1] *Mencius*, Bk. VI, Pt. I, Ch. 11.
[2] Lit, 'When the aim is attained', i.e. the aim of having the opportunity to practise one's principles for the benefit of the people (see *Mencius*, Bk. VII, Pt. I, Ch. 9, Sec. 6; Confucius: *Lun Yu*, Pt. XV, Ch. 8 and Pt. XVIII, Ch. 7, Sec. 5). The words 'in office', in my opinion, bring out in substance the meaning of the text. To translate it as 'when the ambition for office is attained', though closer to the text in its letter, might however be misconstrued as attributing a desire for personal advancement, such as 'Brutus said *Caesar* was ambitious'.
[3] *Mencius*, Bk. III, Pt. II, Ch. 2, Sec. 3.
[4] *Mencius*, Bk. IV, Pt. I, Ch. 23.
[5] *Mencius*, Bk. VII, Pt. II, Ch. 32, Sec. 3.
[6] *Mencius*, Bk. IV, Pt. II, Ch. 8.
[7] *Mencius*, Bk. IV, Pt. II, Ch. 18, Sec. 3.

This is another characteristic of the *Jiun Tze*, a subject that has been treated in the chapter on General Survey. However, in a world where advertisement (must one add the word 'self'?) has become a fine art, one wonders how many persons are hit by this *dictum*.

5. 'If you love others and they do not attach themselves to you in return, examine your own benevolence (to see if it is perfect). [1] If you govern others and they are not well governed, examine your own wisdom (to see if it is perfect). If you behave to others politely and they do not do so to you in return, examine your own respects (to see if they are perfect). Whenever in your action you fail to achieve a desired effect, examine yourself for the cause (of your failure).' [2]

'The man of perfect virtue conducts himself like the archer. The archer first adjusts himself and then shoots. If he misses the mark, he does not complain against those who do better than himself, but examines himself for the cause (of his failure).' [3]

6. 'A person must have first made himself despicable before others despise him; a family must have first made itself destructible before others destroy it; a State must have first made itself assailable before others assail it.' [4]

This saying, like the preceding one, is remarkable both for its completeness and for the wisdom it contains.

7. 'Those who love others are always loved by others; those who respect others are always respected by others.' [5]

This maxim would appear to be only common sense, if it were stated in the reversed form, viz.: Those who do not love others are always not loved by others; those who do not respect others are always not respected by others. But when it is stated in the positive form, it seems very profound. In this, as in many other instances of truth, it is not the rule that is profound but the man's mind that is sometimes shallow.

8. 'There is nothing that is not willed by Heaven. One should accept with resignation what may rightly be attributed thereto. Therefore one who has a right idea of the will of Heaven will not stand beneath a wall that threatens to collapse (for to do so would

---

[1] See *Correct Interpretation of Mencius*, Vol. IV, Bk. XIV, p. 11.
[2] *Mencius*, Bk. IV, Pt. I, Ch. 4, Secs. 1-3.
[3] *Mencius*, Bk. II, Pt. I, Ch. 7, Sec. 5.
[4] *Mencius*, Bk. IV, Pt. I, Ch. 8, Sec. 4.
[5] *Mencius*, Bk. IV, Pt. II, Ch. 28.

only be courting disaster). The death of one who dies in the performance of duties may rightly be attributed to the will of
Heaven; the death of one who dies under shackles (as the result of
a crime) cannot be so attributed.'[1]

9. 'To act without understanding the proper reason for so doing;
to act repeatedly without yet realizing[2] it; and to continue thus
for life without (really) knowing the Way—this characterizes the
majority of man.'[3]

'The *Jiun Tze* (i.e., Noble Man) observes the (natural) law (by
doing his best) and resigns himself wholly to the will of Heaven
(in regard to the result).'[4]

10. 'All (that are required to make oneself perfect) are found
in oneself. Consciousness of being sincere on self-examination is a
form of happiness that is the greatest of all. One who, endeavour-
ing to attain perfect virtue, acts vigorously on the principle of
Shu, that is, acting to others as one would act to oneself (or loving
others like oneself), will get nearer to it in this than in any other
way.'[5]

The second sentence finds an echo in the saying:

'Self-examination in a quiet night
     Finds in heart no cause for shame in any light.'

That is to say, when one searches and researches one's conscience
in solitude and in the calmness of the night, discovering no cause
whatever for shame, one must feel a thrill of joy even 'better than
more honour and more wealth, and more esteem from men'.[6]

SELECTED SAYINGS OF MENCIUS
OF A GENERAL PHILOSOPHICAL NATURE

1. 'Kung Sun Chau (a disciple) said: "Why does not the *Jiun Tze*
(the gentleman)[7] himself instruct his son?" Mencius said: "By
force of circumstances this does not work. He who instructs must
insist on being correct. When such instruction is not observed, it
will be followed by anger. When it is followed by anger, it will,
contrary to intention, hurt (the son, who may sometimes even say):

[1] *Mencius*, Bk. VII, Pt. I, Ch. 2.
[2] The Chinese word *Tschak* here means not 'examining' but 'realizing', i.e. appre-
hending clearly—Commentary.
[3] *Mencuis*, Bk. VII, Pt. I, Ch. 5.
[4] *Mencius*, Bk. VII, Pt. II, Ch. 33, Sec. 3.
[5] *Mencius*, Bk. VII, Pt. I, Ch. 4.
[6] Viscount R. B. Haldane: *Autobiography*, p. 353.
[7] Here the term may be rendered simply as 'gentleman'

'My master insists on my being correct; but he himself is not always correct.' In this way father and son are mutually hurt. When father and son are mutually hurt, it is calamitous. (That is why) the ancients exchanged their sons for purpose of instruction." [1]

That even a question like this has not escaped the attention of the ancients justifies the observation of Goethe that 'Ignorant persons raise questions which have been answered by the wise thousands of years ago'. [2] However, Mencius's words should be understood as referring to the case of regular education rather than ordinary instruction. It would be absurd to imagine that, in ancient days, every time a man, wishing to say something instructive to his son, would call in his neighbour and say to him: 'Please tell this to my son. When you have anything similar to tell to your son, you may send for me and I will do it for you in return.' This cannot be what the Chinese sage intended to mean. What he means is that in general it is impractical for a parent to undertake the education of his own child. It is impractical; because, on the part of the parent, owing to natural affection, there may be an excess of zeal unsustained by corresponding patience, and, on the part of the child, owing either to accustomed indulgence, which 'spares the rod', or to constant contact, which dulls the edge of appreciation, there may be a lack of response coextensive with parental expectation, not to say that, 'A prophet is not without honour, save in his own country, and in his own house.' [3] Moreover, it is one thing to teach the Golden Rule and another to practise it, though it is only right, nay, obligatory, that he who teaches should teach something higher than what he himself has yet been able to attain, hoping that the next generation may do better than the present. To impute, in such circumstances, to the teacher either inconsistency or insincerity would, in the words of an English moralist, 'be so grossly ignorant of human nature as not to know that a man may be very sincere in good principles without having good practice'. [4] However, human nature being as it is, the pupil, while more attentive to instructions that are bought than to what is home-made, may be inclined to expect examples more from one to whom he is bound by a permanent tie than from one to whom he is tied by a temporary relation; but should he ever be critical, less harm would be done in the case of the latter than in the case of the former.

[1] *Mencius*, Bk. IV, Pt. I, Ch. 18.
[2] *Criticisms, Reflections, and Maxims of Goethe*, p. 252. Trans. by W. B. Rönnfeldt, Lond., Walter Scott.
[3] St. Matthew, Ch. XIII, 57.
[4] Boswell's *Life of Johnson*; Ed. G. Birkbeck Hill, Vol. V., p. 259.

There is another reason, which is perhaps peculiar to the Chinese. As has been discussed in the preceding chapter in connection with ancestral worship, and will be discussed again in the next, the Chinese have almost from the dawn of history considered filial piety as the root, or the first step in the cultivation, of virtue—a doctrine which, being equivalent to saying, 'Honour thy father and thy mother, as the Lord thy God hath commanded thee,'[1] could of course be taught with a greater sense of reality and detachment by someone other than the parents themselves.

2. 'There are instances of honour that is unexpected, and of dishonour that results from endeavour to be perfect.'[2]

A man therefore should not be judged entirely by such accidents, nor should a man, having a right sense of the value of things and a clear conscience, allow himself to be unduly affected by them one way or the other. Anyhow, the latter part of the saying must be a consolation to those who sometimes suffer from unspeakable injustice. To give an illustration of it in a lighter vein, I may refer to an instance found in Harris's *Hints on Advocacy*, where a distinguished K.C. had been conducting a cross-examination satisfactorily in a case of homicide and, when he was on the point of resuming his seat, his solicitor sitting behind him suggested an additional question to be put to the witness. He did, and received an answer that was fatal to his case. Thereupon, he turned round furiously to his solicitor, saying: 'Go to hell, and, when you meet your client, beg his pardon!' Has not the solicitor here endeavoured to be perfect?

3. 'If one believes all that the *Book of History* says literally (in its description of events), it would be better to be without the *Book of History*.'[3]

I have been told a story that when Walpole, being too ill to read, was asked what book he would like to be read to him, he said: 'Any book but history, which I know is false.' This, however, is not the meaning of the words of Mencius, who on that particular occasion was referring to a passage, which says: 'So much blood was shed that it floated the implements of war.' This, according to him, could only be figurative. In ancient days, when living was simpler and life less complicated, it was more likely that there were fewer causes and fewer motives for the falsification of history. But the Chinese language is essentially artistic, and, in the description of events, the ancients

[1] Deuteronomy, Ch. V, 16.
[2] *Mencius*, Bk. IV, Pt. I, Ch. 21.
[3] *Mencius*, Bk. VII, Pt. II, Ch. 3, Sec. 1.

were, for the sake of emphasis, fond of using hyperboles or other figurative forms of speech. To take the words too literally in such cases would often miss the point and even be misled. An instance of this was given by Mencius on the interpretation of an ancient Ode, which says:

> 'Of the people left by *Chow*,
> There's not a man remaining now.'[1]

'If you believe these words literally', says Mencius, in referring to that ode, 'it would be that not any person of *Chow* was left—(a state of things that could not be true).'[2]

4. 'A person who covets fame can decline a State of a thousand chariots, but if he is not (really) that kind of man (i.e., a man of such generosity), (even) a matter of a bowl of rice or a dish of soup will affect (lit., be revealed in) his countenance.'[3]

Compare the following passage:

'Nor is it always in the most distinguished achievements that men's virtues or vices may be best discerned; but very often an action of small note, a short saying, or a jest, shall distinguish a person's real character more than the greatest sieges, or the most important battles.'[4]

5. 'Life is what I like, so is righteousness. If I cannot have both, I will forgo life and choose righteousness. Life is what I like indeed, but there is something which I like even more, and so I would not preserve life contrary to righteousness. Death is what I dislike indeed, but there is something which I dislike even more, and so there are dangers which I would not avoid. If in things liked by men none were more liked than life, why would not they employ every means capable of preserving it? If in things disliked by men none were more disliked than death, why would not they do everything capable of avoiding it? From this (we know that) there are occasions on which, though life might be preserved by certain means, men would not employ them, and, though dangers might be avoided by the doing of certain things, men would not do them. Therefore among the things liked (by men), there is something which they like even more than life, and among the things disliked by them, there is something which they dislike even more than

---

[1] *Book of Odes* (*Mow Sche*) Title *Da Yih, Tong Tsee*, Bk. XVIII, No. 2.
[2] *Mencius*, Bk. V, Pt. I, Ch. 4, See. 2.
[3] *Mencius*, Bk. VII, Pt. II, Ch. 11.
[4] *Plutarch's Lives, Alexander.* Translation by Langhorne, Lond., Tegg, 1825, pp. 464-5.

death. Such mentality is not confined to men of worth, but common
to all, it being simply that the men of worth are able not to lose it
(i.e., this mentality).'[1]

This is a high tribute to man's nature, and is one of Mencius's
pronouncements that man's nature is originally good. At the same
time it furnishes an illustration of the meaning of Mencius's own
saying that 'a man must have (made it a principle that there are)
certain things which he would not do before he can act worthily (in
what he would do)'.[2]

6. 'All persons have a heart that feels compassion for others. . . .
For instance, if they were suddenly to see a child going to fall into
a well, none would not feel in his heart a sensation of horror and
anguish. This is due not to any motive for winning the favour of
the child's parents or gaining the approbation of one's neighbours
or friends, nor to any aversion to the repute (of having been un-
affected by such a sight). To judge from this, one who lacks the
feeling of compassion is not a man (i.e., lacks a human quality
essential to man).'[3]

7. 'For nourishing the heart (in order to preserve it in its
natural condition) nothing is better than having few desires.'[4]

In other words, desire without limits is a source of evils.

'A great man is one who does not lose his *child-heart* (i.e., the
innocence and candour natural to a child).'[5]

This is a corollary to the doctrine that man's nature is good. The
heart of the child is pure and free from hypocrisy, but, as he grows
up, is liable to be corrupted by external influence and materialistic
desires. If, in spite of this liability, he is able to retain his natural
purity and, as he advances in age, enlarges it in consequence, he
must be great.[6]

Compare the following passage from the Bible:

'At the same time came the disciples unto Jesus, saying, Who
is the greatest in the kingdom of heaven? And Jesus called a little
child unto him, and set him in the midst of them, and said,
Verily I say unto you, Except ye be converted, and become as little

[1] *Mencius*, Bk. VI, Pt. I, Ch. 10, Secs. 1-5.
[2] *Mencius*, Bk. IV, Pt. II, Ch. 8. See *ante*, p. 149.
[3] *Mencius*, Bk. I, Pt. I, Ch. 6, Secs. 1, 3, 4.
[4] *Mencius*, Bk. VII, Pt. II, Ch. 35.
[5] *Mencius*, Bk. IV, Pt. II, Ch. 12. See Chu Tze's commentary.
[6] See commentary.

children, ye shall not enter into the kingdom of heaven. Whosoever
therefore shall humble himself as this little child, the same is the
greatest in the kingdom of heaven.' [1]

8. 'Kao Tze said (to Mencius): "The nature (of man) is like
the willow, and righteousness is like cups or bowls. To forge
benevolence and righteousness out of man's nature is like making
cups or bowls out of the willow (by transforming it)."

' "Are you able", said Mencius, "without disturbing (Lit., by
conforming to) the nature of the willow, to make cups or bowls
with it? You have first to do fatal injury to the willow in order to
make cups or bowls with it. If you have to do fatal injury to the
willow in order to make cups or bowls with it, then (according to
you), one will have to do fatal injury to the man in order to forge
benevolence and righteousness out of him. If mankind were ever
led to consider benevolence and righteousness as harmful, it would
certainly be due to your words!" [2]

' "The nature of man", said Kao Tze (again), "is like whirling
water. Direct its course eastward, and it will flow eastward.
Direct its course westward, and it will flow westward. The nature
of man does not discriminate between good and evil, just as water
does not discriminate between east and west."

' "Water", replied Mencius, "indeed, does not discriminate
between east and west, but will it not discriminate between
upwards and downwards? A man's nature tends to good just as
water tends to flow downwards. There is no man who (by nature)
does not tend to be good, nor is there water which (by nature) does
not tend to flow downwards. As to water, if you beat it so that it
springs up, you may cause it to rise above your forehead, and, if
you force it up (by some device), you may make it reach the top
of a hill; but do these (results of your action) conform to the
nature of the water? They are only the effect of external force
(applied to it). That men may be prevailed upon to do evil is
likewise the effect of their nature being subjected to the same
treatment." ' [3]

9. 'Kao Tze said (to Mencius): "Life is what is called nature."
' "By maintaining that life is what is called nature", asked
Mencius, "do you mean that (the two are the same), just as (all
things that are) white are white (without any difference)?"

' "Yes, I do," replied Kao Tze.
' "Is the whiteness of a white feather", asked Mencius, "the

[1] St. Matthew, Ch. XVIII, 1-4.
[2] *Mencius*, Bk. VI, Pt. I, Ch. 1.
[3] *Mencius*, Bk. VI, Pt. I, Ch. 2.

same as that of the white snow, and the whiteness of the white snow the same as that of a white gem?"

' "Yes," answered Kao Tze.

' "Then", proceeded Mencius, "is the nature of a dog the same as the nature of an ox, and the nature of an ox the same as the nature of a man?" ' [1]

10. 'Disciple Kung Doo said (to Mencius): "Kao Tze says: 'The nature of man is neither good nor bad'; some say: 'Man by nature may be made to do good or to do evil . . .' and some say: 'There are (men whose) nature (is) good, while there are (others whose) nature (is) bad. . . .' Now you say that nature is good. Are then all these people wrong (in what they say)?"

' "According to the feeling inherent (in man's nature)", answered Mencius, "it can (only) [2] be for doing good. That is what is meant by saying that nature is good. If men do practise evil, this is not a fault due to their natural faculties. The feeling of compassion is found in all men, so are that of shame and aversion, that of deference and respect, and that of approbation and disapprobation. The feeling of compassion argues the existence of (a sense of) benevolence; that of shame and aversion argues the existence of (a sense of) righteousness; that of deference and respect argues the existence of (a sense of) propriety; and that of approbation and disapprobation argues the existence of (a sense of) wisdom. (Senses of) benevolence, righteousness, propriety, and wisdom are not imparted to us from without, but are inherent in us (within). . . . In the *Book of Odes*, it is said:

'Heaven which creates mankind
Gives a law to everything:
Nature constant to man's mind
To lustrous virtue makes him cling.' [3]

(Referring to this Ode), Confucius said: *The author of this Ode knew the way of Nature indeed!*" ' [4]

Mencius's theory that man's nature is good and his invariable association of righteousness with benevolence in the domain of morals are considered by the Chinese as an inestimable contribution to humanity. The theory that man's nature is good is, of course, not free from controversy. Even among Chinese philosophers, there was Hsun Tze (master of Han Fei) who contested it; but his lonely

---

[1] *Mencius*, Bk. VI, Pt. I, Ch. 3.
[2] Commentary.
[3] *Book of Odes* (*Mow Sche*), Title *Da Yah*, *Tsing Min*, Bk. XVIII, No. 3.
[4] *Mencius*, Bk. VI, Pt. I, Ch. 6.

voice has no echo. The Chinese are taught, and the average Chinaman is inclined, to regard every man as good, unless there are grounds for holding a different opinion. This in no way implies credulity or excludes prudence, but is simply the way of the *Jiun Tze* or gentleman; for it is only in that way that one may avoid doing injustice to others, and this is also one way of conforming to the rule, *What you do not wish to be done to yourself do not do to others.* Moreover, they believe that every man has a heart that makes him amenable to reform—a view that necessarily presupposes that man's nature is good. Of course, by maintaining that 'man's nature is good', Mencius does not mean that nature needs no development, or perfection, by instruction or education, which would at least serve against contamination. What he means is that nature tends to good, just as water tends to flow downwards, and he deduces this from the spontaneous feeling of compassion in man. Hsun Tze, who maintains the opposite view, reasons *in effect* that if man's nature were good, there would have been no need for the institution of the ideas of propriety and righteousness, which we call culture. By nature, he argues, men, when hungry, desire to eat, and, when fatigued, desire to rest; but, through culture, men, though hungry, dare not eat first, if in the presence of their elders, and, though fatigued, dare not rest, if taking the toil of their elders. Similarly, by nature, even brothers may quarrel over the division of property, because nature begets the desire to acquire; but, through culture, men may decline even a kingdom in favour of others. From such reasonings and others on similar lines, he concludes that men would be bad, if left to follow their nature, but become good through culture. [1]

As already pointed out, to affirm that man's nature is good is far from saying that culture is superfluous. But it may be observed that, just as the soil that responds to the plantation of delicate plants proves that it is not barren, the fact that man's nature is receptive of such fine ideas as propriety, righteousness, and benevolence rather shows that it cannot be bad. 'Bad', says Carlyle, 'is by its nature negative; whatever enables us to *do* anything is by its very nature good.' [2] Confucius's enunciations on the subject are scanty and indirect. What he says, as already quoted, is: 'By nature men resemble one another; through habit they differ widely.' [3] However, this passage has always been taken to mean impliedly that man's nature is good [4]—a view that is strengthened by his approval of the Ode

[1] See *Hsun Tze*, Ch. 23, Essay on Man's Nature.
[2] *Miscellaneous Essays*, Vol. IV, p. 79; Ed. Chapman & Hall, Lond.
[3] See *ante*, p. 136.
[4] See *Correct Interpretation of Mencius*, Vol. II, Bk. XXII, p. 12.

quoted by Mencius[1] about nature, by his answer about perfect virtue in saying, 'to *regain* (the sense of) propriety (derived from Nature),[2] and by his *dictum* that 'Instruction admits of no class distinction (even based on moral considerations).'[3]

In concluding this question and leaving classical authorities aside, may be added the following modern opinions:

1. From Bishop Joseph Butler:

(a) 'It is from considering the relation which the several appetites and passions in the inward frame have to each other, and, above all, the supremacy of reflection or conscience, that we get the idea of the system or constitution of human nature. And from the idea itself it will as fully appear, that this our nature, i.e., constitution, is adapted to virtue, as from the idea of a watch it appears, that its nature, i.e., constitution or system, is adapted to measure time. . . . Every work of art is apt to be out of order; but this is so far from being according to its system. . . . Thus nothing can possibly be more contrary to nature than vice, meaning by nature, not only the *several parts* of our internal frame, but also the *constitution* of it.'[4]

(b) 'There is no such thing as love of injustice, oppression, treachery, ingratitude; but only eager desires after such and such external goods; which, according to a very ancient observation, the most abandoned would choose to obtain by innocent means, if they were easy, and as effectual to their end. . . . The nature of man, considered in his public and social capacity leads him to a right behaviour in society, to that course of life which we call virtue. Men follow or obey their nature . . . but not entirely: their actions do not come up to the whole of what their nature leads them to; and they often violate their nature; i.e. as they neglect the duties they owe to their fellow creatures, to which their nature leads them; and are injurious, to which their nature is abhorrent.'[5]

2. From Professor Joseph Needham of Cambridge University:

'China has quite as much given to the West as Western culture of machine production and control of natural phenomenon has given to China. I was delighted, when I found that in the eighteenth century some of the ideas, which lie deepest at the root of

---

[1] See *ante*, p. 157.
[2] See *ante*, p. 100.
[3] See *ante*, p. 136.
[4] *Fifteen Sermons*, Preface, pp. 11-12. Printed by Walker & Greig, 1816.
[5] *Fifteen Sermons*, Sermon I, pp. 43-7.

modern progressive thought in the West, were of Chinese origin. Translations of Chinese classics, made about A.D. 1650, brought to Europe ideas of Confucian philosophy that man's nature is fundamentally good, and we know that philosophers of the enlightened periods, who prepared war for the French Revolution and all subsequent advances, pondered much upon this. Hope for human social progress demands belief in fundamental co-operativeness and goodness of human spirit, however much of it may deviate from true nature in individual cases. Chinese philosophy gave us Europeans that belief.' [1]

This chapter is drawing to an end; but I cannot close it without some further observations. What I wish to say is that one searches in vain, in Chinese philosophy or art, for anything that extols physical might or military conquest. Such a doctrine as 'to live dangerously' has no place in Chinese philosophy, nor would the scene of a battle, however glorious, be a suitable theme for the Chinese brush. A *Sung* poem, and perhaps the only one of note, that makes a passing reference to military splendour in glowing terms, does so only with the object of showing its fragility and vanity. It is known as the *First Chak Bek Fu*, a long poem on the ancient 'Trafalgar' of the *Three Kingdoms*. Here is the passage in substance:

A breeze blew gently.
The water was calm.
We raised our glasses to our guests,
singing poetic songs in company of a lustrous moon.
A guest who played the lute sang in response;
But the tune was sad.
We asked why it was in such a mournful tone.
In reply, the guest murmured:
'The moon is bright, the stars are scanty in the sky,
While blackbirds southward fly.'
Is this not from a poem by Tso Meng Tek? [2]
When he swept down from *Ching Chow* [3]
to *Kiang Ling* [4] and onwards to the East,

[1] Press communiqué from *Chengtu*, 31st August 1942. As this was transmitted by wireless, some omissions and clerical errors are possible.
[2] Better known as Tso Chau, who, preparing the ground for the ultimate usurpation, by his son, of the tottering throne of the then crumbling *Han* dynasty, was the real founder of the shortlived *Wei* dynasty (A.D. 220-265). See *post*, 'Fragments from the *Three Kingdoms*'.
[3] Somewhere in *Hupei* Province.
[4] Down the *Yangtze* river.

with his roaring armada, menacingly and proudly
stretched along a thousand miles, [1]
and his waving banners blotting out the sky,
he himself sipping the flowing cup by the riverside
and composing poems on the spot,
with his lance across his shining armour,
he was indeed the great figure of his time.
Alas! where are all these grandeurs now? [2]

There are, however, people who, because China has long suffered from military unpreparedness, are sometimes inclined to think that Chinese philosophy is too pacific in face of a world that often takes force for vitality. Yet in consequence of the fact that she has been able to withstand unflinchingly and without aid for several long years against invasion by one of the strongest modern military and naval powers, they would say that she owes her strength to her civilization. But the civilization of a people cannot be divorced from its philosophy, which is part and parcel of the other. The two opinions, therefore, cannot go very well together, nor can one get over the dilemma by drawing a line between spiritual and physical forces, saying that Chinese philosophy supplies the former, but, since it discourages the latter, is apt to put the nation at a disadvantage in face of others who worship force. From the philosophical point of view, spiritual force is infinitely the stronger. The one is durable and unbreakable, while the other is transient and fragile. Philosophy, which aims at everlasting truth, cannot but see that all that are violent are self-destructive. A philosophy which insists on benevolence, righteousness, propriety, and sincerity, can teach nothing amiss. It is these ideals that form the base of Chinese civilization and culture which took root more than forty centuries ago, and have served as China's *tabula in naufragio* at various times in the course of her history when she was caught in a social or political storm. After all, to be strong in national character, nourished in benevolence, righteousness, propriety, and sincerity, is in no way inconsistent with being strong also in national defence. Weakness in national defence may be due to one cause or another, but cannot be attributed to a philosophy that aims at peace and the elevation of man. Confucius, to whom we largely owe these ideals, has said nothing that may be construed as implying that national defence may be neglected. Indeed, when asked on one occasion about government, he answered: 'Have sufficient food, sufficient military preparedness, and confidence

[1] Chinese mile, which is about one third of an English mile.
[2] By Soo Tung Po. See *Collected Ancient Essays.*

of the people,'[1] though, of course, he aimed at an ideal social order, under which all nations would form a true Commonwealth and there would be no war and no cause for war.[2] Similarly, to be a *Jiun Tze* or gentleman is in no way inconsistent with being at the same time a warrior, scientist, or expert in any branch of knowledge essential to the needs of a modern world. But to have knowledge without being a *Jiun Tze* or gentleman will not do. The 'Chamber of Horrors' in Madame Tussaud's is filled with men of no mean knowledge but mean character.

Lastly, it may be observed that a philosopher like Mencius, for instance, who was sought after by kings and princes ready to heap upon him honours and riches if only he would say 'yes' to them, but who would choose to live in retirement and obscurity rather than budge an inch from his principles, could not have spoken, as he did, without a supreme conviction and a lively sense of the truth of what he said. If this is true of the philosophy of Mencius, it can only be still more so of the philosophy of those sages of whose doctrines he is an ardent and devoted exponent. What has been amiss in the past, as evidenced in the rise and fall of dynasties, is due not to any defect in any of the fundamental doctrines taught by these sages but to the fact that these doctrines have not always been faithfully followed. Chinese people, therefore, should not take lightly, and still less belittle, as some are inclined to do, what their forefathers have treasured for centuries and what has given them wisdom, strength, and capacity for survival. Even a tale that is typical of Chinese sentiment or character should be cherished. There is a story that a man was going to meet a saint on a certain day at a certain place, and had the intention of making a wish for himself on meeting the saint. On his way to keep his appointment he met a stranger, who asked him where he was going and, on being told that he was going to meet a saint, requested him to make a wish for him (the person requesting). He (the person requested) promised. On meeting the saint, he was informed that he could make only one wish, and that, if he made one for others, he could not make any for himself. Faced with this dilemma, he, in spite of the fact that this was his only chance in life to meet a saint, would not break his promise made to the person he had met during his journey, and, after some reflection, made the wish for the latter. But in fact, through his faithfulness and piety, he received his desired blessings from the saint. In other words, the Chinese believe that 'God helps those who help *others*'.

[1] See *ante*, p. 131.
[2] See *ante*, p. 89.

CHAPTER 5

FAMILY

ONE often hears it said that, in the West the social unit is the individual, while in China it is the family. So far as the latter part of
the statement is concerned, this in my opinion can at most amount
only to a point of view. The Chinese referring to themselves speak
always of 400 or 450 million souls and never of such and such a
number of families. In succession, too, one succeeds always to a
definite person and never to a family, though, as a consequence of
the succession, one has to discharge the burden of the family to
which the deceased belonged. 'People', says Mencius, 'have a constant (habit of) saying (things without necessarily comprehending
their proper meaning). They all say "the Empire, the State, and
the family", (without realizing that) the root of the Empire is in the
State, the root of the State is in the family, and the root of the
family is in oneself' (i.e., the individual).[1] This passage, it is true,
has the implied meaning, as given in the *Great Learning*,[2] that the
moral improvement of one's own person is the root or starting point
of all improvements, whether of the family or of the State or of the
Empire; but this only shows that even in the moral domain, it is
also the individual that is, in the last analysis, considered to be the
unit.

Sometimes one also finds in modern legal periodicals attempts to
assimilate the Chinese family to that of the Romans, with all the
doctrines of *potestas* and *manus* of the latter. Such assimilation can
only be misleading. The Chinese have indeed their family council;
but its head does not occupy the position of the Roman *paterfamilias*.
As this is not meant to be a legal treatise, it would be out of place
to go into here the various juridical aspects of the two systems. It
may, however, be said that the Chinese father, though he possesses
great power and influence over his children, has never been accorded
a power so extensive and absolute as the *potestas* possessed by the
Romans. Indeed, Chinese parental power is, as we shall see later,
much softened by the doctrine of parental tenderness, which in
Chinese is called *Chi*. Moreover, both in the domain of law and in
the sphere of morals, the Chinese mother is always linked up with

[1] *Mencius*, Bk. IV, Pt. I, Ch. 5. For words in brackets see Orthodox commentary,
the text of which for the word "meaning" literally means "order".
[2] See *ante*, p. 60.

the father in the term 'father and mother', so that the power of
the mother is equal to that of the father—a fact which makes all the
difference between the Chinese system and that of the Romans,
which placed all the powers over the children in the hands of the
father, or rather the *paterfamilias*. The Roman doctrine of *manus*, that
is, the power or rights collectively of a husband over his wife when
the marriage was in certain legal forms, such as by *coemptio* or
confarreatio, has still less place in the Chinese system; for it put
the woman under perpetual guardianship, whereas, according to the
Chinese system, husband and wife are equals and the power of the
wife, including that over the children, is accentuated by the death
of the husband. The difference between the two systems is at bottom
due to the fact that, while the Romans distinguished themselves in
law, the Chinese cultivated themselves in *Li* (moral rules of correct
conduct or propriety). The XII Tables, the first written law introduced into Rome (451-449 B.C.), allowed the unpaid creditors the
right of cutting up the body of their delinquent debtor, so that one
might receive an arm, and another a leg, to satisfy their legal claims
(Table II). In reading this, one cannot help wishing, for the benefit
of the Roman debtors, that Julius Caesar should have been born a
few centuries earlier, so that he could have invaded the British Isles
at the time of the compilation of the XII Tables and, on his withdrawal from these islands, taken back with him, for the purpose of
heading a commission to revise the Roman code, a Briton who,
in anticipation of the poetic genius of his illustrious countryman
of the Elizabethan era, might, in seasoning justice with mercy, have
introduced a Portia of Rome in advance of the Portia of Venice!
Chinese debtors and even criminals in that period were far more
fortunate. We are told:

'Yang Foo, having been appointed chief judge of criminal justice, consulted (his master) Tseng Tse[1] on his duties. Tseng
Tse said: "The rulers have neglected their duties and, in consequence, the people have for a long time been demoralized. (Therefore in the discharge of your duties as a judge) whenever you have
found out the truth of an accusation, be grieved and compassionate
for the accused rather than jubilant over your success in the
finding."'[2]

The spirit of this advice is quite in accordance with the words of
Mencius, already quoted, that to neglect the welfare of the people
and 'allow them thus to become entangled in crimes and then to

[1] The disciple who composed the *Great Learning*; see *ante*, p. 57.
[2] Confucius: *Lun Yu*, Pt. XIX, Ch. 19.

follow them up with punishments would be to ensnare the people'. [1]
In both cases the blame for the existence of crimes is laid primarily
at the door of those who govern, just as, according to Whichcote,
'the execution of malefactors is no more to the credit of rulers than
the death of patients is to the credit of physicians'. [2] That justice
should be humane is a rule that was as old as Emperor Yu (2205-
2198 B.C.), whose instructions to the judge were:

> 'Punishment should not be extended to one's descendants; re-
> ward should be so extended. Involuntary faults should be pardoned,
> however great they may be; voluntary faults should be punished,
> though they may be small. In cases of guilt when there is doubt
> (as to whether a heavier or lighter punishment should be imposed),
> decide on the latter; in cases of merit when there is doubt (as to
> whether a greater or smaller reward should be given), decide on
> the former. Rather err in letting off a person who is guilty than
> err in condemning to death a person who is innocent.' [3]

Though the Chinese system differs greatly from the Roman
system, it is, however, true to say that the family tie of the Chinese
is, like that of the Romans, very close. Chinese parents, partly
through instinct and partly by habit, would take a deep interest in
their children throughout their lives, while Chinese children, owing
to the doctrine of filial piety, apart from nature, are ever reminded,
if not indeed mindful, of their filial duties towards their parents.
Literature and sayings depicting parental love are abundant. Here
are some instances:

1. 'Parents, showing love to their dear child,
   would do with grace all forms of self-denial.' [4]

2. 'Tender mother holding thread and pin
   Sews the coat of her departing son.
   Stitches after stitches she puts in,
   Lest his return may be a tardy one.' [5]

---

[1] See *ante*, p. 143.
[2] Kenny: *Outlines of Criminal Law*, p. 30. (1929). Whichcote's words have been called
by Prof. Kenny an overstatement; because 'Whereas the death of one patient
never constitutes any step towards the cure of others, the execution of a man,
whom the fear of punishment has not deterred from murder, may help nevertheless to deter others.' In my opinion, Prof. Kenny's comment is correct from the
standpoint of deterrence, but Whichcote's observation is no exaggeration from
the standpoint of government; for a ruler cannot escape responsibility for the
existence of crimes within his dominion. At least, their existence is no credit to him.
[3] *Book of History*, Bk. IV, Record of *Yu*, Title *Da Yu Mu*.
[4] A common saying.
[5] *'Words of a Travelling Son'*, by Meng Chia of *Tang* dynasty.

The last two lines mean that separation between mother and child always seems long to the mother, whose anxiety and care are shown in the close stitching intended to make the garment durable; for she fears, as she always feels, that the child's absence will be long—an apprehension nursed in parental affection.

Filial love is bound up with the doctrine of filial piety, which is not only a salient characteristic of the Chinese family, but also a corner stone of Chinese civilization. In the words of Confucius, 'Civilization commenced with filial piety', [1] a statement that can be well appreciated, if one realizes that the first moment, when the children of men living in the cave began to share willingly their food with their helpless parents, must have been the dawn of civilization and marked the date of distinction between men and lower animals; for 'the man differs from the beast only by a hair's-breadth', [2] consisting in the fact that men are by nature capable of loving their neighbours—a sentiment which is absent in beasts, and, as already discussed in a preceding chapter, [3] must have, in the first instance, been shown to their nearest relatives. There are, however, people who, misapprehending the true nature of the doctrine, think that it gives the parents an excessive control over the children and impedes social progress. Such opinion is, as will be seen, quite unfounded. Still more so is the opinion that 'the root of the Chinese practice of filial piety we believe to be a mixture of fear and self-love'. [4] As observed by one sinologue, 'Confucius taught filial piety as the basis of all happiness in the life of the people'. [5] 'Suppose we view Christianity', says another, 'more particularly through the eyes of the Gospel according to St. John the Divine, to what extent would it be true to say that Christianity is essentially a filial piety religion?' [6]

The doctrine of filial piety has prevailed since the time of the sage Emperor Shun (2255-2205 B.C.), who owed his selection, by Emperor Yao (2357-2255 B.C.) to be the successor to the Empire, largely to his great filial piety, which was heightened by the fact that the conduct of his father towards him was very unnatural. We are told by Mencius that Shun felt that 'the glory and wealth of his Imperial state could not minister to the sorrow of his soul, for which disease he knew that the only remedy was to respect the feelings of his parents and make

[1] *Book of Filial Piety*, Bk. I, Ch. 1.
[2] *Mencius*, Bk. IV, Pt. II, Ch. 28.
[3] See *ante*, p. 54.
[4] Arthur H. Smith: *Chinese Characteristics*, p. 184.
[5] Herbert A. Glies: *Civilization of China*, p. 70.
[6] E. R. Hughes: *Oxford and the Comparative Study of Chinese Philosophy and Religion*, pp. 20-1.

them happy'[1] . . . a sentiment that may be readily understood in the light of the letter which Queen Anne, when still Princess, wrote to her father asking for forgiveness, saying: 'It will be a great addition to the ease I propose to my own mind by this plain confession if I am so happy as to find that it bring any real satisfaction to you, and that you are as indulgent and ready to receive my humble submission as I am to make them, in a free disinterested acknowledgment of my fault, for no other end but to deserve and receive your pardon.'[2] The two cases are of course widely different, for Shun had no cause for asking forgiveness; yet, as in the one case a Princess destined to be Queen felt that she needed her father's pardon for *adding to the ease of her own mind* and, in the other, an Emperor felt that the sole remedy that could 'minister to the sorrow of his soul' was to respect the feelings of his parents and make them happy, there is between them at least some sentiment in common. However, the doctrine of filial piety has never been an instrument of parental tyranny, if such a thing can ever exist. Filial piety, so long as it does not coincide with legal duties, is like all other forms of piety a matter of conscience; for 'love, as an affection, cannot be commanded'.[3] Let the point be illustrated by a well-known and well-founded story. One winter evening, when it was piercing cold, Min Tze Hen, a disciple of Confucius, was sitting in the company of his father and stepmother with her two children. As he was shivering, the father asked him why, and, on receiving no intelligent answer from him, examined his garment and was astonished to discover that it, unlike those worn by the other two children, was lined with some very inferior stuff. Being furious with the wife at this discovery, the father wanted to divorce her, or rather to eject her from the family. Thereupon, Min Tze Hen, though still in his tender age, pleaded in tears with the father, saying: 'If mother remains, one child may be cold; but if mother is gone, three children will be orphaned.' The appeal was so touching that the father was calmed, and the stepmother reformed. This is an instance of filial piety of the purest and simplest nature; because it springs spontaneously from a child; but it is one that shows enough that filial piety, like all other forms of piety, has to proceed from a person of his own accord. It is true that there have been cases, particularly in the past, where persons, believing to be in conformity with the doctrine of filial piety, have made sacrifices that may be deemed excessive or even foolish. But every doctrine worth its name has its martyrs, who themselves never think that their sacrifices are

[1] *Mencius*, Bk. V, Pt. I, Ch. i, Sec. 4.
[2] M. K. Hopkinson: *Anne of England*, p. 126.
[3] Kant. See Edward Westermarck: *Ethical Relativity*, p. 160.

made in vain, and filial piety is no exception. There have also been cases, where a person gives up a high office, in order to live in retirement with his aged father or mother during his or her remaining years. The well-known case of this kind is that of the famous scholar Li Mi of the *Tsin* Dynasty (A.D. 265-419), whose petition for releasing him from office, in order that he might live quietly with his aged grandmother until her death, contains a sentence, which has since become a classic. It reads:

'Your humble minister could not be what he is without his grandmother, [1] nor can she live her remaining years happily without him.' [2]

A reason like this advanced by a high officer of State for relinquishing his post must sound strange to a modern ear; for in these days one would naturally think that the problem can be easily solved, in the case mentioned, by having the aged grandmother to live with the grandson. But the matter then was not so simple. China is an immense country, and, in the days when that sentence was penned, the distance between the Court, where the minister served, and the province, where his native home was, might be thousands of miles, which had to be travelled wholly on foot or horseback. Such a journey would be out of the question for an old woman. Nowadays, such cases are rare, thanks to the modern means of communication. Yet, it is not unusual for a person to decline a diplomatic post abroad, because his father or mother is very old. However, such an act is in no way dictated by the doctrine of filial piety. It is simply a matter of individual sentiment, though it may be said to be very Chinese. Filial piety, as a doctrine, does not require the children to be always with the parents. On the contrary, when children have grown up, parents rather expect them to go out into the world to fulfil their missions of life, and would never allow themselves to be in the way of their achievements. This is quite clear from the following definitions of the term 'filial piety', given in the Classics:

1. 'Filial piety is of three grades. The highest is to honour the parents by achievements, the lesser is not to disgrace oneself, thereby casting reflections on the parents, and the least is to be able to support the parents. . . . Lack of self-respect is want of filial piety; disloyalty in serving the sovereign is want of filial piety; negligence in the administration of office is want of filial piety;

[1] This referred to the fact that he was an orphan in his infancy and had been brought up entirely by his grandmother.
[2] *Collected Ancient Essays*, Standard edition.

insincerity to friends is want of filial piety; and lack of bravery in battle is want of filial piety. . . . Trees should be cut, and animals should be killed, according to season. The Master (Confucius) said: "To cut a tree or kill an animal not according to season is want of filial piety." Petty filial piety consists in exerting oneself for the parents; mediocre filial piety consists in practising benevolence and righteousness; great filial piety consists in conferring extensive benefits on mankind.'[1]

2. 'Filial piety begins with love of parents, matures in service to the sovereign, and ends in establishing oneself according to truth and righteousness.'[2]

It may be asked what filial piety has to do with things like loyalty to the Sovereign or State, conduct towards friends or in battle, service to society or mankind, and cutting of trees or killing of animals, none of which has any visible connection with being 'filial'. The answer is that parents, naturally or presumably, intend or wish that their children should first of all fulfil their duties as good citizens and, if possible, have achievements, so that any conduct conforming to this parental intention or wish is filial piety and, conversely, any conduct contrary to it is lack of filial piety. As to the cutting of trees or killing of animals not according to season, this is considered to be wanton or cruel, and wantonness or cruelty of any kind is repugnant to virtue, of which filial piety is only one form. Thus seen, filial piety only in its first stage and elementary nature, means mere love of parents, its ultimate purport being the formation of character, attainment of virtue, and service to society and mankind.

Filial piety, moreover, never means blind obedience to one's parents, for instance, to the extent of doing something unrighteous. In English law, when a crime is committed by the wife in the presence of the husband the rule of 'presumed compulsion'[3] is applied in favour of the wife. But in Chinese law no such rule ever exists in favour of the son, in spite of the doctrine of filial piety. Indeed, Confucius even says: 'A father has a disputant son,'[4] which means that one may and should reason with one's parents when their orders are contrary to righteousness, such as the commission of a crime or sin; for in such circumstances blind obedience would only do the parents a bad turn, contrary in fact to filial piety.

[1] *Book of Li*, Bk. XLVIII, Title *Tse Yee*. In modern phraseology, particularly as sovereignty now resides in the people, the word 'sovereign', occurring in this and the next passages, may well be rendered by the word 'State'.
[2] *Book of Filial Piety*, Bk. I, Ch. I.
[3] Kenny: *Outlines of Criminal Law*, p. 72 (1929).
[4] *Book of Filial Piety*, Ch. 15.

Filial piety, even when confined to mere love of parents, is some-thing worthy of man as man. 'The assassin', says Edmund De Amicis, 'who respects his mother has still something good in his heart.' Life is also so much sweeter, if a person having brought up his children finds, in his days of old age and failing health, that he can rely on their affection. For what would be the state of society, if men, when they have grown up and ceased to be dependent on their parents, should also cease to be attached to them, as they did when they were young? Surely, the sacred relation between parent and child means more than 'cupboard love'. From the social stand-point, the doctrine of filial piety throws no unequal burden on any section of the community, as some people may think; for every person may have children and is bound in time to become old, so that in turn he will receive what he gives. It is Goethe, I think, who says: 'He who does not respect the aged when he is young will himself not be respected when he is old.' In China the doctrine in fact confers an inestimable benefit on those who observe it; because, filial piety being universally deemed to be a high virtue, those who are known for it are always accorded a marked social esteem—a fact that often entails no little material advantage, or at least shows that the performance of no other natural duty is so handsomely rewarded as filial piety. From the moral standpoint, it is only reciprocal that children who, in the normal case, receive so much from their parents in care and affection, should, in turn, show them care and affection, when most needed. To be otherwise would be ungrateful. While ingratitude like a stab from behind is one of the worst forms of sin, gratitude, like the payment of a just debt, is only an elementary form of virtue, and, if we remember the already quoted saying:

'Parents, showing love to their dear child,
Would do with grace all forms of self-denial,'

filial piety is but an elementary form of gratitude. In other words, filial piety, so far as it is a duty, is a duty dictated by Nature and, so far as it is a virtue, is a virtue that, like charity, should begin at home. That is why it is said that 'filial piety is the root of virtue', [1] and that 'no sin is greater than conduct that is unfilial' [2] because it poisons the spring of nature. According to the English poet, Caesar died immediately from a burst heart caused by ingratitude rather than from the wound caused by the stab received from his assassin; for has not Shakespeare said:

[1] Book of Filial Piety, Ch. 1; Confucius: Lun Yu, Pt. I, Ch. 2, Sec. 2.
[2] Book of Filial Piety, Ch. 11.

. . . 'When the noble Caesar saw him stab,
Ingratitude, more strong than traitor's arms,
Quite vanquish'd him: then burst his mighty heart'? [1]

If the heart is so vulnerable even in the case of a man who 'rather tells thee what is to be feared than what *he* fears', [2] how easily it must be capable of being shattered by the unfilial conduct of one's own children. Lastly, let us hearken to the words of Philo on the Ten Commandments:

'But if we fail to draw our proper lesson from the things of earth, let us pass to the realm of winged creatures that make voyage through the air, that from them we may learn our duty. Aged storks, unable to fly, stay in their nests, their offspring fly, so to say, over all lands and seas, seeking sustenance in all places for their parents; these, in consideration of their age, deservedly enjoy quiet, abundance, even comforts. And the younger storks console themselves for the irksomeness of their voyaging with the consciousness of their discharge of filial duty and the expectation of similar treatment on the part of their offspring, when they too have grown old. Thus they pay back, at the time when needed, the debt they owe, returning what they have received; for from others they cannot obtain sustenance either at the beginning of life, when they are small, or, when they have become old, at life's end. From no other teacher than nature herself have they learned to care for the aged, just as they themselves were cared for when they were young.' [3]

To the above words of Philo may be added the following extracts of two letters written by Dr. Johnson to Boswell:

1. 'The longer we live, and the more we think, the higher value we learn to put on the friendship and tenderness of *parents* and of friends. *Parents we can have but once;* and he promises himself too much, who enters life with the expectation of finding many friends.' [4]

2. 'Your resolution to please your father I sincerely approve. . . . We all live upon the hope of pleasing somebody, and *the pleasure*

[1] Shakespeare: *Julius Caesar*, Act III, Sc. II, Ls. 189-91.
[2] Shakespeare: *Julius Caesar*, Act I, Sc. II, Ls. 300-1.
[3] Hugo Grotius: '*De Jure Belli Ac Pacis*,' Bk. I, Sec. 7, *note 2*, Trans. by Francis W. Kelsey, Vol. II, p. 11.
[4] Boswell's *Life of Johnson*; Ed. G. Routledge & Sons, Vol. II, pp. 3 and 13. Letters dated 14th January 1766 and 21st August 1776 respectively. The italics are mine.

of pleasing ought to be greatest, when our endeavours are exerted in conse-quence of duty.' [1]

The doctrine of filial piety has its counterbalance in the doctrine of *Chi*, which, as an adjective, meaning tender, kind, gentle, or merciful, may here, as a noun, be translated as parental tenderness. The latter doctrine is based on the idea that tenderness or lack of tenderness to one's own children is, apart from other considerations, in fact tenderness or lack of tenderness to the grandchildren of one's own parents. On one occasion, Confucius, hearing that his disciple Tseng Tze had allowed himself to be beaten unconscious by his father, reproved him severely, saying to his fellow disciples that 'he was quite wrong in not running away from violence; because, if he had allowed himself to be killed, he would have been guilty of gross unfilial conduct by involving his father in the stigma of unrighteous-ness and, what is more serious, in the crime of killing a subject of the Emperor'. [2]

In conventional language, however, it is the mother who is called *Chi*, the 'Tender or Gentle One', while the father is called *Yen*, the 'Grave or Severe One'. But this must not be taken to imply that the father is in any way unkind or hardhearted. 'Chinese parents', says a well-known sinologue, 'are, if anything, over-indulgent to their children. The father is, indeed, popularly known as the "Severe One" and it is a Confucian tradition that he should not spare the rod and so spoil the child, but he draws the line at a poker. The mother, the "Gentle One", is, speaking broadly, a soft-hearted, sweet-natured specimen of humanity, one of those women to whom hundreds of Europeans owe deep debts of gratitude for the care and affection lavished upon their alien children. . . . Among other atro-cious libels which have fastened upon the fair fame of the Chinese people, first and foremost stands the charge of female infanticide, now happily, though still slowly, fading from the calculations of those who seek the truth. . . . Illegitimate children, the source of so much baby-farming and infanticide elsewhere, are practically un-known in China; and the same may be said of divorce.' [3]

The relation between parent and child is, no doubt, considered sacred in every country. But it is possible that the degree of reaction of popular sentiments to that sacredness varies. An instance of this may be drawn from two well-known fictions, one of which is the

[1] Boswell's *Life of Johnson*; Ed. G. Routledge & Sons, Vol. II, pp. 3 and 13. Letters dated 14th January 1766 and 21st August 1776 respectively. The italics are mine.
[2] *Family Sayings of Confucius*, Bk. IV, p. 3.
[3] Herbert A. Giles: *The Civilization of China*, pp. 96 and 99.

comedy *L'Avare* by Molière, the other being the Chinese historical romance, the *Three Kingdoms*, written in the *Ming* Dynasty (A.D. 1368-1644). In the comedy mentioned, father and son wooing the same woman are portrayed in a comic scene as follows:

Harpagon: Oh! sus, mon fils, savez-vous ce qu'il y a? C'est qu'il faut songer, s'il vous plaît, à vous défaire de votre amour, à cesser toutes vos poursuites auprès d'une personne que je prétends pour moi, et à vous marier dans peu avec celle qu'on vous destine.

Cléante: Oui, mon père, c'est ainsi que vous me jouez! Eh bien! puisque les choses en sont venues là, je vous déclare, moi, que je ne quitterai point la passion que j'ai pour Mariane, qu'il n'y a point d'extrémité où je ne m'abandonne pour vous disputer sa conquête, et que, si vous avez pour vous le consentement d'une mère, j'aurai d'autres secours peut-être, qui combattront pour moi.

Harpagon: Comment, pendard! tu as l'audace d'aller sur mes brisées?

Cléante: C'est vous qui allez sur les miennes, et je suis le premier en date.

Harpagon: Ne suis-je pas ton père? et ne me dois-tu pas respect?

Cléante: Ce ne sont point ici des choses où les enfants soient obligés de déférer aux pères, et l'amour ne connaît personne.

Harpagon: Je te ferai bien me connaître avec de bons coups de bâton.

Cléante: Toutes vos menaces ne me feront rien.

Harpagon: Tu renonceras à Mariane.

Cléante: Point du tout. [1]

[1] Molière: *L'Avare*, Act IV, Sc. III. Translation:

Harpagon: Oh! now then, my boy, do you know what's the matter? You must, if you please, think of getting rid of your love-affair by ceasing all your overtures made to a person whom I claim for myself, and of marrying in the near future one who is destined for you.

Cléante: Yes, my father, it is in this way that you have been playing against me! Well, since things have got to such a state, I tell you frankly that I will not give up the passion I have for Mariane: there is no limit to which I will not go in disputing your conquest, and though you have in your favour the consent of a mother, I shall have, perhaps, other forces that will work in my favour.

Harpagon: What! rascal, you have the audacity to be my rival?

Cléante: It is you who are my rival, and I was the first in the game too.

Harpagon: Am I not your father, and must not you respect me?

Cléante: These are not things in which children are bound to respect their fathers. Love knows nobody.

Harpagon: I will make you respect me with my stick.

Cléante: All your threats will mean nothing to me.

Harpagon: You shall give up Mariane.

Cléante: Not at all.

In the story of the *Three Kingdoms*, Sun Chuan, uncrowned king of State *Wu* (about A.D. 200) contrived to eliminate Lew Bei, [1] his rival for the Empire. The latter, being a widower, was to be lured to *Wu* on a feigned proposal from Sun Chuan to be suitor to his younger sister. It was planned that after Lew Bei had arrived in *Wu*, he should be confronted with certain territorial demands and, on their rejection, be made prisoner. However, contrary to the intention of Sun Chuan, the news of a possible happy event reached the ears of the 'royal' mother, who, on Lew Bei's arrival in *Wu*, granted him an audience as her prospective son-in-law. As he won her approval, she took him under her wing. From that moment Sun Chuan was simply paralysed in face of the unexpected situation so created, because he could not, and would not, do anything that might shock the feelings of his mother.

The sentiment thus incidentally revealed is the more remarkable; because the story was intended to illustrate a political dilemma rather than filial piety. The novelist in devising something to frustrate the plot must have instinctively felt that the sacredness of parental relation is such that it must be respected even in a political drama. To be otherwise, and, *a fortiori*, to put mother and son in a comic light, such as parent and child wooing the same person, would make the story un-Chinese and strange in the eyes of its readers.

The term 'filial piety' (*Hsiao*) is often used together with the term *Di*, which means behaving like a dutiful younger brother. As already mentioned, [2] it is a Confucian doctrine that a youth should fulfil, in the best manner, at home, his filial duties to his parents (*Hsiao*) and, abroad, his brotherly duties to his elders (*Di*)—a doctrine that has for centuries been taught to Chinese youths almost from the days they quitted their cradles. Such conduct is deemed not only as essential to the formation of good character but also as a practical contribution to good government. Confucius, when once asked why he took no part in the Government, replied:

'The *Book of History* thus speaks [3] of filial piety "You fulfil your filial and brotherly duties and so render (*pro tanto*) your service to the Government." [4] He who fulfils these duties, therefore, contributes in effect his share to good government. What is then the necessity of actually taking part in the government (so long as one fulfils these duties).' [5]

[1] See *post*, *Fragments from the 'Three Kingdoms.'*
[2] See *ante*, p. 85.
[3] This part of the reply is not a question, though it seems to be so in form. See commentary.
[4] *Book of History*, Bk. XVIII, Records of *Chow*, Title *Tsun Chun*, No. 23.
[5] Confucius: *Lun Yu*, Pt. II, Ch. 21.

Mencius has spoken even more plainly in this respect as follows:

'The path of duty is (in fact) near, but some people (are apt to
neglect the duties that are immediate and pretentiously but
vainly) seek what is remote. The fulfilment of duty is (in fact)
easy, but some people (are apt to neglect the duties that are plain
and pretentiously but vainly) seek what is difficult. If every person
would love his parents and respect his elders and superiors (to
whom respect is due), the whole world would be peaceful.' [1]

The main ideas of the two passages are substantially the same. A
political community has its unit in the individual. If every person
plays his part, the community or its government will fare well. But
in order to play one's part, one must first of all fulfil one's elementary
and immediate duties; for without such elementary virtue and discipline it would be vain to talk of the fulfilment of others that are
of a more exacting nature. How far such ideas are still intelligible to
a modern world may conceivably be a question capable of being
answered in various ways; but they have been perfectly compre-
hensible to the Chinese for many centuries. If I may mention, in a
lighter vein, an anecdote, a Western friend of mine has, in reference
to the saying quoted from Mencius, observed: 'With us it would
certainly be correct to say that if every man loves his wife and respects his mother-in-law, the whole world will be peaceful!' Though
the observation was meant to convey rather wit than wisdom, I for
one cannot see in it anything amiss, and even venture to think that
in these days, when women's votes count so much in election in
some countries, the observation is fraught with political sagacity!
However, this is only by the way; but it furnishes a convenient break
for the discussion of the position of the Chinese woman.

It may be helpful to quote here a passage from a foreign author in
order that some points therein raised may be elucidated, and that
an avenue may thus be cleared for a better understanding of Chinese
institutions:

'The Chinese doctrine has nothing to say on behalf of its
daughters but everything on behalf of its sons. If the Chinese eye
had not for ages been colour-blind on this subject, this gross out-
rage on human nature could not have failed of detection. By the
accident of sex the infant is a family divinity. By the accident of
sex she is a dreaded burden, liable to be destroyed, and certain to
be despised. The Chinese doctrine of filial piety puts the wife on

[1] *Mencius*, Bk. IV, Pt. I, Ch. 11. For words inserted in brackets see commentary and
'*Correct Interpretation of Mencius*', Bk. XV, p. 3.

an inferior plane. Confucius has nothing to say of the duties of wives to husbands or of husbands to wives. Christianity requires a man to leave his father and mother, and cleave to his wife. Confucianism requires a man to cleave to his father and mother, and to compel his wife to do the same. If the relation between the husband and his parents conflicts with that between the husband and his wife, the latter, as the lesser and inferior, is the relation which must yield. The whole structure of Chinese society, which is modelled upon the patriarchal plan, has grave evils. It encourages the suppression of some of the natural instincts of the heart that other instincts may be cultivated to an extreme degree. It results in the almost entire subordination of the younger during the whole life of those who are older.'[1]

In regard to the passage above quoted, it may first be observed that, as all doctrines teach the fulfilment of duties, they know no sex, though in their application the condition of *mutatis mutandis* is necessarily implied. For instance, filial piety being a virtue to be expected from one's children, its application cannot, by its very nature, have any sex limitation. Things like 'bravery in battle', as a form of filial piety, are of course inapplicable to women, except, perhaps in these days of total war, where women equally play their part. But others, such as 'Honour thy father and thy mother' and be virtuous, are obviously no less applicable to daughters than to sons. The apparent misunderstanding of the author just quoted may be due to the fact that Chinese pronouns have no gender, and especially to the fact that the Chinese word 'son' (*tze*) was often used to mean both daughter and son, for its original meaning was 'descendant' or 'child', while the word 'brother' was sometimes used to mean sister as well, e.g.:

  1. 'The Master said that Kung Yair Cheang was fit to be a son-in-law; for though he had been in prison, he was not guilty. Accordingly, he (Confucius) had his own *tze* [which would now mean son] married to him (Kung Yair Cheang).'[2]
  2. 'The wife of Ni Tze[3] and the wife of Tze Loo are brothers (*hsung di*).'[4]

In language of the present day the term for sisters is *tsia mei*; yet in literary composition one still frequently employs the term 'female

---

[1] Arthur H. Smith: *Chinese Characteristics*, p. 183.
[2] Confucius: *Lun Yu*, Pt. V, Ch. 1, Secs. 1-2.
[3] Here *Tze* in capital letters means Master, as explained before.
[4] *Mencius*, Bk. V, Pt. I, Ch. 8, Sec. 2.

brother' for sister. All these may be a little complicated, but common sense uninfluenced by preconceptions should guard one against gross misunderstanding. It would not do, for instance, to say, even without being acquainted with the above text of Mencius, using the term 'brother' for 'sister', that the Chinese saying, 'Within the four seas all are brethren' applies only to men and not to women, or to say that Anglo-Saxon people ignore the existence of women, because their word for the human race is 'mankind', or that the English poet Pope has not given due honour to the fair sex in his line: "The proper study of mankind is man.'[1] Nor should the use of the pronoun 'he' lead one to think that only the male sex is meant. The fact that it was not until 1889 that English Parliament passed a Statute,[2] providing that 'words importing the masculine gender prima facie include females', shows that even English lawyers, whose legal phraseology is as a rule very precise, never thought until 1889 that the use of the pronoun 'he', instead of the phrase 'he or she', might cause any confusion. In Chinese an expression like 'he or she' would be literary barbarism. As to the allegation that female children are liable to be destroyed, one need only refer to the words already quoted from Professor Giles.[3]

It is also incorrect to say that 'the doctrine of filial piety puts the wife on an inferior plane'. Her status, as daughter-in-law, is simply assimilated to that of her husband—a fact that implies no more inferiority than a wife's taking the nationality or the surname of the husband, as is the case in most civilized countries. Inferiority in kinship is not the same thing as inequality. Very often it is a privilege; for the 'inferior' is free from the principal responsibilities of the family and, on the death of the superior, succeeds, as a rule, to what the latter has saved in a lifetime. That is why the Chinese sometimes say that one prefers to be a *Shao Yer* (young lord) to being a *Lao Yer* (old lord). On the marriage of a male child, for instance, the custom is that the parents, as a token of affection and recognition of the bride as an ultimate successor to the mother's position in the family, would, apart from giving the bride part of the best jewels of the family, if any, move out from their room, then the best in the family, and give it to the new couple, as the father's parents once did, when he was married. Thus it can hardly be said to be wrong that the wife, while she lives with her husband's parents, should respect their wishes in the same way as her husband. In practice, if the husband earns his living far away from home, the wife would,

[1] *Essay on Man*, II, L. 2.
[2] Interpretation Act, 1889.
[3] See *ante*, p. 172.

if circumstances permit, live with him, as the parents would like them to have children. In that case, no possible 'conflict' could arise. But the wife would feel it a highly moral duty to visit the husband's parents as often as possible and feasible, especially when the latter are getting old and there are no younger members of the family to look after them.

The remark that 'Confucius had nothing to say of the duties of wives to husbands or of husbands to wives' is, to say the least, inaccurate. Confucian doctrines about conjugal relation are many, the following being only a few instances:

1. 'It is said in the *Book of Odes*: "Harmony with wife and children is sweet like the music of the lute or the harp. When concord prevails among brothers, life is delightful. *Conduct thus thy family and be happy with thy wife and children!*" Reciting this Ode with praise, the Master said: "This will make the parents happy!" '[1] In other words, this is the fulfilment of a great filial duty.

2. 'Confucius, in answer to the Ruler of his State about government, said: "The ancient enlightened Kings made it a rule of government to (set the example of) respecting (i.e., being affectionate to) their wives and children. There are good reasons for this; because the wife forms the principal link of parental relation, while the children form the succeeding link of it." '[2]

3. 'The Master said: "The constant duties of universal application in human relations are five, and the requisite virtues for their fulfilment are three. The duties between sovereign and subject, between parent and child,[3] between *husband and wife*, between elder brother and younger brother, and between friends are the five constant duties of universal application. Wisdom (sense of those duties of human relations), benevolence (sympathetic conception of those duties of human relations), and courage (vigorous application of one's mind towards those duties of human relations) are the three requisite virtues of application, while the sole means of attaining these virtues is to be true (to one's soul)." '[4]

Mencius has also spoken on the subject as follows:

'Between parent and child,[5] there should be affection; between sovereign and subject, there should be righteousness; *between hus-*

[1] *Doctrine of the Consistent Mean*, Ch. 15.
[2] *Book of Li*, Bk. L, Title *Duke Aoi Asks*, No. 27.
[3] Lit., father and child.
[4] *Chung Yung* (*Doctrine of the Consistent Mean*), Ch. 20.
[5] Lit., father and child.

band and wife, there should be respective duties; between the elders and
the young, there should be order; between friends, there should be
sincerity.' [1]

The ancient dictionary *Shui Wen* defines the word 'wife' as 'one's
equal'. There is a common saying: 'The husband sings, the wife
follows.' In the *Book of Li* it is said that *'between husband and wife
there should be (mutual) devotion'*, [2] and that 'a woman, when young and
unmarried, follows the father and (after his death) the elder brother;
after marriage, follows the husband; and during widowhood, follows
her son'. [3] The latter part of this passage has often been mistaken
by persons, acquainted more with Roman law than with Chinese
institutions, for the Roman *manus*, which put the woman under
perpetual guardianship. But, as it has already been discussed, [4] this
Roman institution, or anything like it, has never existed in China.
By the doctrine of filial piety, with which my readers must be
familiar by this time, it is always the son who should respect the
wishes of the mother. That part of the passage is therefore simply
a rule of exhortation to woman, who seeking advice should look, as
her 'next friend', first to her father or elder brother, then to her
husband, and, lastly, to her son, as the case may be.

It is, however, true that, in principle, the Chinese husband always
leads the wife, and is never led by her. This is, after all, only in
accordance with the command of the Lord, who 'unto the woman'
said: 'Thy desire *shall be* to thy husband, and he shall rule over thee.' [5]
But, in principle, in which country is this not supposed to be the
case? Indeed, the principle is so universal that rarely, if ever, would
a woman like to hear her husband openly called 'henpecked',
although she is in fact leading him; merely because she would not
like others to think that her mate lacks that masculine quality that
nature assigns to men. Yet, after all, form is never the substance. To
be supposed to lead is one thing, while to lead is another. It may
indeed be that 'the husband sings first' and then 'the wife follows',
according to the common saying, already quoted; but this does not
mean that he may not have to choose a song that is agreeable to her
in order to enjoy 'the sweet music of the lute or the harp', as the
ancient Ode calls it. Nature has yet not failed to endow a species
with some strong point for its protection. According to Lao Tze,
as already quoted, 'the female always conquers (the male) by being

[1] *Mencius*, Bk. III, Pt. I, Ch. 4, Sec. 8.
[2] Bk. LXI, Title *Meaning of Marriage*, No. 44.
[3] Bk. XXVI, Title *Chia Tek Sang*.
[4] See *ante*, p. 163.
[5] Genesis, III, 16.

passive'.¹ In less philosophic parlance one may say that the tenderness and tears of a woman can melt the heart of man. The early
English Chancellor who put 'kisses' after 'kicks' in the phrase
'kicks and kisses', used in the introduction of the Equitable doctrine
of 'restraint in anticipation', must have thought that if women were
ever conquered by men, it was the 'kisses' and not the 'kicks' that
had administered the 'knockout' blow. At any rate, 'The Chinese
woman', says Professor Giles, 'has by no means such a bad time as
is generally supposed to be the case. . . . The Chinese woman often,
in mature life, wields enormous influence over the family, males
included, and is a kind of private Empress Dowager.'² Indeed,
China has twice been ruled by a woman with an iron hand, the first
instance being in the *Tang* dynasty, the second in the *Ching*.

It is true that, in the days when the words of the English sinologue
just quoted were written, the Chinese woman was still disqualified
for any public office, as it was considered that it was more suitable
for her to rule in the family than in the State, yet this disqualifica-
tion was indirectly compensated by the fact that she was, on the one
hand, entitled to share, by right, the rank and honour of her husband
and sons and, on the other, exempted from certain services and
punishments to which men alone are liable. But in the matter of
political enfranchisement for women it will be found that China is
not the only country that has been 'slowly wise' or 'meanly just',³
and that even a country so advanced in politics as England is apt 'to
buried merit raise the tardy bust';⁴ for, if I have been rightly informed, it was only some years after the death of Mrs. Pankhurst,
leader in the movement for women suffrage, that a statue was
erected in her honour. However, Chinese women of to-day are found
in the legislature, the judiciary, the executive, and the diplomatic
service, and, what is more, they play such a notable part, active or
passive, in the present war of resistance that, when its history is to
be written, the historian will have to pay them no less homage than
to their heroic brothers or husbands. De Lolme commenting on the
British Constitution has said that the English Parliament 'can do
everything but make a woman a man, and a man a woman'.⁵ Modern
legislation in China has certainly not attempted to do that, for
nature forbids; but, so far as equal rights are concerned, it has vir-
tually obliterated the distinction between man and woman. Neverthe-

¹ See *ante*, p. 109.
² Herbert A. Giles: *The Civilization of China*, pp. 100 and 104.
³ Dr. Johnson: *Vanity of Human Wishes*.
⁴ Dr. Johnson: *Vanity of Human Wishes*.
⁵ Dicey: *Law of the Constitution*, p. 43, 9th ed.

less, it is still the general belief of the Chinese, which has prevailed since ages past, that the proper function of a woman, as destined by nature, is to be 'a good wife and good mother' (*sen chee leang mu*). Education, and especially family instruction, for women, therefore, still largely aim at that goal. To begin with, social convention commends the chaperonage of women and frowns on the free mixing of women and men. When a man hands a thing over to a woman, or *vice versa*, the rule is that they should avoid touching each other's hand. [1] This rule is known to every educated Chinese, and, though in these days the introduction of certain customs, such as dancing, in certain circles renders inevitable in such circles a modification of this convention, people in general still observe it. A convention like this may sound strange in the twentieth century; but it is no stranger than seeing women in some parts of China, such as Peking (now called Peiping), still curtsy in the street. However, certain Chinese conventions, tending to draw a 'moral cordon' between men and women in their social intercourse, are often mistaken by people, unfamiliar with Chinese culture, for a sign of subjection of women. In fact, the Chinese, having a great reverence for womanhood, the source of future generations, consider feminine purity as something sacred, comparing the woman to flawless jade. She is taught from her days of the nursery to conduct herself always according to propriety (*Li*)—to be more than 'Caesar's wife', to be above *criticism*. [2] The Chinese word for the habitation of a woman is '*kwei*' (閨), which is composed of two words: *jade* (圭) inside a *door* (門). This conception of womanhood with its attendant rules of propriety is not without fruits of a salutary nature. As already quoted from an English author, 'illegitimate children are practically unknown in China, and the same may be said of divorce'. [3]

As to the remark that 'Christianity requires a man to leave his father and mother and cleave to his wife', [4] a Chinese would, with profound respect, think that cleaving to one's wife need not entail the leaving of one's parents, nor would cleaving to one's parents necessarily involve a diminution of one's affection for one's wife, and that life would be so much sweeter, if parents, wife, and oneself should cleave together. As a whole nation can do this in time of war, there is no reason why one's closest relations cannot do this in time of peace. It would be presumptuous on my part to try to interpret the Bible, of which I have only a reverential knowledge; but, with

[1] *Mencius*, Bk. IV, Pt. I, Ch. 17.
[2] For some interesting views read *Autobiography* of Margot Asquith; p. 35.
[3] See *ante*, p. 172.
[4] See *ante*, p. 176.

respect, I venture to observe that the text on which the passage concerned is based does not seem to be wholly incompatible with filial piety. The said passage is apparently taken from St. Matthew, ch. xix, where it is said:

'The Pharisees also came unto him, tempting him, and saying unto him, Is it lawful for a man to put away his wife for every cause?

'And he answered and said unto them; Have ye not read, that he which made *them* at the beginning made them male and female,

'And said, For this cause shall a man leave father and mother, and shall cleave to his wife: and they twain shall be one flesh?

'Wherefore they are no more twain, but one flesh. What therefore God hath joined together, let not man put asunder.'

It seems to me, if I may say so, that the gist of these passages lies in the words '*What God hath joined together, let not man put asunder*'— an injunction that concerns divorcement rather than parental relation. After all, so far as I know, the phrase, 'shall a man leave father and mother, and cleave to his wife', occurs only once in the Bible, whereas the words, 'Honour thy father and thy mother', is repeated no fewer than five times. [1]

It is also incorrect to say that 'Confucianism requires a man to cleave to his father and mother, and to *compel* his wife to do the same'. [2] The fact is that husband and wife are bound by the doctrine of mutual devotion to 'cleave' together; but, as the husband does not in consequence leave his parents, the wife follows him as a matter of course—true to the doctrine that 'husband and wife are one person'. It is, however, true that in China the mother is accorded more respect and consideration than the wife both in the family and in society and, in the light of what has been said in this chapter, it is regarded by the Chinese as rightly so, for at least four other reasons:

1. The wife with her youth and other attractions, together with the tie of children in most cases, is in the nature of things a more powerful competitor for the man's affection than his aged parents. Mencius, who had a profound knowledge of human nature, said: 'When a man is young, he turns his thoughts to his father and mother. When he begins to feel the attraction of beauty, he turns his thoughts to the young and beautiful. When he is married and

---

[1] Exodus, Ch. XX, 12; Deuteronomy, Ch. V, 16; St. Matthew, Ch. XV, 4; Ch. XIX, 19; Ephesians, Ch. VI, 2.

[2] See *ante*, p. 176.

has children, he turns his thoughts to his wife and children. A man of great filial piety turns his thoughts to his father and mother for life.'[1] In other words, a man would naturally cleave to his wife, whereas the parents, as they advance in age and gradually in time become dependent, are in danger of being neglected, unless there are doctrines or customs to maintain a just balance, not to mention that the days with the wife are long, while those with the parents, from the day when one is married, may be short.

2. It is only a question of time when the wife will attain the position of the mother. The temporary identification of her status with that of her husband towards his parents only paves the way for the future, when the doctrine or custom, which seemingly works against her for the present, will operate in her favour.

3. There is no guarantee that a marriage is always happy. For instance, a woman may become a widow while her children are still young; but if she knows that her 'widow-comfort and sorrows' cure'[2] is brought up, he will continue to cleave to her, she will have hope for a brighter future and her grief will be so much softened.

4. A doctrine or custom which protects the aged, making their lives pleasant, cannot fail to promote pure unselfishness on the part of the individual and confer incalculable benefits on society. Thanks to such a doctrine or custom, an aged Chinese father or mother would seldom be, to borrow a line from Goldsmith,[3] 'remote' (because their children no longer cleave to them), 'unfriended' (because he or she is too old to have friends), 'melancholy' (because he or she is obliged to live alone or only with a companion), and 'slow' (because he or she being aged and infirm is shunned by the young). He would be called *Lao Tai Yer* (Honourable Old Man) and she *Lao Tai Tai* (Honourable Old Lady), privileged persons, universally respected and accorded special considerations, so much so that it is good form in China, when one calls on a friend, to pay respects, either by leaving a card or by words of mouth, to his parents. If a person attains eminence, his parents will be the first to be honoured both at home and in society. Thus the Chinese approach old age with no apprehension, knowing that they will not be shunned, deserted, or abandoned, but will, on the contrary, be humoured, respected, and honoured. Indeed, old age to them is a dignified 'pension' in itself, which, though only moral in character, is sure, fair and square.

[1] *Mencius*, Bk. V, Pt. I, Ch. 1, Sec. 5.
[2] Shakespeare: *The Life and Death of King John*, Act III, Sc. IV, L. 105.
[3] *Traveller*, Line 1: 'Remote, unfriended, melancholy, slow.'

To close this chapter and by way of illustration, let me relate a few personal experiences:

1. Once I was invited to an informal dinner in a renowned city of the world, at which I was expected to say a few words, the only other speaker on the occasion being an eminent writer. I was placed on the left-hand side of the host; but to my surprise I was called upon to speak first—an unexpected honour that nearly upset the mental arrangement of my speech. However, at the end of the dinner, seeing that my fellow-speaker was an older man, I went over to salute him in order to have a short conversation, in the manner that every educated Chinese would do in such circumstances, and, thinking that he might be pleased, I said: 'I had the pleasure of reading some of your books when I was a student.' To this he replied: 'You mean that I am getting old' or something to that effect. This unlooked-for answer put me somewhat in the position of Boswell on his first meeting with Dr. Johnson.[1] I was simply *nonplussed* and, after a while but not without an awkward silence, I said: 'No sir, this is not my meaning. But do you think that old age is something to be dreaded or despised? In my country old age is everywhere respected and universally honoured.'

2. Some years ago I happened to be one afternoon at the house of a friend in Peiping (then known as Peking), who was disposing of some surplus objects of art. He, I may mention, was a scholar of the old school, though he had subsequently received a modern education. In the room where the objects were displayed there was a foreign couple of the globe-trotter type with a touch of the commercial agent. In the course of conversation the woman said to the man: 'George, my shoelace is undone. Tie it for me, dear.' Thereupon, she raised her foot upon a chair without ceremony, and the man tied the shoelace without a murmur. This incident did not strike me as anything very extraordinary; because I had lived a long time abroad.

[1] As some of my readers may not know this story, I beg to give it here. Dr. Johnson had prejudices against the Scotch, and Boswell, being a Scotchman, though proud of his country of birth, took care, on his first meeting with the man whom he admired and whose friendship he wanted to cultivate, not to kindle the latter's whimsical sentiments by putting forward his nationality as a claim to the latter's acquaintance. But in introducing him, his friend Davis roguishly coupled his name with the words 'from Scotland'. Thereupon he said: 'Mr. Johnson, I do indeed come from Scotland, but I cannot help it,' in order to soothe Johnson's well-known prejudices against the Scotch; but he received, to his mortification, the witty retort: 'That, sir, I find, is what a very great many of your countrymen cannot help,' seizing the expression 'come from Scotland' and wittily interpreting it, as if Boswell had meant having *come away from it* instead of merely *being of that country*. (See Boswell's *Life of Johnson*, Ed. George Routledge and Sons, Lond., Vol. I, p. 225.)

But my compatriot, in spite of his modern education, was, while this conjugal service was being meekly performed, visibly affected, as if the dignity of his whole sex had been at stake. Had gallant George been the son of the woman, I believe that my compatriot would have been so favourably impressed by the man's filial conduct that he would have 'hugged'[1] him.

3. A place like Shanghai would be the last place in China that one would select as a specimen of her civilization or culture. Yet I have seen there more than once a man of the working class with a saddened face but a resigned look, riding on a rickshaw and holding carefully and tenderly in his arms a sick old woman wrapped in dilapidated blankets or thick garments. What does all this mean? To me it means a great deal. It is the sight of a man of some age but apparently of little education who, though too poor to be able to afford the expenses of an ambulance, would, without a murmur, as evidenced in his look, carry affectionately, as evidenced in his way of holding and wrapping, his sick old mother to the hospital. The poor woman, indeed, may die; but who does not? What matters is, she will die with a peaceful and contented heart, because the person of her own blood whom she has nursed and brought up is by her bedside at the last moment of her life; and the latter will live with an eased conscience, because he is able to perform his last duty to the woman whose hand has rocked his cradle. I often think that this is a beautiful example of humanity, and that, if I were an artist, I would have the scene sanctified by the brush and the picture hung in my study. But, after all, I am expressing only a common Chinese sentiment.

4. I know a self-made man who often thought affectionately of his deceased parents and, in doing so, would drop a tear. I asked him why, and his answer was: 'I owe everything to my parents. As you know, my grandfather was a farmer without a farm, whose only property was his integrity and implements. It was my father who through years of toil and thrift founded a moderate family estate, thanks to which I was able to acquire an education that helped me to attain my present position. But he died while I was still an infant, and it was my mother who brought me up and, by her virtue, inspired me with a right ambition. Without them I would probably be earning my daily bread in the field. Alas! they are no longer in this world, and I have no means of performing to them my filial duties. Now, I comprehend that saying of Confucius: "The age of parents

---

[1] 'Sir, I was once in the company with Smith, and we did not take to each other; but had I known that he loved rhyme as much as you tell me he does, I should have *hugged* him.'—Johnson. Boswell's *Life of Johnson*; Ed. G. Birkbeck Hill, Vol. I, pp. 427-8.

should never be left out of memory. In one respect, it makes one feel happy (because they have attained years); in another respect, it makes one feel apprehensive (because they are getting old and the days of performing one's filial duties to them may be numbered)." '[1]

Lastly, to the Chinese the family is a social factor for peace, as no one who has a family would think lightly of war, and is the happy medium through which nature breeds in man the sense of love, affection, duty, and responsibility.

[1] Confucius: *Lun Yu*, Pt. IV, Ch. 21. The words in brackets are based on orthodox commentary. They do not form part of the quotation.

CHAPTER 6

MARRIAGE

THE Chinese have been depicted by others as a people one of whose chief desires is, when they reach the marriageable age, to get married and have children and, when they have children, to have grandchildren. This, like many other descriptions, is of course an exaggeration, if not misinterpretation; yet, broadly speaking, it is only an exaggeration. In the West, every man is a soldier; in China, with moderate exceptions, every man is a husband and every woman a wife. It has long been a guiding principle in Chinese sociology, to which China owes her high degree of morality, that 'there should be no murmuring woman within nor lonely man without' (*nei wu yuern nue vy wu kang foo*).[1] According to the Sage, Mencius, with whose philosophy my readers must by now be familiar, this accords with the natural desires of man—at least a Chinaman. 'On the birth of a boy', says he, 'it is wished (by the parents) that he shall have a wife and, on the birth of a girl, it is wished (by them) that she shall have a husband. This parental feeling is possessed by all.'[2] In other words, the philosophic *dictum* that 'the honest man who married, and brought up a large family, did more service to mankind than he who continued single, and only talked of populations',[3] or 'marriage is the best state for a man in general; and every man is a worse man, in proportion as he is unfit for the married state',[4] fits in well with Chinese sentiments, which may echo with the words:

> Though a single woman may do much,
> A married woman can do even more.

Anyhow, modern legislation in some European countries encouraging, and even compelling, by various means, people to have children shows that the Chinese in this respect have not been wrong. If one reads the pathetic words of Marshal Pétain in his speech of 20th June 1940: '*Trop peu d'enfants, trop peu d'armes, trop peu d'alliés, voilà les causes de notre défaite,*'[5] putting the lack of children as the first

---

[1] For origin of this rule, see *ante*, p. 128.
[2] *Mencius*, Bk. III, Pt. II, Ch. 3, Sec. 6.
[3] Goldsmith: *Vicar of Wakefield*, Ch. I.
[4] Boswell's *Life of Johnson*; Ed. Everyman's Library, Vol. I, p. 624.
[5] 'Too few children, too few arms, and too few allies . . . these are the causes of our defeat.' Le Maréchal Pétain: *Paroles aux Français*, p. 44.

cause of the late national catastrophe of France, one cannot help feeling that the Chinese in this respect are also wise. Indeed, it is to her teeming millions that China owes her present existence as an independent power, and the world is indebted for being its vanguard in the Second World War in saving its civilization.

As to Chinese marriages, there are some people who, having heard of the term 'go-between', think that he is like a middleman in commercial transactions, ready to arrange matches on the spot, as it were, while there are others who, having read novels written by authors supposed to 'know' China, burlesquely describing, in hardly a dozen words, what purports to be the marriage 'ceremony' of Chinese servant girls, believe by analogy that marriage in China must be a very simple affair. This impression is so general and so deep that the writer himself has, during his sojourn in Europe, been delicately asked more than once by persons of culture whether their impression is correct, and his answer is: 'To believe in this would be like pursuing truth by such means as climbing up a tree to look for a fish.' If there is anything in which the Chinese may be said to attach much to form and ceremony, it is certainly marriage. Even in the case of the humblest person, marriage is a very solemn affair and is so regarded by the public. Consequently, its celebration, divided into stages, often lasts for days, and the bridal chair, with the bride in it, has always the right of the road in precedence over everybody, including the Prime Minister of the day. In the matter of the courtesy of the road, as noted in *John Chinaman at Home*,[1] 'respect is always paid to a burden. Should even a Mandarin,[2] when walking, meet a porter carrying one, he will step aside and make his retinue do the same'. But in the case of the bridal chair, the rule is not that consideration is given to the carriers, but that honour is accorded to the bride, who, respected as the mother of future generations, is saluted by everyone, including her parents and elder brothers, on the day when she assumes the duty of womanhood, for which mankind is ever grateful, and which Nature dictates. This unique respect paid to the bride and the universal honour accorded to the mother, as described in the last chapter, speak eloquently for the position occupied by the woman in the orbit of Chinese social system. With these observations, I may now introduce my readers step by step to a Chinese wedding. First of all let me begin from the very beginning.

'When Heaven and Earth harmonize', says the *Book of Li*, 'everything prospers. Marriage is the origin of all generations. That it should be a union of two persons of different family names is in-

[1] By the Rev. E. J. Hardy, pp. 212-13.
[2] An official, so called by foreigners in the old days.

tended to maintain a wise barrier between persons of close relations.
. . : (The wife) being one with her husband is his equal.' ¹ 'Marriage
is the happy union of two persons of two different family names
with a view, in the upward way, to performing ritual duties to the
ancestors and, in the downward way, to continuing the future
generations. It is considered so important that its ceremony (at every
stage) . . . is performed with a reverential solemnity.' ² 'Co-habitation
between man and woman', says Mencius, 'is one of the most important relations of man.' ³ 'If, without waiting for the approval of
the parents and the arrangement of a go-between, the young man
and the young woman were to bore holes in the wall in order to
steal a sight of each other, or climb over it in order to be with each
other, then the parents as well as all other people of the country would
despise them.' ⁴

What has been quoted above may be said to be the Chinese historic
conception of marriage and its form. At a very early stage of their
history, at least in the time of Yao and Shun (2357-2255 B.C.), ⁵ it
was conceived that co-habitation between man and woman was a
sacred relation, which should originate in a proper form, making
it a marriage and the man and woman husband and wife. This form
was found in parental consent of the parties and in the intervention
of a third party, called the go-between, testifying to the propriety
of the relation, as a matter of public interest. The necessity of
parental consent must be of a very ancient origin; for even in the
Book of Odes, which consists largely of folk-songs reflecting deep-
rooted customs and sentiments of the people, there appears the
following verse:

> 'To espouse a woman how should one proceed?
> One must inform one's parents then indeed.' ⁶

Other aspects of form, such as various ceremonies, could have grown
up only gradually as material civilization advanced, though it may
be remarked that they were well developed and reached a high
stable state many centuries before the Christian era, as evidenced in
the Book of Li, compiled in the Han Dynasty (206 B.C.-A.D. 196).

However, as in China modesty is one of the first things that are

---

¹ Book of Li, Bk. XXVI, Title Chia Tek Sang. The word 'equal' is defined there as
'same as superior and inferior'.
² Book of Li, Bk. LXI, Title Meaning of Marriage, No. 44.
³ Mencius, Bk. V, Pt. I, Ch. 2, Sec. 1.
⁴ Mencius, Bk. III, Pt. II, Ch. 3, Sec. 6.
⁵ See Mencius, Bk. V, Pt. I, Ch. 2, Sec. 1.
⁶ Book of Odes (Mow Sche), Bk. V, No. 2, Title Kuo Feng, Chi. Quoted in Mencius,
Bk. V, Pt. I, Ch. 2, Sec. 1.

taught to women, and custom excludes the free mixing of women and men, the chance of self-matching is practically *nil*. Indeed, except among a limited number of persons who have lived abroad or received a highly modern education, wooing or courting is unknown in China. Therefore parents (and in case there are no parents, those who are *in loco parentis*) conceive it as their duty to take the initiative. When a child reaches the marriageable age, unless there are reasons for postponing the question, which are many in the case of men on account of economic burden, or unless the parents have already some young friend or relative in view, the father or mother would request a friend or relative to recommend a suitable young person of his or her knowledge or acquaintance as a prospective son-in-law or daughter-in-law, as the case may be. If such a recommendation is made and considered *prima facie* agreeable, in the light of the account given regarding the person and the family concerned, the parents of the latter will, through a friend or relative known to them, be sounded as to the possibility of a 'matrimonial alliance'. Should the sounding yield a positive result, the two families will, according to custom, exchange a pink card, in which are stated the exact hour, day, month, and year of birth of the person concerned, together with the names of his or her father, grandfather, and great-grandfather, and which, for want of an English term, may be called *horoscopal testimony*. Having received this, each family makes careful inquiries about the young man or the young lady, as the case may be, and the moral and hygienic history, up to three generations, of his or her family. In general, inquiries are directed, in the case of the man, first to his character, health, and ability, and, in the case of the lady, first to her virtue, health, and temperament. Nowadays, education forms a distinct feature of the inquiry; but in olden days, when the system of awarding diplomas, marks of modern education, did not exist, it was implied, as regards the man, in the term 'ability' and, as regards the lady, in the term 'virtue', the best proof of education. The question of means of the male party or his family naturally would not be omitted from a prudent inquiry; for on this depends much of the material happiness of the woman. But the same question is not looked at in the same light as regards the family of the female party; for a man marries a woman for her qualities and not for her means, at least according to true Chinese traditions. It can be said that fortune hunting has never been looked upon as a noble game in China. Indeed, people used to go to the other extreme. Marquis Tseng Kwoh Fan, the well-known scholar-statesman of the Taiping Rebellion period, whose position might be compared with that of Duke of Wellington at the peak of his glory, and whose philosophy had a profound influence on Chinese thought for the last hundred years, advised his son to choose as wife 'a girl from an agricultural and literary family,[1] possessing none whatever of the habits of the rich or the high-stationed'.[2] His matrimonial philosophy may be summed up as: 'I choose my wife as she did her wedding gown, not for a fine glossy surface, but such qualities as would wear well.'[3] A popular saying, commonly observed, is: 'Bamboo gates match with bamboo gates, and wooden doors with wooden doors.' In other words, one should in general marry one's peer; for, just as 'disproportioned friendships ever end in disgust',[4] unequal life-partnership runs the risk of sharing the same fate.

After the necessary inquiries have been made, if the parents are not satisfied with the result, they will, through a friend or relative, inform the other family that the connubial destinies of the two parties are not in harmonious accord according to a study of their *horoscopal testimonies*—a delicate way indeed of ending a 'matrimonial *démarche*'! If, however, they are mutually satisfied with the result, meetings between the young man and the young lady are discreetly arranged, always, of course, in the gathering of friends or relatives. After a few of such meetings, the parents, finding no ill reaction from them, would sound the child's opinion. In the case of girls, silence with a deep blush is, after a reasonable lapse of time, as a sort of *locus poenitentiae*, usually taken as signifying consent. Among better-off people in these days, particularly those who live in town, the time-honoured process is reversed. Parents would extend invitations to suitable young people so as to afford their children of marriageable age opportunities to meet, and form an opinion of, them, before any actual matrimonial project is conceived. Very often, friends or relatives would offer these opportunities; for the Chinese in general think it a pleasant duty to be instrumental in bringing about a happy event. They would say that 'the *Jiun Tze* would help others to accomplish what is good',[5] and probably also think that they are thus rendering a handsome service to mankind. Thanks to modern life, such opportunities are now many in the normal course of existence, though the traditional 'moral cordon' between men and women still remains—a custom which pays a handsome dividend in good morals, forming a great asset of Chinese culture and civilization.

[1] In other words, 'a well-educated girl of the middle class'.
[2] *Tseng Kwoh Fan's Letters to His Family*, letter dated 16th April, 29th year of Tao Kwong (1850).
[3] Goldsmith: *Vicar of Wakefield*, Ch. I.
[4] Goldsmith: *Vicar of Wakefield*, Ch. V.
[5] See *ante*, p. 39.

In days of old no such meeting was arranged as a rule, and the young people to be married had to trust to the wisdom and judgment of their parents. There are still such cases; but these are found chiefly among people of the rural district, who generally marry their distant relatives or persons of neighbouring villages, so that in many cases the parties themselves are in fact acquainted with each other, or have the chance of being so. A marriage where the parties never saw each other until the wedding is nowadays called a 'blind marriage'. Yet in the light of what has been described about the steps taken leading to the conclusion of a marriage, even without any meeting, it is not really so blind as it is supposed to be, though this must not be taken as a plea for the old custom. The parents who, apart from possessing experience, have the advantage of being interested without the disadvantage of being 'blinded by love', may, like bystanders, in fact see more of the game. It is of course always easy to judge harshly of the past. But the fact that marriages in the past have generally been happy, as divorce was almost unknown,[1] at least shows that they have fared well in the annals of matrimony. At any rate the past had its laurels, which the present and the future have still to win. However, as life has for its own preservation to adapt itself to circumstances, which are always changing, life changes too. Yet, whatever changes there may be to come, parental aid, in various degrees according to circumstances, in the matter of marriage of one's children is, in the eyes of many a Chinese, not without its wisdom and ethical value. A system, as incidentally revealed in Jane Austen's *Pride and Prejudice* and *Sense and Sensibility*, would seem to impose on the woman a strain, which a little judicious aid and care of the parents may sensibly ease. From the ethical and social standpoint, if the parents may choose the form of religion for their child, as is the case in all countries, there can be nothing wrong in the fact that they should play some part in the choice of his or her mate. The very fact that in all systems of law parental consent is required in marriage as an essential element either of form or of capacity[2] shows also that, historically, the parents are never considered as a disinterested party.

Now, a word about the go-between. As has been said, he (or she) is not a common agent for arranging marriages for others, but a third party considered since time immemorial as an essential element to the form of marriage. In most cases he is actually a friend or relative of the family of one or both of the parties. Very often he slips out of the scene after the match has been arranged, and, on the approach

[1] See *ante*, p. 172.
[2] See *Rules of Private International Law Determining Capacity to Contract*, by the present author; (Stevens & Sons, Lond.)

of the happy event, somebody else, having in fact nothing to do with the arrangement of the match, is requested to fill the role as a matter of formality. A person entrusted with the misson of a go-between always acts with great consciousness of his moral responsibility, so much so that there is a popular saying:

> 'Wise is he who is no middleman
> Or even guarantor or go-between.'

It is not within the scope of this book to go into the details of the celebration of a marriage event or its ceremony, interesting though they are. What is to be given here is only an outline, but may be said to be, in substance, a form that has been, and still is, generally followed, though custom, like life, is constantly moving towards simplicity.

A marriage consists of two parts: the betrothal and the wedding, both of which are celebrated by the sending of presents from the man's family to that of the woman. On the occasion of the betrothal, something, intended for the personal use of the man, is given in return by the woman's family. It is obvious that on the occasion of the wedding no present of any kind is given in return by the woman's family; because it already gives a great deal, in the form of a bride with a dowry, though, as we shall see, the bride herself has something to offer to each member of the family on the first day of salutation. The presents sent by the male party consist chiefly of viands and other eatables intended for the feasts of the occasion and for distribution among neighbours, friends, and relatives, as celebration of the event in both the social and the legal senses of the term. With these presents are usually added some jewels and silks intended for the bride. Between the betrothal and the wedding some time must elapse, which may be days, weeks, and even years, depending on the circumstances. When it is wished that the wedding should take place, one party sends a representative to the other for consultation regarding the date to be fixed. When it is fixed, it is written on a special ceremonial documentary paper sent by a special messenger of the family of the male party to the family of the female party. As this is a solemn affair, it is done with some formality. Jewels intended for the bride elect are sent on this day. It is always for the bridegroom's family to provide for the bridal-chair to be sent to the family of the bride, the idea being that it is the bridegroom who goes to fetch the bride, and not the bride who comes to his home. Ancient custom required the bridegroom, under order of his father, to accompany the bridal-chair to the house of the bride and escort her back in person. But in modern days this formality is simplified, and only the bridal-chair, accompanied by the go-between and a wedding band,[1] if one can afford it, is sent. When the bridal-chair arrives at the house of the bride and the bride is ready to leave, she is solemnly escorted by her mother to the bridal-chair—a formality that signifies that the parting is a marriage with parental consent. At this moment the mother and the daughter always break down in the midst of music and of joy. In the *Book of Li*[2] it is said: 'The family which has a daughter married will not extinguish its lights for three consecutive nights; because its members anxiously think of the absent one' (as if she might by chance come home in darkness)—a passage which conveys a sentiment at once tender and poetic. The parting words said by the mother to the daughter generally are: 'Be a good wife and good mother and be happy and in harmony with your husband for ever', or something to that effect. In ancient days the parting maternal instructions were: 'When you arrive in your (new) home, be respectful and careful in your behaviour and do not disobey your husband.'[3]

When the bridal-chair arrives at the gate of the house of the bride-groom, its arrival is announced by a strain of music. Thereupon the bridegroom in his ceremonial robe proceeds to the bridal-chair, opens its door, bows, as a mark of equality, to the bride, and escorts her into the house. This is not merely a formal welcome, but repre-sents, in a simplified form, the 'conjugal pilgrimage' formerly made by the bridegroom to the house of the bride. When inside the house, they, with the help of attendant matrons, proceed to worship Heaven and the family ancestral tablets—a formality that represents the religious element of the marriage ceremony. This being ter-minated, the couple is led by the attendant matrons into the bridal chamber, where they drink the Loving Cup and partake of 'The Feast of the Warm Matrimonial Bed'.[4] All these ceremonies, as they have been expressly provided in the ancient *Book of Li*,[5] must have been observed in substance for more than twenty centuries, though they may vary in details according to local and personal con-ditions. The Loving Cup, properly speaking, consists of two vessels

[1] According to the *Book of Li*, Bk. XXVI, no band should be employed; because, as marriage implies very solemn duties, the liveliness of music might prevent one from realizing in full the solemn duties that are implied. What solemnity the ancients attached to marriage may be gathered from this passage. Modern life, however, makes a departure from this ancient custom.
[2] Bk. XVIII, Title: *Tseng Tze Asks*, No. 7.
[3] *Mencius*, Bk. III, Pt. II, Ch. 2, Sec. 2.
[4] This is so called in Canton. In other parts of China it may be known by other names, such as 'Feast of Harmony'.
[5] *Book of Li*, Bk. LXI, Title *Meaning of Marriage*, No. 44.

made from one dried gourd cut into two. But in modern days cups
specially made in a shape that permits them to be formed into one
are generally used. However, a little wine is poured into each of
these, one being given to the bride, and the other to the bridegroom.
The bridegroom takes a sip from his, and one of the attendant
matrons takes up that of the bride, and holds it to her lips, she being
too shy and embarrassed to do so herself. At this moment her cheeks
go red, her heart throbs, and leaning more and more heavily on the
arms of the attendant matrons, as if she were going to drop, she is
a dear indeed! While Nature whispers in her bashful ears: 'Now,
thou art a wife and wilt be a mother, the personification of tenderness and of love,' Modesty, with Youth, by a wave of the wand,
transforms her into Venus on the spot! If I might embody the scene
and sentiment in a stanza, I would do so as follows:

> With trembling hand the Loving Cup she sips.
> 'Tis rather pressed close to her virgin lips.
> Behold her maiden blush with throbbing heart!
> Modesty plays the part of Cupid's dart.

She trembles not with fear, nor even with joy, but with modesty
and a deep sense of the solemn duty into which she is entering.
Marriage is indeed an occasion for joy; but, like the giving birth of
a child, though followed with joy, the very moment, that means so
much in one's life—in the one case the woman becomes a wife, in
the other she becomes a mother—is not one for light-hearted feelings.
She therefore trembles. Her modesty plays the part of Cupid's dart.
For, though it is proverbial that 'Venus creeps out of the lover's
eyes', Handsome is that Handsome does, modesty being a form of
beauty that is pure and sure and endures. Beauty remains where
Modesty is, even though Youth may have departed, as the Chinese
would say:

> Despite that she is near her *cinquantaine*,
> Modesty makes her maiden charm remain. [1]

Moreover, 'love-making' between persons not yet married to each
other, even though betrothed, is unknown in China. It commences
after the sipping of the 'Loving Cup'. Such a process may seem
strange to Western people, who may justly observe:

> Truly, 'East is East, and West is West'. [2]
> Their love-making epochs are reversed.

[1] A well-known saying, a little paraphrased or adapted.
[2] Rudyard Kipling: *Ballad of East and West*.

The Chinese process, however, wears well. Shakespeare in his *As You Like It* put into the mouth of Rosalind these lines:

> 'Men are April when they woo,
> December when they wed:
> Maids are May when they are maids,
> But the sky changes when they are wives.' [1]

To these lines the Chinese may well respond with the following stanza:

> In China people share a blessèd lot.
> They start love-making with the nuptial knot,
> So married life withstands all kinds of weather;
> Wives are ever May, men ne'er December.

The last two verses have their justification in the fact that divorce was and is extremely rare in China, though it could and can be effected by mere mutual consent. A man named Sung Hung of the later *Han* period, who had risen from a humble family to be a high official, was much admired by the Emperor for his personal charm and ability and, in consequence, was asked, as he was already married, to divorce his wife, a simple woman of the peasant stock, in order to marry one of the Imperial princesses. To this overture he replied: 'Your Majesty, the woman of my humble meal shall never go down from my hall.' These words, now spoken in the elliptical form, 'the woman of humble meal' (*jow kang tsee chee*), have since become proverbial. However, let me resume the description. After the Loving Cup has been drunk or rather pressed to the lips of the bride, a little wine from the bridegroom's cup is poured into hers and a little wine from hers is poured into his. The wine thus mingled is sipped by both—a ceremony symbolic of affection and oneness, while the partaking of the 'Feast of the Warm Matrimonial Bed', which is a formal affair and not a substantial meal, means equality, harmony, and the sharing of joy and sorrow in common for life. After this ceremony, they are, morally as well as legally, husband and wife in the fullest sense of the term. Then they proceed to the hall to salute the bridegroom's parents, relatives, and friends. On this occasion, the parents, as a token of affection, would, as a rule, give the bride some forms of jewels, the value of which varies, of course, with their purse. At the same time the bride would, as a mark of respect, present them and other members of the family with something useful, the value of which varies with the fortune of her own family.

[1] Act IV, Sc. I, Ls. 153–6.

What remains now to be mentioned is the Wedding Feast, to which near neighbours, close relatives, and intimate friends, apart from persons who have sent in presents, are, generally, invited. At the end of the feast some friends of the bridegroom would stay on for a few joyous hours in the house of the new couple in order 'to see the bride'. At a gathering, with the new couple in the centre, and the household and neighbours sitting or standing round here and there, the guests display their wit by making appropriate jokes or, if they are scholars, air their scholarship by launching out verses composed, or supposed to be composed, on the spot, much to the enjoyment of some and the amusement of others. Very often, want of wit is made up in laughter. The gathering does not break up until the small hours of the morning. In fact, the longer the guests stay, the greater is deemed the honour done to the family.

Normally, the celebration of a wedding lasts from two to three days. In cases where one can afford the expenses, it lasts much longer. For weeks after the wedding, the bride is still called by that sweet name—a fact that enhances her conjugal festivity in no small degree—and custom permits friends of the family to come at any convenient time 'to see the bride', with the consequence of being entertained in some suitable way. All this is a form of conviviality, welcome by the family; because it brightens rather than blights the 'domestic honeymoon'. It is 'domestic'; for the new couple do not go away after the wedding to enjoy themselves, but remain at home to keep up the joy of the parents, who see in the marriage of their children the fulfilment of one of their principal parental wishes and duties—a feeling that begets in them a large measure of happiness.

What has been described is the customary or historic form of ceremony, which is in substance common throughout the country. During the last two decades a modern form similar to what prevails in the West has grown up. It is less picturesque and less solemn, because it is less historic; but it can be less expensive and certainly takes up less time.

To conclude this chapter, let me offer a translation of two well-known poems of the *Tang* period (A.D. 618-906), which throw a poetic light on the bride and women in general in China.

    1. She shyly passed the bridal night with lights suppressed,
       And waited dawn to greet her husband's honoured parents.
       After toilet she in low voice him addressed:
       'Are my eyebrows painted in the latest fashion?' [1]

[1] *Tang Poems*, Standard Ed.

2. She tours the kitchen three days after wedding,
   And cleans her hands to do the homely cooking.
   For knowing not the taste of husband's mother,
   She gives a bit first to his little sister. [1]

The first poem, it may be remarked, though it has the 'Bride' as the theme, was in fact one addressed by a poet, before himself becoming famous, as a homage to a Lord of Literature whose authoritative taste he wanted to ascertain, just as the bride would, in the words of the poet himself, consult the bridegroom in painting her eyebrows. However, as it is, the poem depicts modesty, good manners, filial piety, care for personal appearance, and love, while the second poem imparts the idea of attention to domestic duties, care in their performance, devotion to the husband's parents, and good sense, all of which are qualities that a Chinese woman is taught to cultivate and expected to possess.

[1] *Tang Poems*, Standard Ed.

CHAPTER 7

FRIENDSHIP

A MAN may have no wife, such as the case of a bachelor or widower, and a woman may have no husband, such as the case of a spinster or widow, but neither he nor she can have no friend. A person may have no parents, because they have died, and no children, because he is unmarried or childless; but he must have friends. These simple truths show how important is the part that friendship plays in the life of man.

> 'Friendship, peculiar boon of heaven,
> The noble mind's delight and pride,
> To men and angels only given,
> To all the lower world denied.'[1]

These Johnsonian lines may be echoed or, to use a Chinese term in poetry, 'harmonized in response'[2] by adding the following stanza:

> It forms a sacred link[3] in men or women,
> And serves for all as the most precious guide.
> As it is with life so closely woven,
> It should always 'lean to Virtue's side'.[4]

The ancients, who might be simpler-minded but were, for that reason, truer to nature, had often a deeper sense of the meaning of human relations than the moderns, who are apt to be influenced more by interests than by sentiments, particularly where material civilization is advanced; for the rapid growth of the materialistic, multiplying in its train man's needs and desires, rarely fails to tend to overshadow the spiritual. Hence it is always easier for men to share their lot harmoniously in adversity than in felicity, as the two World Wars have eloquently shown. In adversity, the man's soul is stirred, and he thus sees things in a clearer light and a truer perspective; whereas

---

[1] Boswell's *Life of Johnson*; Ed. G. Routledge & Sons, Vol. I, p. 82.
[2] The Chinese term is *Whaw*, which means composing a poem in response to another with the same rhymes.
[3] This is a Chinese idea, according to which friendship forms one of the five most important human relations. See *post*, p. 200.
[4] The words in inverted commas are from Goldsmith's *Deserted Village*; but they fit in well with Johnson's idea of friendship: 'The greatest benefit which one friend can confer upon another, is to guard, and excite, and elevate his virtue.' See *post*, p. 200.

in felicity, Interest, the Maid of Materialism, begins to intrigue and exercises an influence from which only the wise can be immune. This does not, of course, mean that adversity is something desirable while felicity is not. That would be absurd. It is simply a fact bearing the semblance of fate, with the additional aspect of a warning, just as it is calamity, and not prosperity, that affords the test of loyalty or other virtue, and it is common danger, and not common safety, that tightens the bond of friendship or brotherhood. The Chinese say:

> 'A poet's at his best,
> When he is poorest.' [1]

This, similarly, does not mean that poverty is the ideal lot of the poet. But it does happen, more often than not, that it is in darkness that he is most luminous, and this is true no less in the West than in the East. Savage, if he had not been destitute, would probably not have written the line: 'No tenth transmitter of a foolish face.' [2] The English Lexicographer, if he had had enough means to pay for a night's lodging instead of loitering in the street like a homeless soul, could not have uttered the phrase: To 'stand by their country'. [3] Possibly, too, the literary world would have been deprived of a treasure, the *Vicar of Wakefield*, if its author had not been so poor as to be arrested by his landlady for rent. [4]

However, the Chinese being of an ancient race, cling, in the matter of friendship, still to their old traditions. At a very remote period, their sages classified friendship among the five most important human relations: sovereign and subject, parent and child, elder brother and younger brother, husband and wife, friend and friend. In their sacred books guidance is found about the meaning, the basis, the choice, and the duty of friendship, as well as the way of maintaining it.

MEANING OF FRIENDSHIP

'It is on the path of culture that the *Jiun Tze* (the gentleman) [5] meets and makes friends, and he regards friendship as a means of advancing his virtue (through mutual instruction).' [6] The idea is, to use the words of an English philosopher, that 'the greatest benefit which one

---

[1] A saying from Ou Yang Sou, eminent poet and writer of the *Sung* dynasty. See *Collected Ancient Essays.*

[2] Boswell's *Life of Johnson*; Ed. G. Routledge & Sons, Vol. I, p. 88.

[3] *Ibid.*, p. 87.

[4] See *ibid.*, p. 241.

[5] Here the term may be rendered simply as 'gentleman'.

[6] See Confucius: *Lun Yu*, Pt. XII, Ch. 24.

friend can confer upon another, is to guard, and excite, and elevate, his virtue'. [1] At any rate, friendship, being one of the most important relations of man, is not formed merely for the sake of gain or profit, but has a higher meaning. Hence an association of persons for the purpose of poaching or gaming can hardly be called friendship. Indeed, it is doubtful whether political association, however close, can *per se* be regarded as real friendship. I have heard it observed that 'the strangest thing in life is that politics can make a man's best bed-fellow his deadly enemy'. It is rather instructive to read in the *Autobiography* of Lord Haldane that, when he was once asked by a distinguished statesman and man of the world whether, even with the aid of such knowledge as experience had brought, he would like to try to begin life anew, he answered in the negative, and that, when he posed the same question to his interlocutor, he received a like reply. The reasons given by him for his own answer are that 'we are apt greatly to underrate the part which accident and good luck have really played in the shaping of our careers and in giving us such successes as we have had'. [2] Yet as these questions and answers have come from the mouths of two eminent men in politics, one of whom has 'sat in Parliament for over forty years, ten of which have been spent in successive Cabinets', [3] one cannot resist at least a subsidiary impression that politics are rather a field where one seeks and snatches one's laurels than a 'path of culture' where one meets and makes friends.

BASIS OF FRIENDSHIP

What has a meaning in human relations must have a basis. As regards friendship, the Chinese find it in sincerity and equality. Tseng Tze, the disciple of Confucius whose saying on friendship has just been quoted, had the habit of examining himself three times a day. In these daily self-examinations he would ask himself three questions of a pious nature, one of which was: 'Have I been insincere in my intercourse with friends?' [4] Confucius himself, when he was once asked by his disciples to express his cherished desires, said, *inter alia*, 'To treat friends with sincerity', [5] while Mencius, in speaking of the five most important relations of man, laid it down that 'between friends there should be sincerity', [6] and, as already referred to, 'lack

---

[1] Boswell's *Life of Johnson*; Ed. G. Birkbeck Hill, Vol. II, p. 248.
[2] *Autobiography* of Viscount Haldane, p. 353.
[3] *Ibid.*, p. 2.
[4] Confucius: *Lun Yu*, Pt. I, Ch. 4.
[5] See *ante*, p. 89.
[6] *Mencius*, Bk. III, Pt. I, Ch. 4, Sec. 8.

of sincerity towards friends is contrary to the doctrine of filial piety'.[1] So much do the Chinese attach sincerity to friendship that the imputation of insincerity to a friend is, in their eyes, worse in moral implication than the accusation of a breach of trust. The charge of 'selling (i.e., betraying) a friend' is no less serious than that of Petty Treason in the Middle Ages. Of course, a person may break off a friendship that is deemed undesirable. As divorce is permissible, there is no reason why friendship may not be broken off. The English have the expression, 'to cut one's acquaintance'. A Chinese would say 'to cut one's seat' (*ghaw shih*) when he breaks off his friendship with someone, the metaphor, which means that he would not sit together with the latter, being based on the following story:

Two well-known scholars, Kwan Ning and Hwa In, of the *Wei* dynasty (A.D. 220-265) in the period called *The Three Kingdoms*, were intimate friends. They would work together in the field and sit together in the library. One day when they were digging together in the field, they found a piece of gold. Kwan Ning took no notice of it and continued to dig; but Hwa In picked it up, and gazed at it before he threw it down. Another day when they were studying in the library and sitting together as usual, there were shouts in the street that a nobleman riding in a fine carriage was passing by. Kwan Ning took no notice of this and continued to read; but Hwa In, attracted by the splendour, abandoned his study and rushed out to have a look. Since this incident Kwan Ning had a low opinion of Hwa In and separated his own seat from his, saying to him: 'You are no friend of mine.' Hence the expression 'to cut the seat'. Subsequent events proved that Kwan Ning was right; for while he absolutely refused any office successively and earnestly offered to him by the usurper of the throne of *Han*, Hwa In, on the contrary, played a prominent part in the usurpation to the disgust of posterity.

In the *Autobiography*[2] of Lord Haldane we are told that on one occasion there was, between three eminent English statesmen, Rosebery, Randolph Churchill, and Chamberlain, a slight scene, in consequence of which Randolph Churchill beckoned to the waiter and said: 'Waiter, put a flower-pot there,' indicating a spot between himself and Chamberlain. Would this amount to a 'breach *ad hoc*' or a 'breach *nisi*' or a 'breach *cum loco poenitentiae*'? However, though a Chinese may 'cut the seat' with a friend, he would consider it at least bad taste to speak ill of him afterwards. It is a well-known

[1] See ante. p. 169.
[2] See p. 84.

saying that 'the *Jiun Tze* (the gentleman)[1] of old, though he might have broken off his friendship with a man, would not for that reason utter an ill word against him'.[2] This, it may be mentioned, is another characteristic of the *Jiun Tze* and a principle which the Chinese have always been taught to observe.

That equality forms part of the basis of friendship is well voiced by the sage, Mencius. 'In friendship', says he, 'there should be no pretension to superiority because of age, rank, or (the position of one's relatives, such as) brothers. Friendship with a person is friendship with him for his virtue: there cannot be any pretension to superiority.'[3] Any air of superiority, on the part of the one or the other, would make genuine friendship impossible. Even age, which is universally respected in China, does not warrant such pretension, though in practice the younger man would, according to Chinese culture, voluntarily play the part of the younger brother. What the Chinese call 'age-forgotten friendship' is a friendship between two persons whose years are greatly unequal, but who have forgotten their disparity in age. Such friendship is very common among the Chinese, who have since ages past realized the necessity and wisdom of 'keeping friendship in constant repair'. [4]

If between friends no pretension to superiority is permissible, still less so would be snobbery, which is always considered as despicable by the Chinese, though in China it is the rich or the high-stationed that are sometimes snubbed. Kings and princes in the past were often snubbed by the learned and the virtuous. An interesting instance of this kind is the case where the famous First Emperor of the *Chin* Dynasty (221-206 B.C.) was snubbed by the scholarly envoy of a very small State. It happened in this way. *Chin* having arbitrarily proposed to the small State to exchange a piece of territory, the latter, being unwilling, commissioned an envoy to *Chin* to explain matters to the Emperor, who was then at the height of his power. At the audience, which seemed to be a *tête-à-tête* conference, the following incident took place:

> The Emperor, suddenly losing his temper, said: 'Have you ever heard of the anger of an Emperor?'
>
> 'No, Your Majesty,' replied the Envoy.
>
> 'When an Emperor is in anger,' said the Emperor, 'there will be a million corpses lying about with blood flowing a thousand miles.'

---

[1] Here the term may be rendered simply as 'gentleman'.
[2] See *Collected Ancient Essays*, Title *Memorial to the King of Yen*.
[3] *Mencius*, Bk. V, Pt. II, Ch. 3.
[4] Boswell's *Life of Johnson*; Ed. G. Birkbeck Hill, Vol. I, p. 300.

'Has Your Majesty', asked the Envoy, 'ever heard of the anger of a plain scholar?'

'The anger of a scholar', answered the Emperor, 'can mean no more than taking off his hat and shoes, and knocking his head against the ground.'

'No, Your Majesty,' said the Envoy. 'This is the anger only of a fool, not that of a scholar.' After saying this, and in highly poetical diction, he recited graphically three well-known but not far distant historical instances, where unworthy reigning princes were openly slain by scholars. At the end of the citation he calmly exclaimed: 'Now, I am going to add my name as the fourth to the list. When a scholar is in anger, there will be only two corpses lying about with blood flowing within five steps. To-day is the day when the whole Empire shall be in mourning.' Thereupon he rose with his sword in hand. The Emperor, visibly affected, forthwith knelt [1] before his interlocutor, saying: 'Please sit down, Master. Why should things be like this? I understand now. The fact that (larger States like) *Haan* and *Wei* have perished, while (a small State like) yours survives, is merely because it has (men like) you, Master.' [2]

This is from a historical record entitled '*Tang Chu brought peace with honour to his sovereign*'. To borrow a phrase used by Burke in praising Boswell in his successful *negotiation* with Johnson to dine with John Wilkes at the house of Mr. Dilly, 'there was nothing equal to it in the whole history of the *Corps Diplomatique*'. [3] As to the way in which the Emperor tactfully extricated himself from the impasse, posterity paid him the tribute of being worthy of one who succeeded in founding the first Empire in supersession of the long and chaotic period of the *Warring States*. For, instantly realizing the weak point of his own impulsiveness and impetuosity, he, instead of persisting in his error, as many a smaller man would have done, lost no time in remedying it by being sublimely humble and magnanimous—an attitude which, on account of the very fact that he was then the most powerful, he could well afford to adopt—thus not only restoring his dignity, but also turning the incident from a momentary oral defeat into a permanent moral victory in the eyes of both the then excited world and the future calm-minded historian.

[1] In those days kneeling was a much simpler affair than it would be in these days; because people sat on the ground covered with mats. It was equivalent to a deep bow in these days.

[2] Records of the *Warring States*, 481-205 B.C. See *Collected Ancient Essays*.

[3] Boswell's *Life of Johnson*; Ed. G. Routledge & Sons, Vol. III, p. 49.

CHOICE OF FRIENDSHIP

In the words of Mr. Churchill, 'how much easier it is to join bad companions than to shake them off!'[1] This is true no less in time of peace than in time of war, just as the saying 'a man is judged by the company he keeps' is no less Chinese[2] than English. We are told:

1. 'Have no (man as) friend who is not (morally) equal to you.'[3]
2. 'There are three (kinds of) friendship that are beneficial and three that are detrimental. Friendship with the upright, friendship with the sincere, and friendship with the enlightened are beneficial. Friendship with the insincere, friendship with the flattering, and friendship with the flippant are detrimental.'[4]

The Chinese, who believe much in the influence of examples, think that one's conduct may easily be affected by those of one's friends, particularly when one is young. It was due to this belief that in the old days the Emperor used to select with care young men of well-known good conduct to keep company with his princes in their studies. This practice has become a matter of history with the passing of the monarchy in China; but the phrase still remains. It means now spending a few idle, yet pleasant, hours or days with a person of some social distinction purely for easing his solitude or heightening his amusement. If, therefore, you ask a Chinese what he has been doing lately and he replies: 'I have been keeping company with princes in their studies' (*pei tai tze doo shoo*), his words must not be taken literally.

A common saying, relating to the influence of example, reading in Chinese as:

> 'Jin joo jair chak
> Jin moh jair hak,'

may be rendered as:

> You will be pink,
> When you are near what's red;
> But you'll be black,
> When you are near the ink.[5]

---

[1] Spoken at Quebec on 31st August 1943.
[2] The Chinese saying is: 'Before judging the man himself, judge first the company he keeps.'
[3] Confucius: *Lun Yu*, Pt. I, Ch. 8, Sec. 8.
[4] Confucius: *Lun Yu*, Pt. XVI, Ch. 4.
[5] Chinese ink is black.

There are, of course, always exceptions to the rule. Fagin tried in vain to convert Oliver Twist into a thief. This is called in Chinese 'Going through the mud without a stain'. That is why Kwan Yin, Goddess of Mercy, the highest Buddhist Goddess in Chinese mythology, is represented sitting on a lotus, which is a plant that grows in the mud, like one born in a dirty world, but rising high above it, with flowers that are beautiful, stems that are straight and firm, and leaves that are even *water*-proof—a noble plant indeed!

DUTIES OF FRIENDSHIP

All human relations imply certain duties. Friendship, being one of the most important relations of man, naturally means something more than an occasional entertainment or exchange of letters of mutual regard. Confucius, in reply to a question about the duties of friendship, said: 'Admonish your friends faithfully, and guide them with tact. If you find this impossible, stop, and do not let yourself be disgraced.' [1] For, while it is one's duty to correct one's friends when they are at fault, admonition without tact is apt to be fruitless. There is also a limit in duties of this kind. It would be unwise for a friend to resort to constant reproof, which might impose a strain on friendship and constitute one of those 'unhappy chances' to which 'human friendships are liable'. [2] 'Nagging (which has been wittily defined by an English lawyer as 'the constant re-iteration of the unpleasant truth') between friends', says a disciple of Confucius, 'makes friendship distant'. [3]

Another duty incidental to friendship is obviously that of mutual aid. This must be so in all countries and in all ages; but it is possible that a people with older traditions has a deeper sense of this duty. Chinese history furnishes many instances where men gave up their lives for the sake of friendship. The very saying that 'When parents are living, a man should not promise his life to his friends (as a pure sacrifice outside the scope of duty)' [4] shows that such cases have been not infrequent. It may appear that this idea of friendship is exaggerated. But has not Sydney Carton willingly gone to the guillotine to save Charles Darnay? It is true that this is only *A Tale of Two Cities*; but life, we know, is sometimes even stranger than fiction, and nobler things have been accomplished by man than what the novelist

---

[1] Confucius: *Lun Yu*, Pt. XII, Ch. 23.
[2] Boswell's *Life of Johnson*; Ed. G. Routledge & Sons, Vol. III, p. 227.
[3] See Confucius: *Lun Yu*, Pt. IV, Ch. 26.
[4] *Book of Li*, Bk. I, Title *Chue Li*, No. 1. For correct interpretation of this passage, see *Complete Works of the Two Chings*, Vol. II, Bk. XVIII, p. 22.

has ever yet been able to create by his pen. Indeed, the three historical instances alluded to by the Envoy who snubbed the Emperor of *Chin* are just in point. They all were cases where a scholar sacrificed his life, not for fame or honour and still less for gold, but for friendship. If we leave out the question of merit and ethics involved in those political dramas, which we are not to judge here after some twenty and odd centuries, the spirit of sacrifice therein displayed gives us some idea of how far a Chinese may be prepared to go for the sake of friendship. Cases where a man accepts and faithfully carries out the request of a dying friend to take care of his family and bring up his children are numerous. 'The Chinaman's words are his bonds'[1] when made to a living person. They are a sacred trust to him, when made to a dying one. Generosity is also a feature of Chinese friendship. If you go to a restaurant, or a place of amusement, with a Chinese friend without a previous understanding as to who will foot the bill, you will in most, if not all, cases find he will contend for the privilege of being your host. A 'Dutch treat' is unknown in China; because it would appear strange to a Chinaman for friends to eat together in enjoyment and pay separately. Confucius once asked a disciple what his cherished desire was, and the latter answered: 'I desire, (when I have) carriages, horses, and light fur coats, to share the use of them with my friends, feeling no regret in case they are spoiled.'[2] These words express well a Chinese sentiment. One frequently hears them repeated by the Chinese in the elliptical form, 'to share the use with friends', (*eu peng yau gung*), in pressing others to accept a loan of things.

WAY OF MAINTAINING FRIENDSHIP

'Familiarity breeds contempt' is an English saying, and it is an English poet who has said: 'I always thought fit to keep up some mechanical forms of good breeding without which freedom ever destroys friendship.'[3] Whatever may be the applicability of the first saying in friendship, the second certainly fits in with Chinese culture, which has its base in the observance of *Li* (moral rules of correct conduct and good manners). Confucius, praising a worthy man of his time said: 'Yen Ping Chung knows well how to maintain

---

[1] 'That the word of the Chinese merchant is as good as his bond has long since become a household word, and so it is in other walks of life. The amount of solid honesty to be met with in every class, except the professionally criminal class, is simply astonishing.' (*The Civilization of China*, by Herbert A. Giles, p. 75).
[2] Confucius: *Lun Yu*, Pt. V, Ch. 25.
[3] Goldsmith: *Vicar of Wakefield*, Ch. IV.

his friendship with others. Though their friendship may be of long duration, he continues to treat them with respect.'[1] In other words, friendship should be maintained with constant respect, which is a precept and not mere form or ceremony.

To conclude this chapter, it may be added that in China, just as in other lands, and in all ages, there are friends and friends. The date of friendship or its duration, though a sign of intimacy, is not necessarily the test of its value. Sometimes, friendship, like 'love at first sight' ripens at the first meeting. The Chinese call this *E jen yu gu* (first sight as old). But, as has been quoted, 'it is only when the time of the year becomes cold that one knows that the pine and the cypress are the last to wilt'.[2] Adversities therefore are the golden test. The Chinese who have a long history cannot be without experience, telling them:

'The world blows hot and cold',[3]

or, as the Latin poet Ovid said in his *Sorrow*, composed on his exile:

'Donec eris sospes, multos numerabis amicos:
Tempora si fuerint nubila, solus eris.'[4]

That is to say:

'So long as you enjoy a happy fate,
You may be sure to find your friends abound.
But if the sky is in a cloudy state,
You'll be alone and also lonely found.'

However, as poverty, in Chinese eyes, is no cause for shame[5] and still less for scorn, even if not 'the mark of the elect', and as the Chinese put learning and knowledge above wealth and vulgar honour[6] and respect virtue even more, Chinese friendship generally cannot fail to be made of 'sterner stuff'[7] and, like Chinese marriage, can withstand rough weather.[8] Indeed, the Chinese are always taught, and regard it as a virtue, 'not to neglect or abandon old friends'.[9] It is said that, when Walpole became Prime Minister, he asked a friend what the latter would wish from him, and the latter

---

[1] Confucius: *Lun Yu*, Pt. V, Ch. 16.
[2] See *ante*, p. 135.
[3] A saying: *Si tai yen liang*.
[4] *Ovid*, Bk. I, IX, Ls. 5-6. Ed. S. G. Owen; Oxford University Press.
[5] See *ante*, p. 94, for words of Prof. Giles.
[6] See *ante*, pp. 95, for words of Grotius and others.
[7] Shakespeare: *Julius Caesar*, Act III, Sc. II, L. 98.
[8] See *ante*, p. 196.
[9] See Confucius: *Lun Yu*, Pt. VIII, Ch. 2, Sec. 2.

replied that all he wished was that Walpole should bow to him at his levee. [1] The story has a touch of Chinese humour, except that, to a man of virtue or learning, a Chinese Walpole would bow without being told.

The Chinese expression for bosom friend is *Tsee-tsue* (Lit., knows-me), a term meaning much more than mere intimacy, in the sense of close contact or association, or merely that 'my friend should approve of my aims and I of his'. [2] It lays stress on true understanding and appreciation, coupled, of course, with loyalty and sincerity. There are friends who flatter or please you. There are those who praise or even adore you. But there are few who really understand and rightly appreciate you. The well-known classical instance of friendship of the last category is that between a man named Bow Shoo and Kwan Chung, famous Prime Minister of *Chi* of the *Spring and Autumn* period (722-481 B.C.), who said: 'The persons to whom I owe my existence are my parents; the person who understands me is Bow Shoo.' And a well-known popular saying of the same purport is:

'In drinking, when you are with bosom friends,
A thousand flowing cups are no excess;
But when you talk to one who has no sense,
E'en half a phrase from you is utter waste.'

As an illustration, the devotion shown by Boswell in his writing the life of Dr. Johnson may be only a matter of hero-worship; but his words in the defence of Johnson concerning the remark '*Non equidem invideo, miror magis*' [3] could only be those of a bosom friend. 'No saying of Dr. Johnson's', says he, 'has been more misunderstood than his applying to Mr. Burke, when he first saw him at his fine place at Beaconsfield, *Non equidem invideo, miror magis*. These two celebrated men had been friends for many years before Burke entered on his parliamentary career. They were both writers, both members of the Literary Club; when, therefore, Dr. Johnson saw Mr. Burke in a situation so much more splendid than that to which he himself had attained, he did not mean to express that he thought it a disproportionate prosperity; but while he, as a philosopher, asserted an exemption from envy, *non equidem invideo*, he went on in the words of the poet, *miror magis*; thereby signifying either that he

[1] Boswell's *Life of Johnson*; Ed. Everyman's Library, Vol. II, p. 64, 'Letter to Sir Joshua Reynolds'.

[2] Goethe: *Criticisms, Reflections, and Maxims*, p. 195. Trans. by W. B. Rönnfeldt, Lond., Walter Scott.

[3] 'My admiration only I exprest, No spark of envy harbours in my breast.' This line was from Virgil translated by Johnson in his youth.

was occupied in admiring what he was glad to see; or, perhaps, that considering the general lot of men of superior abilities, he wondered that Fortune, who is represented as blind, should, in this instance, have been so just.' Let us now pause and ask: Could such words be uttered by a man for his friend whom he merely admired or adored? No. They could come only from the mouth of one who really understood and appreciated the other. No less so was Boswell's lament of the temper once shown by Johnson, when out of humour; for he grievously felt it not so much an injury to himself as *an injustice to Johnson*, 'because it gave persons (not in sympathy with him) an opportunity of enlarging upon his supposed ferocity, and ill-treatment of his best friends.'[1] Such words and affection like those displayed on the other occasion can come only from the heart of a *Tsee-tsue*, and with these words, too, I conclude this chapter.

[1] Boswell's *Life of Johnson*; Ed. G. Routledge & Sons, London, Vol. III, p. 227.

CHAPTER 8

LITERATURE

PART I

ON the question whether Chinese literature should be treated in this work, I was at first rather wavering, recalling the soliloquy of Hamlet, not that there is no place for it, but that, as its field is so wide and its volume so colossal, I wondered how it might be intelligibly introduced so as to enable my readers to have a glimpse of it without finding it too tedious. However, it must be done. The literature of a country is a unique specimen of its civilization and culture, being the channel through which its people express their ideas and thoughts, and forming what they rightly consider to be their just pride and most precious heritage. The art of a country may be lost or perish; its literature remains. In this respect, literature has a value even more permanent than art. Happy therefore are the Chinese, whose country, if rich in art, is even richer in literature. 'There are', says an English author, 'probably more books stored and sold in Peking (old capital of China) than in any other city of the world.'[1] In a long street, named Lou Li Chong, well-known to foreigners, practically nothing but books and objects of art are sold. For as, in the words of a sinologue, 'the Chinese were a remarkably civilized nation some time before Greek civilization can be said to have begun',[2] and as China is the country that first invented paper and printing, holding, always, scholarship and learning in high esteem, the amount of her literature must be enormous. As an instance, her encyclopaedia, Sze Ku Chuen Shoo, compiled under the patronage of the Emperor Chien Lung (A.D. 1736-1796) by a small army of eminent scholars, consists of 79,582 books[3] bound in 36,378 volumes[4] of 30 cm. in length, 19 cm. in width, and 1·2 cm. in thickness. It contains, after selection and revision, all that had been written up to the time of its compilation in the following four departments:

1. Sacred books, comprising the whole Confucian Canon and its commentaries, together with all the ancient books associated with it.

[1] The Rev. E. J. Hardy: *John Chinaman at Home*, p. 209.
[2] Herbert A. Giles: *The Civilization of China*, p. 239.
[3] See List of Index to '*Sze Ku Chuen Shoo*'; Ed. Great Eastern Book Co., Bk. IV, p. 77.
[4] See *Chekiang Library Pamphlet*, April 1933.

2. History, general and local, including biographies or bio-graphical notes of eminent persons.

3. Philosophy of various Schools other than what is classified in the first category, including agriculture, art, astronomy, astrology, botany, Buddhism, calligraphy, cosmogony, divination, drawing, economy, geography, handicrafts, law, lexicology, mathematics, medicine, military strategy, music, oratory, painting, sports, sur-gery, Taoism, and other branches of art or science or useful knowledge.

4. Literature, comprising high-class poetry, essays, and songs of various forms and styles, as well as miscellaneous writings of recognized merit and historical interest.

The 79,582 books, compiled out of 173,187 books, are divided as follows:[1]

1. Sacred Books	10,255 out of 20,365
2. History	21,950 out of 38,278
3. Philosophy	17,877 out of 59,478
4. Literature	29,500 out of 55,066
	79,582 173,187

Books are so many and the field of literature is so wide that, even in an advanced examination for literature, it would be unfair to confront a candidate with passages taken from books that are not usually read, though they may not be of a special nature. In the old days of classical examination the term 'Classics' was generally understood to mean only those subjects that are classified in the first category, including some branches of general history and general literature. The various schools of philosophy classified under the third category, for instance, were considered to be special branches of knowledge. Just as a priest of the Christian church is not required to know Buddhism or Mohammedanism, so a Confucian scholar was not expected to know, as a matter of course, much in the province of philosophy beyond the Confucian School, which is already a great deal. Chinese literature is not only vast in its bulk but also pure in its content. 'Throughout the Confucian Canon, there is not a single word which could give offence, even to the most sensitive, on questions of delicacy and decency. Chinese poetry, of which there is in existence a huge mass, will be searched in vain for suggestions of im-propriety, for sly innuendo, and for the other tricks of the unclean.'[2]

[1] See List of Index to 'Sze Ku Chuen Shoo'; Ed. Great Eastern Book Co., Bk. IV, p. 77.
[2] Herbert A. Giles: The Civilization of China, pp. 128-9.

OLD PALACE SPECIAL LIBRARY
For Sze Ku Chuen Shoo

Literature is so bound up with the history, philosophy, customs, traditions, and ways of thinking of the people to which it belongs, that it rarely fails to lose its charm, when it loses its nationality through translation. This is specially true in the case of highly literary Chinese with its classical allusions which, though full of relish to those who know, are meaningless to those who do not. Some years ago I was requested by a man to translate into English a draft telegram purported to be sent to the then Labour Government in England in connection with some incident in China. It was penned evidently by a person eager to display a knowledge of the Classics; for, apart from several highly literary passages, it contained the phrase 'I would cry bitterly at the Court of *Chin*'. This is an allusion to the well-known history of a minister of *Cho*, named Sin Bow Shoo, who obtained, in the year 505 B.C., military aid for his ruler from *Chin*, by crying seven days and nights successively at its Court. The ruler of *Chin* was moved by the appeal, because he felt that, as *Cho* could have a minister so loyal as Sin Bow Shoo, it should not be ignored. This is the historical basis of the allusion. The phrase now simply means, in a literary sense, 'making a strong appeal for urgent aid'. For instance, when Reynaud broadcasted his appeal to the United States on the eve of the collapse of France, this phrase would be highly appropriate. But it would make no sense, if it were literally translated. Therefore, to the man who requested me to do the translation, I said: 'When the Right Honourable Englishman reads in the telegram the words, "the Court of *Chin*", he will surely think that there must be an error in transmission, believing that it is the Court of St. James that is meant, and, when reminded by his learned colleague, the Lord Chancellor or the Attorney General, of the constitutional aspect of the question, will say: "If the Chinaman wants to come, he should come to Downing Street and not the Court of St. James!" '

As instances of allusion, the following may be given:

1. '*Under foot*'.

This is a well-known term of friendly endearment daily used in letters, equivalent to the English word 'dear' in addressing a male friend. Instead of saying 'Dear Smith', the Chinese may write 'Smith under foot'. It is an historical allusion based on the following story:

A virtuous man, named Jer Tsee Tuo, of the seventh century B.C., had loyally accompanied with others a feudal Prince in exile, during which he was perhaps the one who experienced the greatest hardship. When the Prince ultimately succeeded in returning to his State and became ruler, he handsomely rewarded all those who had been with him in exile, but, through inadvertence or otherwise, he left out Jer Tsee Tuo, who, being a virtuous man, also expressed no desire for reward. He retired to lead a hermit life in the forest on a mountain. After some time the Prince thought of him and his past services, and consequently offered him a high post; but he firmly declined and even refused to come out from the forest, in spite of repeated attempts at persuasion. In order to induce, or rather compel, him to come out, fire was set to the forest where he was living. But, to prove that his retirement was not due to any chagrin and that he was firm in his intention, he put his arms round a tree and was thus burnt to death. Immensely grieved at this sorrowful result, the Prince ordered the tree to be cut down and a pair of shoes made of it. Every day he would wear these shoes, and every moment he thought of the past, he would weep bitterly, looking downward at his shoes, and calling 'under foot', 'under foot'. Since then, this term has become one of friendly endearment.

2. 'Upwardly, to support and, downwardly, to maintain'.

This is an elliptical expression for 'means of maintaining one's family'. It is an allusion to Mencius, who said that the minimum condition of livelihood that a good ruler should ensure for his people was that every man should be able to have 'enough means, upwardly, to support his parents and, downwardly, to maintain his wife and children'.[1] A Chinese trade unionist, therefore, in order to show that he is an educated man, may well, on demanding a minimum wage for his fellow-workers, say, 'The wages we receive are not enough, upwardly, to support, and downwardly, to maintain.'

3. 'Pressing the golden thread'.

This means doing things not for oneself but for others, and in consequence making no progress in one's career. It is an allusion to a celebrated poem of the *Tang* Dynasty, entitled 'A Poor Girl'. The lines referred to are:

'I hate to press the golden thread year after year,
For making wedding gowns for other girls to wear.'

If Edmund Burke were a Chinaman, it would be quite conceivable that, in the days when he was serving Hamilton as a secretary[2] he might, in talking to Johnson or his other fellow-members of the Literary Club, say: 'I am quite well but still pressing the golden thread.'

[1] See *ante*, p. 143.
[2] *Dictionary of National Biography*, London, 1886, Vol. VII, p. 347.

Briefly, 'Old rain' means old friend—an allusion to a poem by the famous poet Doo Fu; 'Resting cloud' means thinking of intimate friends—an allusion to a *Tang* poem; 'The sorrow of gathering wood' means illness—an allusion to the ancient *Book of Odes*; 'A switch of the autumn wave' means a glad eye given by a woman—an allusion to a poem by Soo Tung Po; 'Crying wild geese' means refugees—an allusion to the ancient *Book of Odes*; 'Ching Chow' (name of a city) means not returning a thing borrowed—an allusion to the history of the 'Three Kingdoms'; 'The evening cloud and the spring tree' means thinking of intimate friends—an allusion to a poem composed by the poet Doo Fu in thinking of his friend, the Poet Li Tai Po. Allusions exist of course in every language, but the Chinese tongue has a rich mine of them.

Chinese literature is not without wit or humour. There are many books which can keep one awake in a way even more powerful than strong coffee. The following story is one of many from these volumes, but I am quoting it only from memory:

A man harbouring an intense enmity against another consulted a sorcerer, who said: 'I can have your enemy killed by spirits summoned from the underworld.' 'This is splendid', answered the man; 'but his property would still remain.' 'Then I will call fire down from heaven to have all his goods and belongings destroyed,' said the sorcerer. 'Even this would leave his lands untouched,' replied the client. 'Now', said the sorcerer finally, 'as your hatred against your enemy is so extreme, I am going to give you something that is most destructive of all. If you can only induce him to use it, he will be absolutely finished.' After saying this, he handed a small sealed packet to the man, who, on opening it, found there contained nothing but a pen. Rather surprised, the man asked the sorcerer what mysterious power of destruction there could be in that. 'Ah!' exclaimed the sorcerer, with a sigh, 'you seem not to know how many persons have brought utter ruin upon themselves and theirs by the use of this precious thing.'

Chinese novels are many, and there are good ones too. But they have not yet been accorded the honour of high literature. The reason is not that even the good ones are not good enough to deserve that honour, but that, in my opinion, while the Chinese love poetry and history, both of which they have in abundance, the novel in their eyes rarely reaches the level of the one in beauty or of the other in excitement; for in poetry one finds beauty crystallized, while in history one finds life even stranger than fiction. However, there is a novel called the *Three Kingdoms*, an historical romance, already referred to in the Chapter on Family. It may be said to be one of the best known and most widely read books in China during the last three hundred years, particularly among the masses. Though it belongs to the lighter branch of literature, yet, as it may for that reason, apart from its own merits, give my readers a more vivid picture of things and, at the same time, a bird's eye view of Chinese novels in general, I propose to furnish, as a supplement to literature, a translation of a selected chapter of it, in which will be found, incidentally, a glimpse, through Chinese glasses, of the illustration of benevolence, culture, filial piety, fraternal deference, friendship, hermitage, humour, loyalty, patience, philosophy, politics, righteousness, scholarship, sincerity, wisdom, wit, and womanhood.

PART II

FRAGMENTS FROM THE 'THREE KINGDOMS'

ONE day Lew Bei, still at the beginning of his career destined to make him King of a third of the Empire, was fleeing for his life. He arrived on horseback before a wide stream, while pursuing troops were hot at his heels. In this painful dilemma, which may aptly be expressed as 'between the devil and the deep sea', the only thing he felt he could possibly do was to run the risk of crossing the stream at any cost. But after proceeding a few paces the horse fell on its forelegs, making part of his clothes thoroughly wet. In this plight he called the horse by its name: 'Dee Lo! Dee Lo! You are bringing disaster upon me to-day.' Suddenly, the horse rose from the water and jumped thirty feet over to the other side of the stream. Thus he was saved. While he was contemplating the danger that had confronted him and the luck that he had in escaping it, the sun was setting, and a boy on cow back, playing a flute between his lips, was slowly coming his way. 'I am not equal to him,' murmured Lew Bei with a sigh. He then stopped and looked admiringly at the boy, as he approached.

The boy also stopped and fixed his eyes on Lew Bei, ceasing to play the flute. 'Are you General Lew Hsuan Tek[1] who crushed the *Yellow Turban Rebellion*?' asked he.

'How do you, a boy of a far-hidden hamlet, know my name?' replied Lew Bei, rather surprised.

---

[1] Lew Bei's courtesy name, that is, the name not given to him at birth by his parents, which is called one's 'nursery name', but adopted by himself to be used by others in addressing him.

'I often wait on my master,' said the boy. 'One day he had guests who talked about a certain Lew Hsuan Tek. They said that his height was seven foot five, his hands reached his knees, and his ears were so large that he could see them with his own eyes, and that he was the hero of the day. As you answer this description, I think it must be you.'

'Who is your master?' asked Lew Bei, more surprised.

'His name is Sze Ma Fay. His courtesy name is Water Mirror,' replied the boy. [1]

'Where does he live?' asked Lew Bei once more.

'There, in that forest,' said the boy, pointing to a bungalow afar.

'I am indeed Hsuan Tek,' said Lew Bei. 'Will you take me to see your master?'

The boy consented and led the way. The journey was about two miles in distance. When they arrived at the bungalow, they dismounted. Lew Bei followed the boy into the bungalow. As they just reached the middle gate, Lew Bei heard someone playing beautifully on an ancient harp. He told the boy not to announce his arrival for the moment, and remained outside, listening attentively to the music. Suddenly, the music ceased, and a man was heard laughing and saying as he came out. 'The music was smooth and calm. All of a sudden it rose to a high pitch. There must be a distinguished man listening.'

'Here is my master, Mr. Water Mirror,' said the boy to Lew Bei, pointing to the man who just appeared.

Lew Bei glanced at the man, and was much impressed by his uncommon and arresting demeanour. Forthwith he stepped forward to greet him respectfully, his clothes being still partly wet.

'Sir', said the man, 'you have escaped from a mortal danger today.'

Lew Bei was quite taken aback by this unexpected remark, marvelling how on earth the man could have known the accident. He was received into the hall, where he saw books heaped on shelves, an ancient harp lying on a stone sofa, and bushes of pine-trees and bamboos, waving outside the window, while a refreshing air pervaded the whole country house.

'Sir', said Water Mirror, 'how is it that you are here?'

'By chance I passed here,' answered Lew Bei. 'Through the kindness of your boy I seized the opportunity of paying you my respects. I am grateful for your kind reception.'

---

[1] Sze Ma Fay and Water Mirror are therefore the same person, though he may be referred to as the one or the other.

'Sir,' said Water Mirror, smiling, 'to be frank, you have been fleeing from danger.'

Lew Bei, feeling that it would be better to take his host into his confidence, unfolded the whole story of his flight.

'I know this by your countenance,' said Water Mirror. 'I have heard of your great name for a long time. But why are you still in such a plight?'

'It is Fate that makes it so,' answered Lew Bei.

'It is not Fate,' said Water Mirror, 'but the fact that you have no competent men to help you that is responsible for it.'

'Although I myself am incompetent,' said Lew Bei, 'I have Sun, Mee, Kan, and others, as my advisers, and Kwan, Chang, Chao, and others, as my generals. They all have rendered me invaluable services.'

'Kwan, Chang, and Chao are no doubt generals of the first order in directing campaigns,' said Water Mirror; 'but, unfortunately, they do not know how to direct men. Sun, Mee, and Kan are only book scholars; they are no statesmen.'

'I have always tried to secure men of talent,' said Lew Bei, 'but as I have not had the fortune of meeting one, what can I do?'

'Have you not heard of the saying of Confucius,' said Water Mirror, 'that "even in a hamlet of only ten houses there will surely be found men who are loyal and sincere"?[1] By analogy, how can you say that men of talent are not to be found?'

'I am very ignorant', said Lew Bei, 'and earnestly desire to be enlightened by you.'

Water Mirror repeated a popular song sung by children in certain districts, and explained to Lew Bei the omen conveyed by each line of the song, which indicated that he was the man of the hour.

Lew Bei, not a little startled by this, thanked his host for the compliment, saying: 'How dare I have that honour?'

'All the most wonderful talents of the world are in this district,' said Water Mirror. 'You only have to find them.'

'Who are these wonderful persons, and where do they live?' asked Lew Bei.

'There are two persons: The Sleeping Dragon and The Wakeful Phoenix,' replied Water Mirror. 'If you can secure the service of even only one of them, your empire will be assured.'

'The Sleeping Dragon and The Wakeful Phoenix, who are they?' asked Lew Bei again.

Water Mirror laughed, and clapped his hands, saying: 'Well, well.' Lew Bei asked once more; but Water Mirror said: 'It is get-

[1] Confucius: *Lun Yu*, Pt. V, Ch. 27.

ting dark. You had better spend the night here. We shall talk about the matter again to-morrow.' He then ordered the boy to have the table laid for dinner, after which Lew Bei retired.

During the night Lew Bei revolved in his mind the words of Water Mirror, and was unable to sleep. Suddenly, in the depth of the night, he heard someone knock at the front door of the bungalow and then enter, followed by the voice of his host: 'Yuen Chih, it is you! How is it that you are here?' He thereupon rose from his bed and listened attentively. 'I have for a long time heard', said the visitor, 'that Lew Ching Sing liked men of merit and disliked men of demerit. I made a special call on him, but found that he had only a false reputation. He could neither employ men of merit, nor get rid of men of demerit. I therefore left him, taking leave by a letter, and came here.' 'You have the abilities', replied Water Mirror, 'great enough to help one to found an empire. You should try to find a worthy man to serve. Why should you have stooped to see the man Ching Sing. A hero is just in your presence. It is merely that you do not know him.' Then the visitor said: 'You are quite right.'

Lew Bei was delighted with this conversation overheard, thinking that the visitor must be either The Sleeping Dragon or The Wakeful Phoenix. He wanted badly to come out to meet him, but feared that his appearance might be an intrusion. Therefore he waited until dawn, when, on seeing his host, he asked him who the night visitor was. The latter replied that the visitor was a friend of his. Lew Bei expressed a desire of meeting him, but was told that he had gone to look for a worthy chief whom he could serve. Disappointed, Lew Bei asked for the name of the visitor, but received in reply only a smile and the words 'Well, well', nor was he any more successful in his request for further information about The Sleeping Dragon and The Wakeful Phoenix. Finally he begged Water Mirror to give up his hermit life and honour him with his services in his effort to restore the *Han* Dynasty. To his entreaties, Water Mirror replied: 'I am a lazy man of the wilderness, unworthy of any such honour as you suggest. There are, however, persons ten times abler than myself, who will aid you in your great task. You should go and try to find them.'

All of a sudden there were shouts of men and neighings of horses outside the bungalow, and the boy ran in to say that a general with troops was at the gate. Lew Bei, rather agitated, hurriedly went out to see what happened. To his joy and relief, he found that the general was his famous Chao Yun, who had been looking for him. Therefore he took leave of Water Mirror. On his way back to his Headquarters he saw in the market a man in scholarly attire coming along, while singing:

> The world is in its dotage; [1]
> Fire's about to rage; [2]
> The Gigantic House [3] is cracking;
> A single log gives little backing. [4]
> There lives a man of merit in the valley,
> Who desires to serve a master worthy.
> A worthy master seeks a man of worth;
> But he alas! does not know me on earth.

Greatly impressed by the veiled meaning of the song, which seemed to depict aptly the then situation both politically and personally, Lew Bei wondered if the man was 'The Sleeping Dragon' or 'The Wakeful Phoenix' mentioned by Mr. Water Mirror. He therefore dismounted, and, after a formal salutation, courteously invited the man to accompany him to his Headquarters.

'My name is Darn Fuoo,' said the man to Lew Bei. 'I have always heard that you, Sir, have a high esteem of scholars. It has long been my wish to offer you my services; but fearing that a direct self-introduction might be construed as an intrusion, I sang in the market in order to attract your attention.'

Lew Bei was pleased with what Darn Fuoo had said, and treated him as a guest of distinction.

'Sir', said Darn Fuoo, 'may I have another look at the horse on which you were riding?'

Lew Bei gave order that the horse be unsaddled and brought in.

'Is not this the famous horse called Dee Lo?' asked Darn Fuoo. 'Although it is a horse that can run a thousand miles, it is one that will bring disaster upon its master. It should not be used.'

'What you said has already happened,' answered Lew Bei. He then told Darn Fuoo the accident that he had, while crossing a stream in fleeing from a pursuing army.

'No, no,' said Darn Fuoo. 'This is saving its master, not doing him harm. It must sooner or later bring harm to one master. I have a suggestion to make that may prevent it.'

'I desire to hear your instruction,' said Lew Bei.

'If you have in mind', said Darn Fuoo, 'any person for whom you harbour a grudge or any enmity, you may give him that horse. After

---

[1] This means that the Empire is in great turmoil.
[2] This means that a revolution is going to break out.
[3] This refers to the *Han* dynasty.
[4] This means that a leader, however capable, cannot save the situation without the help of other men.

he has answered the ill omen, you may then use it again without fear of evil.'

Lew Bei at once changed his countenance and said sternly: 'Sir, you have only just come here. You do not teach me to follow the righteous path, but teach me things that will benefit myself at the expense of others. I dare not follow your advice.'

Darn Fuoo burst into laughter and congratulated Lew Bei on his noble-mindedness. 'I have heard much of your virtue,' said he; 'but, to tell you frankly, I desired to see it demonstrated. Hence what I said.'

Lew Bei again changed his countenance, and, rising to thank Darn Fuoo, said: 'How dare I think that I possess any virtue? It is you, Sir, who will impart it to me by your instruction.'

'In my journey to this district', said Darn Fuoo, 'I heard the people of *Sin Yere* sing:

> Long live the Prefect of *Sin Yere*,
> Our Royal Uncle Lew!
> E'er since his arrival here,
> People's wants are few.

'This, Sir, shows not only that you have virtue, but also that your virtue is renowned.'

Lew Bei was inwardly delighted, and, after a discussion with Darn Fuoo on the military situation, made the latter his military adviser. From that day onward, Darn Fuoo, by a course of brilliant strategy turned the fortune of war in favour of his chief against Tso Chau, the usurper. While Tso Chau was smarting over his unexpected defeats, he asked his men if they knew who had been planning the latest campaigns for Lew Bei.

'The man who has recently been acting as Lew Bei's military adviser is named Darn Fuoo,' replied a general.

'The man's real name is not Darn Fuoo,' interposed Ching Ue, a civil adviser. 'This is only his assumed name. His real name is Chu Shu. His courtesy name is Yuen Chih.'

'How is his ability compared with yours?' asked Tso Chau.

'Ten times of mine,' answered Ching Ue.

'Alas!' exclaimed Tso Chau. 'All talented men rally to Lew Bei. His wings are formed. What shall be done?'

'Although Chu Shu is with Lew Bei,' said Ching Ue thoughtfully, 'it will not be difficult to have him here, if Your Excellency wants him.'

'How will this be possible?' asked Tso Chau.

'Chu Shu is a man of great filial piety,' answered Ching Ue. 'He lost his father when he was young, and his only brother died recently. His mother is now very old and living alone. If Your Excellency send someone to induce her to come here and then persuade her to write a letter to her son, calling him back, he will obey for certain.'

Tso Chau, exceedingly pleased with this advice, dispatched at once a special messenger travelling day and night to secure Chu Shu's mother. In a few days she arrived. Tso Chau treated her very respectfully, saying: 'Madam, I have heard with unbounded admiration that your son, Yuen Chih, is a world talent. He is now at *Sin Yere*, aiding a rebel against the Imperial Government. This is like a piece of fine jade fallen into the mire. It is a great pity. May I request you to write a letter to call him back? You may be sure that I will petition the Emperor to honour him with a high office.' Having said this, he ordered the attendants to bring an ink-grinding stone and other writing instruments for the old lady to write.

'Who is Lew Bei?' asked Chu Shu's mother.

'A man of no consequence of the city of Bei, pretending to be a descendant of the Imperial Family, but possessing no merit whatever,' replied Tso Chau. 'He is what is called a gentleman outwardly but a mean fellow inwardly—a hypocrite.'

'How false and deceitful you are!' exclaimed she, raising her voice to a high pitch. 'I have for a long time heard that Lew Bei is a direct descendant of King Chung San and the son of the great-grandson of Emperor Shao Tsing. He is universally known for his modesty, for his esteem of men of merit, and for his kindness to the people —a true hero of the hour. My son in serving him has found the right master. You, though bearing the name of Prime Minister of *Han*, are a traitor. It is sheer shameless audacity that you call Lew Bei a rebel, and venture so far as to suggest that my son should forsake the righteous and rally to the wicked. What a shame!' Thereupon she snatched the ink-grinding stone and struck Tso Chau with it. The latter, being furious, ordered his guardsmen to have her seized to be summarily executed. Ching Ue intervened, whispering to Tso Chau: 'She insulted Your Excellency with the intention of provoking Your Excellency to kill her. If Your Excellency killed her, you would court an odious name and make her a martyr. After her death, her son would serve Lew Bei in dead earnest with the additional spur of revenge. It is therefore better to spare her life and retain her here, making Chu Shu's attention divided, so that, even though he may continue to serve Lew Bei, he will not be able to concentrate his energy. Moreover, so long as she is here, I shall be able to find means to make him come.'

Tso Chau, in consequence of this advice, withdrew the order and

LITERATURE   223

sent Chu Shu's mother away to be confined in a separate building. Henceforth, Ching Ue would call on her every day, treating her kindly like his own mother. He also frequently sent her presents, accompanied with a courteous note, to which she sometimes replied in writing. In this way he obtained her handwriting, and, by imitating it, he forged a letter to be sent by a trusted messenger to Chu Shu. The letter was worded as follows:

'Since the recent death of your brother, I am quite alone. In the midst of misery and sorrow, which is still green in my memory, I was kidnapped to Hsu Cheong by someone acting on the order of Prime Minister Tso, who said that you had become a rebel and has consequently had me imprisoned. It was only through the kind and timely intervention of Ching Ue that I was released. If you give yourself up by coming back, my life will be spared. When this letter reaches you, think of the filial debt that one owes to one's mother, and start for home at once for the sake of filial piety. After you have returned here, thus saving my life, we shall retire to our old farm, and spend our remaining days there quietly. Just now my life hangs on a hair. Help! Help!'

Chu Shu, having received this letter, was in tears. He forthwith went to see Lew Bei and, showing it to him, said:

'I am a native of Yuen Chuen. My real name is Chu Shu, and my courtesy name Yuen Chih. It was to escape from personal danger that I assumed the name Darn Fuoo. Once, as I had heard that Lew Ching Sing was a man who esteemed scholars, I made a special call on him; but as I found in my conversation with him that he was not a man of much worth, I left him, taking leave only by letter, and went in the night to see Mr. Water Mirror at his bungalow, informing him of my experience with Lew Ching Sing. He reproached me bitterly for my ignorance of men, and told me that you were there, suggesting that I should serve you. Consequently, I composed a fanatic song, and sang it in the market in order to attract your attention. Thanks to your kindness and confidence, I was able to offer you my humble services, the performance of which required great trust. For this I feel highly honoured and shall ever be grateful. But alas! Tso Chau has by treacherous means kidnapped my aged mother to Hsu Cheong, and had her imprisoned, threatening to put her to death. She has now written to me, asking me to go back to save her life. I must go, not because I do not wish to be always with you in order to show my gratitude for your kindness and my appreciation of your friendship, but because my mother's life is at stake. It is with a heavy heart that I have come to take leave of you. Farewell.'

Lew Bei, on hearing this, almost broke down, saying:

'The affectionate relation between mother and child is one dictated by Nature. Yuen Chih, [1] please do not worry yourself about me. After you have rejoined Madam, your Honoured mother, Fortune may still favour me with the chance of receiving your instruction.'

Chu Shu, thanking him, expressed the wish to depart.
'Pray, remain with us one more night,' said Lew Bei, still in tears. 'To-morrow, we shall partake of a farewell meal.'
Then a man named Shuen Chuen whispered to Lew Bei:

'Yuen Chih is a rare genius of the world. He has long been with us in *Sin Yere* and knows all our military secrets. If you allow him to go over to Tso Chau, Tso Chau will for certain offer him a high post and make good use of his services. This will endanger our safety. We should, with all our means and power, make him remain and not let him go. When Tso Chau realizes that his effort to secure him is in vain, Tso Chau will certainly have his mother put to death; and, when he learns of his mother's fate, he will no doubt do his best to avenge the crime done to her by Tso Chau.'

'No, no,' answered Lew Bei gravely. 'To cause people to take the life of someone's mother in order to secure the services of her son is repugnant to the notion of benevolence. To insist on a man remaining with you and not let him go, thus barring the path between parental and filial affections is repugnant to the sense of righteousness. I would rather die than do anything of that kind.' [2]

All who heard these words were deeply moved with feelings of gratitude.
Lew Bei afterwards pressed Chu Shu to drink a cup of wine.
'Having heard that my aged mother is being in prison', said Chu Shu, 'I cannot force down my throat even a golden or jady drop.'
'Hearing that you are going to leave us', responded Lew Bei spontaneously, 'I feel as if I had lost an arm. Though the food might be as delicious as dragon's liver or phoenix's marrow, it would be tasteless to me.'

[1] Yuen Chih, it will be remembered, is Chu Shu's courtesy name.
[2] '(The ancient sages) would not commit a single unrighteous act or kill a single innocent person even for acquiring an empire.' (*Mencius*, Bk. II, Pt. I, Ch. 2, Sec. 24.)

The two men sat up *tête-à-tête* until dawn. In the meantime officers and ranks had prepared a grand farewell feast laid in the outskirts of the town. Lew Bei and Chu Shu were both on horseback, proceeding side by side to the place where the feast was laid. When they reached the Long Pavilion, they dismounted. Holding a cup to drink to the health of Chu Shu, Lew Bei said: 'Bei,[1] not being favoured by Fate to enjoy for long the company of those whom he admires and to whom he is attached, is now forced to part with you. It is his sincere wish that you, Sir, will find a worthier Chief in future and attain great eminence.'

'My ability is limited', responded Chu Shu, overwhelmed with emotion, 'and my knowledge small. But, in spite of this, I had the privilege of being entrusted by you with affairs of the utmost importance. I am grateful to you. Unfortunately, I have to part with you in the midst of my task. But I can assure you that this painful decision has been taken entirely on account of my mother. Even if Tso Chau should force me, I will never, until the end of my life, do a single thing for him.'[2]

'When you are away, Sir', rejoined Lew Bei sadly, 'I will also retire to the wilderness.'

'In serving you in the task of founding an empire', said Chu Shu, 'what I relied on in myself was my presence of mind. Now, on account of my mother, this presence of mind has been completely shaken. Therefore even if I were to remain here with you, I would no longer be able to render you any useful service. Sir, you should look for other and abler men to help you. Why should you be in such despair?'

'There is not another man in the world who is equal to you,' said Lew Bei.

'I am a man of only mediocre ability,' said Chu Shu. 'How dare I accept the honour you thus accord me?' Then, turning to the officers and ranks, he addressed them thus: 'I hope you all will serve your Chief faithfully and loyally in the common cause, so that your names will go down to posterity and shine in history. Never act like me, who desert my task in the midst of it.'

All officers and ranks who heard these words were immensely touched. Lew Bei, who could not bear the thought of separation, accompanied Chu Shu in his departing journey farther and farther.

'Pray, Sir, do not tire yourself by accompanying me too far,' said Chu Shu to Lew Bei earnestly. 'Let me say farewell now.'

'Sir,' replied Lew Bei, 'after to-day we shall be in different parts

[1] Speaking in the third person as a high form of politeness.
[2] A promise, it may be mentioned, which was afterwards faithfully kept.

of the world, and I do not know when we shall meet again.' While he was saying this, he was no longer able to withhold his tears. Chu Shu's eyes were also wet as he parted. Standing by his horse on the bushy wayside, Lew Bei watched Chu Shu on horseback, with a few attendants, rapidly disappearing in the distance. He sorrowfully murmured to himself: 'Yuen Chih is gone. What shall I do?' He looked ahead, but a forest prevented him from seeing far. Thereupon he pointed his whip to the forest and said to his men: 'I would like to have all the trees there cut down.' On being asked why, he replied: 'Because they prevent me from seeing Chu Yuen Chih.'

As Lew Bei was thus looking afar, he saw Chu Shu suddenly whip his horse and turn back. 'Yuen Chih is returning,' muttered Lew Bei. 'Is it that he does not want to go?' Highly pleased with this prospect, he forthwith mounted on his horse, and whipped it to run forward to meet Chu Shu. On seeing Chu Shu, he said: 'Master, on returning, you must have made up your mind.'

'My mind', replied Chu Shu, pulling tight his horse, 'has been so disturbed, like a bundle of yarn in confusion, that I have forgotten a word that I meant to say to you. In this neighbourhood there is a wonderful genius, living in fact not very distant from here. Sir, I suggest you should try to find him and beg him to offer you his services.'

'May I ask you', said Lew Bei, 'to arrange with him for a meeting with me?'

'This man', answered Chu Shu, 'cannot be asked to come to see you. Sir, you have to call on him personally. If you can secure his services, he will be to you like the great statesman Lu Vang to the *Chow* dynasty or the great statesman Chang Leong to the *Han* dynasty.'

'Master', asked Lew Bei, 'how are his ability and virtue in comparison with yours?'

'To compare me with him', replied Chu Shu, 'would be like comparing an ass with a *Chi Lin*[1] or a crow with a phoenix. He often compares himself to Kwan Chung and Yerk Yee.[2] In my opinion, they are not his equals by a long way. His ability is immense: he is *the* man.'

'I would like to know his name,' said Lew Bei, delighted.

'His name is Tsu Ghaw Liang. His courtesy name is Kung Ming,' replied Chu Shu. 'In the place where he lives, there is a mount, known as "The Sleeping Dragon". Consequently, he calls himself

---

[1] A fabulous noble animal whose appearance is a sign of great prosperity for the world.

[2] Great statesmen of the *Spring and Autumn* period (722-481 B.C.).

"The Sleeping Dragon". He is the greatest genius that has ever lived. I suggest that you, Sir, should go and call on him without delay. If you can persuade him to serve you, what worries will you have in your ambition and attempt to found an empire?'

'Once Master Water Mirror said to me', rejoined Lew Bei, recalling something to his memory, 'that if the services of either "The Sleeping Dragon" or "The Wakeful Phoenix" could be secured, the empire would be assured. Do you mean the same persons?'

'The Wakeful Phoenix is another person,' said Chu Shu. 'The Sleeping Dragon is Tsu Ghaw Kung Ming.'

'It is only to-day', exclaimed Lew Bei, 'that I understand the phrase "The Sleeping Dragon and the Wakeful Phoenix". How wonderful it is that a great genius should be so near! If not for you, Master, I would be blind in spite of my eyes.'

The two men finally said farewell to each other. Chu Shu, feeling grateful for Lew Bei's friendly attachment, and fearing that Kung Ming might refuse to emerge from his hermit life to serve Lew Bei, went direct to the Sleeping Dragon Mount to see him in order to put in a few words for Lew Bei. He found Kung Ming at his cottage and, on being asked about the object of his visit, first told Kung Ming the cause of his sudden departure, and then mentioned his recommendation, and finally begged his friend not to refuse Lew Bei, when he should call, but to avail himself of the opportunity to give the benefit of his wonderful knowledge and talents to a yearning world.

'You mean to make a sacrifice of me,' said Kung Ming, changing his countenance. After saying this, he turned his back and left Chu Shu, who felt rather remorseful and departed at once for his maternal home.

When Tso Chau heard of Chu Shu's arrival, he ordered a group of men of high rank to welcome him outside the city. He was given a handsome reception and then conducted to see Tso Chau, who on seeing him said: 'Master, you are a scholar of the highest merit. Why should you have stooped to serve Lew Bei?'

'I had to flee from personal danger', replied Chu Shu, 'when I was still young. In consequence, I was stranded in a friendless world. That was why I went to *Sin Yere*, where I met Lew Bei. My mother, I understand, is here, and has been kindly looked after by you. I am grateful.'

'Master, as you are now here', said Tso Chau, 'you will have the opportunity of attending on Madam, your Honoured mother, both day and night, and I shall also have the opportunity of receiving your instructive advice from time to time.'

Chu Shu, after thanking Tso Chau, hurriedly left him and went to see his mother. On seeing her, he knelt down before her in tears.

'Why are you here?' asked she with horror, thinking that her son had come over to the side of Tso Chau.

'Recently, I have been serving Lew Bei,' answered Chu Shu; 'but as I have received a letter from you, I immediately came home.' Thereupon he handed her the letter.

'Poor child!' exclaimed she with horror, after having read the letter. 'You have been drifting in the world for years. I thought you had learned something by this time. On the contrary, you are more ignorant than before. Do you think that I would ever have written you such a letter—to call you back to serve a traitor even for the sake of saving my life? As an educated man, you should understand that the duty of serving one's country has a higher claim than the duty of serving one's home. You know very well that Tso Chau is a traitor, and that Lew Bei is a man whose benevolence and righteousness are renowned throughout the country, apart from being a direct descendant of the *Han* Imperial Family. As you have been serving him, you have indeed found the right master. But relying simply on a letter the forgery of which is self-evident, and without exercising any judgment, you have, at least as the world will judge you, forsaken the righteous for the wicked, thus, by your own folly, acquiring an ignoble name for yourself and bringing dishonour on your ancestors. What a terrible responsibility I must bear for having failed to bring you up wiser! Poor child, you have wasted your life in the universe!'

Listening to this painful reproach, and realizing his own tragic blunder, Chu Shu, still kneeling on the ground, dared not raise his head. His mother, overwhelmed with grief, was unable to utter a word more; but seeing that her son was now within the clutches of the traitor who could easily continue to use her as a weapon, so that her existence would remain only a source of danger to her son and the cause of righteousness, she in a moment of despair slipped behind the screen, and in an instant it was announced that she was dead. Chu Shu, on hearing this, fainted, without recovering his consciousness until after a long time. As soon as Tso Chau learned this news, he sent representatives with funeral presents to tender Chu Shu his condolence, and afterwards went personally to pay respects to the dead body before burial. Chu Shu escorted the coffin of his mother to his native district declining all the presents sent by Tso Chau.

While this family tragedy was taking place, Lew Bei was making preparation to call on Kung Ming. Just before his departure it was announced that a man of uncommon appearance was at the door. Lew Bei murmured to himself: 'Can the visitor be Kung Ming?' He at once put on his proper clothes, and went to the door to receive his visitor. On finding that the visitor was Sze Ma Fay (Mr. Water Mirror), he gladly invited him to step in.

'Since I saw your saintly face last', said Lew Bei, 'I have been so busy with my military affairs that I have not been able to call on you. To-day being honoured by your visit, I am delighted.'

'I have heard that Yuen Chih is here,' replied Sze Ma Fay.

'Recently', rejoined Lew Bei, 'because Tso Chau had Yuen Chih's mother imprisoned, she has written to call him back to his native district.'

'Ah! He has fallen into a trap!' exclaimed Sze Ma Fay, with a sigh. 'I have always heard that his mother is most virtuous. Even if she had been imprisoned and her life put in danger, she would never have sent for her son. The letter must have been a forgery. If Yuen Chih did not go, his mother may live. Now, as he is gone, she must be dead.'

Lew Bei, horrified by this remark, asked why.

'Yuen Chih's mother,' replied Sze Ma Fay, 'actuated by a high sense of righteousness, must feel ashamed to see her son back *under the circumstances*.'

Then Lew Bei told Sze Ma Fay that Yuen Chih on leaving recommended Kung Ming to him. 'What kind of man is he?' asked Lew Bei.

'Yuen Chih wanting to go, go he might,' said Sze Ma Fay, smiling. 'Why should he try to dig him (Kung Ming) out to offer "blood, toil, tears, and sweat"?'[1]

'Why, Master, do you say this?' asked Lew Bei.

'Kung Ming often compares himself to Kwan Chung and Yerk Yee,'[2] said Sze Ma Fay. 'His ability cannot be measured.'

'Why are there so many worthy men in this neighbourhood?' asked Lew Bei.

'Once an eminent astronomer learned in the science', replied Sze Ma Fay, 'observed that as a group of brilliant stars assembled above this part of the earth, this neighbourhood was destined to be the home of the worthies.'

[1] Spoken by Mr. Winston Churchill on 13th May 1940. I must beg pardon for this anachronism. But it may be remarked that, curiously enough, this is almost an exact translation of the original, and that there is much in common between the two cases, the one called to build an empire, the other to save one.
[2] See *ante*, p. 226, note 2.

During this conversation, it happened that one of Lew Bei's two sworn brothers,[1] Kwan Yun Cheong,[2] a general of the highest repute and a man of many virtues, was standing by. He observed: 'I have heard that Kwan Chung and Yerk Yee were both great statesmen of the *Spring and Autumn* period, whose merits were as immense as the universe. Kung Ming compares himself to these two men. Is not this rather too much?'

'In my opinion', said Sze Ma Fay, 'not only he is equal to them, but I would compare another two men to him.'

'Who are these two men?' asked Kwan Yun Cheong.

'He is equal', replied Sze Ma Fay, 'to Jenk Tze Yar, whose genius was responsible for the foundation of the *Chow* dynasty that lasted eight hundred years, and to Chang Tze Fong, whose genius contributed to the foundation of the *Han* dynasty that prospered for four hundred years.'

Everybody present listened to this with amazement. Sze Ma Fay then took leave of Lew Bei, who tried to detain him but in vain. When he was out in the street, he looked up to the sky, laughing loudly, and said: 'The Sleeping Dragon, although he has found the right master, has not lived in the right time. It is a great pity!'

Having uttered these words, he walked away quite unconcerned. Lew Bei observed: 'A true hermit and worthy!'

Next day Lew Bei and his two sworn brothers started on their journey to call on Kung Ming. On their way they saw at some distance a few farmers digging and singing:

> Blue sky is like a round-shaped cover;
> Flat earth is like a vast chess-board.
> As black from white men always differ.
> They fight for fame of vulgar sort.
> The winner is content and happy;
> The loser's lot is sad and rough.
> Wise is the man of *Nan Yang* Valley,
> Who sleeps head-up and ne'er enough.

Profoundly impressed by the philosophic wording of the song with

---

[1] 'Sworn brothers' are persons who are not brothers by blood but swear to be brethren for life. In their words, 'they wish not to be born, but to die, on the same day of the same month of the same year'.

[2] He was celebrated particularly for heroism, loyalty, magnanimity, and righteousness, and is now generally known as Kwan Gung, 'Gung' being a term of veneration. His personality, largely through the influence of this historical romance, makes a special appeal to the masses, who worship him not merely as a hero but as a god, considering him also as the symbol of brotherhood. Temples built in his honour are found in most parts of China.

all its delicate and shrewd allusions, Lew Bei pulled up his horse, and asked the farmers who had composed it. They replied that it had been composed by Master The Sleeping Dragon. Lew Bei then asked where Master Sleeping Dragon lived, and was told that he lived in a cottage on a small mount known as *The Sleeping Dragon*, not far away. After thanking them, Lew Bei's party continued their journey. At last, they arrived at the gate of the cottage indicated. They dismounted, and knocked at the gate. A boy appeared.

'Will you announce', said Lew Bei to the boy, 'that Lieutenant General of *Han*, Marquis of *Yu Ching*, Prefect of *Yu Chou*, Royal Uncle Lew Bei, has come to call on your master?'

'I cannot remember all these titles,' said the boy looking rather puzzled.

'In that case', said Lew Bei, 'you simply say that Lew Bei has come.'

'Master was out this morning,' answered the boy.

'Where has he gone?' asked Lew Bei, somewhat disappointed.

'I cannot tell,' answered the boy laconically.

'When will he be back?' asked Lew Bei again.

'It may be three or four days, or it may be weeks,' answered the boy.

Lew Bei was bewildered. Chang Fei,[1] his youngest sworn brother, who was also a general of the highest repute and courage but a man of impetuous temper, said: 'Since he cannot be seen, we had better go home.'

'Wait a moment,' said Lew Bei, suspecting Chang Fei's impatience.

'Let us go home *now*,' said the other younger brother, Kwan Yun Cheong. 'We may afterwards send someone from our Headquarters to find out things for us, and then we shall be able to decide what to do.'

Lew Bei, seeing that this was a reasonable course to take, finally said to the boy: 'When your master returns, please inform him that Lew Bei has called.'

The party then started to return to their Headquarters. After proceeding some distance, Lew Bei pulled up his horse and looked back. The beautiful natural scenery of the hill, where he had just been, drew from him immeasurable admiration. While he was in-

[1] He was originally a wine seller and butcher by profession, possessing a physical strength that 'could defy 10,000 persons'. Exceptionally brave, loyal, frank, impatient, and outspoken, he could not stand what he himself believed to be pretence or pretext; but he was very deferential to his sworn elder brother. Throughout this historical romance, he is a well-drawn character.

dulging in this contemplation of nature, a man of hermit countenance emerged from a by-path. 'He must be Master The Sleeping Dragon,' muttered Lew Bei to himself. He therefore dismounted and bowed respectfully to the man, saying: 'May I take it that you are Master The Sleeping Dragon?'

'Who are you, General?' asked the man.

'I am Lew Bei,' replied Lew Bei.

'I am not Kung Ming, but a friend of his,' said the man. 'My name is Chuoo Jou Ping.'

'I have for a long time heard of your eminent name,' said Lew Bei. 'As Fortune has enabled me to meet you here, will you sit down for a moment, so that I may benefit by your instruction?'

The two men then sat face to face on a stone in the forest, while Kwan and Chang stood by.

'General, may I ask what you want to see Kung Ming for?' said Chuoo Jou Ping.

'As the country is now in a state of commotion,' replied Lew Bei, 'I desire to secure Kung Ming's help in restoring it to peace and order.'

'Sir,' said Chuoo Jou Ping, smiling, 'though your intention to substitute order for disorder is good and praiseworthy, you must not forget that since the dawn of history, order and disorder are never permanent factors of life. When *Han* supplanted the *Chin* dynasty, it was a change from disorder to order. After two hundred years of peace and tranquillity, there came the short period of usurpation by Wang Mang. That was a change from order to disorder. After that, came the Restoration. That was a change from disorder to order. Since then, the people have enjoyed peace and prosperity for two hundred years. Therefore war commences again. It is time for order to relapse into disorder. This is fate and cannot be averted by human agency. Even though you may succeed in persuading Kung Ming to take up the task of restoring the Empire to order, I do not think he will succeed. It will be only a waste of energy. Have you not heard of the saying:

> He who conforms to Nature's law is happy;
> He who does not do so will soon be sorry?'

'Sir, what you have said is certainly philosophy of the highest order,' replied Lew Bei. 'But as I am a descendant of the *Han* family, who has the imperative duty to save the *Han* dynasty, how can I evade this duty by resigning myself to fate?'

'I am only a plain man of the wilderness, quite unfit to participate in the discussion of world affairs,' said Chuoo Jou Ping. 'It was only because you did me the honour of asking me of my opinion that I ventured to express it.'

'I appreciate, Sir, your instruction,' said Lew Bei. 'Do you know where Kung Ming has gone?'

'I also want to see him,' replied Chuoo Jou Ping. 'But I do not know where he is.'

'May I ask you to give us the pleasure of your company at our humble quarters?' asked Lew Bei.

'Thank you,' replied Chuoo Jou Ping. 'I love idleness, having no desire for worldly honour for ages. Good-bye.' After saying this, he bowed deeply to Lew Bei, and walked away.

Lew Bei and his two sworn brothers resumed their journey for home.

'We have not found Kung Ming', observed Chang Fei, 'but met that wretched scholar, wasting a lot of time!'

'His words are those of a learned hermit,' said Lew Bei in answer to Chang Fei's observation.

A few days afterwards reports were received by Lew Bei that Master The Sleeping Dragon had returned. He therefore ordered horses to be ready for a second journey.

'I think Kung Ming is only a country clown,' said Chang Fei. 'Why should you, my Elder Brother, go personally? We can send someone to fetch him here.'

'Have you not read Mencius', said Lew Bei, 'who says: "If you desire to see a man of great merit and do not do so in the proper way, it is like asking someone to come in and bolting the door at the same time"?[1] Kung Ming is a genius of world-renown. How can you summon him? Having said this, he mounted on his horse, and proceeded in his second attempt to find Kung Ming. His sworn brothers, Kwan and Chang, followed him. The weather of the year was just at its worst. A northerly wind was blowing violently. Snow was falling heavily. It was piercing cold.

'In beastly weather like this', said Chang Fei, 'even military campaigns have to be suspended. Why should we come such a long way in order to see a man of no consequence? I think we had better return to our Headquarters to take shelter from these shattering wind and snow.'

'On the contrary', said Lew Bei, 'I just want Kung Ming to know that I am truly in earnest to make his acquaintance. If you, my younger brother, fear the weather, you may go back first.'

'I do not fear even death,' replied Chang Fei. 'How can I fear the weather? What I fear is that you, my Elder Brother, may tire yourself out for nothing.'

[1] *Mencius*, Bk. V, Pt. II, Ch. 7, Sec. 8.

'Then be quiet and follow me,' said Lew Bei sharply.

When they were not far from the cottage to which they were proceeding, the singing of a song was heard coming from a tavern by
the roadside. As soon as the song ended, another began. Both were
poetically phrased, displaying profound scholarship and penetrating
knowledge of current events. When the second song terminated, two
men were heard laughing loudly, while clapping their hands. Lew
Bei, wondering, murmured to himself: 'Is The Sleeping Dragon
here?' He therefore dismounted, and went into the tavern. He saw
two men sitting face to face at a table with cups in hand. One of
them had a white face with a long beard, while the other had classical
features, looking like a venerable ancient. Lew Bei bowed to them
and said: 'Which of you, Sirs, is Master The Sleeping Dragon?'

'Who are you, Sir?' replied the man with a long beard. 'What do
you want in asking for The Sleeping Dragon?'

'I am Lew Bei,' replied Lew Bei. 'I look for Master The Sleeping
Dragon in order to secure his services for restoring peace and order
to the country.'

'Neither of us is The Sleeping Dragon,' said the man with a long
beard. 'We are only his friends. My name is Shih Kwong Yuen,
and that of my friend yonder is Meng Gung Va.'

'I have heard a great deal about you, Sirs,' said Lew Bei, delighted.
'What a chance it is to me to see you here! There are two spare
horses outside. May I ask you to go with me to see The Sleeping
Dragon and have a talk together?'

'We both are vagabonds of the mountain and the forest, quite
ignorant of high politics,' replied the man with a long beard. 'Pray,
don't waste your time on us. You had better go yourself.'

Lew Bei, seeing that he could do nothing further, took leave of
them, and resumed his journey towards *The Sleeping Dragon Mount.*
When he arrived with his party at the gate of the cottage, he asked
the boy whether his master was in.

'He is reading in his study,' replied the boy.

Lew Bei was evidently pleased. He followed the boy into the cottage. When he reached the middle gate, his eyes caught sight of the
following couplet written on it:

Simplicity brightens the aim;
Composure attains what's afar. [1]

[1] This means, as I would interpret it, that a simple life unencumbered with desires
is conducive to clear and pure thinking essential to a noble aim, while a mental
equilibrium undisturbed by passions is necessary for the achievement of what is
great or profound.

While he was meditating on the philosophy of these words, he suddenly heard someone composing a poem orally. He stood by the gate listening, and saw a young man with his hands round a small stove, singing as follows:

> The phoenix flies a thousand feet above.
> It cannot rest but on the highest tree.
> The scholar who may shelter in a cove
> Would serve no man who shall not master be.
> I till my fields and love my cottage humble,
> To pride my harp and books without a grumble.

He took care not to disturb him; but as soon as the singing had ceased, he went up and bowed to him respectfully, saying: 'Master, I have heard of your illustrious name through many channels, but never had the opportunity of making your acquaintance. Recently, thanks to the introduction of Mr. Yuen Chih, I have been here once to pay you my respects; but you were not in. To-day I call again specially, in spite of the weather. How fortunate I am to be able to see you now!'

The young man hurriedly returned his bow, saying: 'General, are you Lew Bei? You want to see my brother, I believe.'

'You too, Sir, are not Master The Sleeping Dragon?' exclaimed Lew Bei, bewildered and surprised.

'I am his younger brother,' replied the young man.

'Is Master The Sleeping Dragon in?' asked Lew Bei.

'He went away with some friends on a pleasure trip,' answered the young man courteously.

'I am truly out of luck!' said Lew Bei. 'Twice I have been unable to see a great worthy.'

'Please stay for a cup of tea,' said the young man apologetically.

'As the man we want to see is not here,' interposed Chang Fei, looking impatient, 'let us go.'

'I understand that your brother, Master The Sleeping Dragon, is well versed in military science,' said Lew Bei to the young man, ignoring the remark of Chang Fei. 'May I hear something of this from you?'

'I know nothing about it,' answered the young man.

'What is the good of asking him?' interposed again Chang Fei, looking more impatient. 'It is blowing and snowing hard. We had better return to our Headquarters at once.'

Lew Bei reprimanded Chang Fei for talking in this manner. He then asked Kung Ming's brother for pen, ink, and paper to write a letter to be left for Kung Ming. It was worded as follows:

'Having heard of your illustrious name with profound admiration, I have called on you twice. But not being favoured by Fortune, I found you were away on both occasions. As a descendant of the Imperial Family of *Han*, witnessing the *Han* dynasty crumbling to pieces, while law and order are trampled down, with rebels and traitors springing up in the four corners of the Empire, I am truly heart-broken. Alas! though I have the ambition to save the Empire, I have not the ability to do so. I therefore earnestly beg you, Sir, will, for the sake of benevolence and righteousness, and in the interest of the people and country, generously allow your talents to be available, like the great Lu Vang of the *Chow* and the great Tze Fong of the *Han*. The Empire will be deeply indebted to you.'

Lew Bei handed the letter to Kung Ming's brother, and took leave of him. Just on the point of departure, Lew Bei saw the boy waving his hand outside the fence and shouting: 'Old Master is back.' Lew Bei naturally thought that Kung Ming was coming home. He eagerly looked afar. A man warmly clad, riding on a colt and followed by a boy carrying a gourd of wine, was seen. He was crossing a small bridge, covered with snow, while he was orally composing a poem on the spot, as follows:

> One night there blew a bitter northern gale;
> Thick purple cloud veiled thousand miles of space;
> Then everywhere snow flakes rained down like hail;
> As if the world had wholly changed its face.
> I turned my eyes up to the angry sky,
> Believing there must be a dragons' fight [1]
> What looked like dragons' scales flew low and high.
> They soon were seen all over left and right.
> Just riding on a colt across a bridge,
> I wailed the thin plum blossoms by its edge.

Much struck by the poetic diction of the poem and the veiled meanings it graphically conveyed, as regards both the prevailing conditions of the country and the detached attitude of the saintly-minded man towards all that are worldly, Lew Bei exclaimed to himself delightfully: 'He must be The Sleeping Dragon!' He at once dismounted, and made a deep bow to the man, saying: 'Master,

[1] The dragon is a fabulous animal, certain types of which are, according to Chinese popular mythology of uncertain origin, capable of causing convulsions in the sky. Here, the verse refers metaphorically to political convulsions in the country, that is, civil war.

this weather must be rather trying for you. I have been waiting here for some time.'

The man, somewhat surprised, immediately alighted from his colt to return Lew Bei's courtesy, while Kung Ming's younger brother, who was standing behind, said: 'He is not my elder brother, The Sleeping Dragon, but his father-in-law, Mr. Huang Chunk Yen.'

'The poem just composed by you orally on the spot is exquisite,' said Kew Bei to the man, politely, suppressing any display of disappointment.

'Once in my son-in-law's house', replied Huang Chunk Yen, 'I heard several poems orally composed. But I remember only this one. As, on crossing the bridge a little while ago, I saw the plum blossoms nearby were falling down, I was touched, and therefore repeated the poem. I never thought that it would be overheard by you.'

'Have you, Sir, seen your son-in-law?' asked Lew Bei.

'I have just come to see him,' replied Huang Chunk Yen.

Lew Bei, seeing that it was no good to remain any longer, took leave of Huang Chunk Yen, and proceeded homeward, rather downhearted—a situation which was reflected in the following poem:

> A snow storm bars no visit to the wise.
> Fruitless tries to woeful thoughts give rise.
> Frozen streams and slippy rocks make tortures
> For the lengthy trip and chilly horses.
> Ahead pear blossoms fly in ceaseless gust.
> My face is daubed with scattered willow dust.
> Resting my whip to look behind, I've found
> A heap of silver [1] on the Dragon Mount.

A few days afterwards Lew Bei again wanted to call on Kung Ming, hoping that his third attempt might be more successful.

'Elder Brother,' said Kwan Yun Cheong, 'you have called on him personally twice. The courtesy extended to him is already excessive. I think Kung Ming has only an empty name but no real merit, and therefore had not the courage to meet you. Why do you, Elder Brother, have so much confidence in him, which after all may be misplaced?'

'No, no,' replied Lew Bei, 'formerly the Duke of Chi [2] had to wait on a simple man of Tung Kwok five times before he could see him.

[1] This means the snow, of course.
[2] This was the Duke whose political achievements Mencius was asked by King Suen of Chi to relate (see ante, p. 138), and who had as Prime Minister the famous Kwan Chung (see ante, pp. 124, 128, and 209).

Naturally, in order to see a great worthy, I must be even more humble.'

'Elder Brother is mistaken,' interposed Chang Fei, unable to control his temper any longer. 'How can this country clown be a great worthy? This time Elder Brother need not go. I will go alone to fetch him. If he does not come, I will put a rope round him to bring him here.'

Lew Bei severely reprimanded Chang Fei for his rudeness, saying: 'Have you not heard of the story of how the sage King Wen of *Chow* waited on Jenk Tze Yar?[1] Even King Wen had to show such humility to a worthy, why are you so lacking in civility? This time you need not go. I will go with Yun Cheong.'

'Since two Elder Brothers go,' said Chang Fei submissively, 'how can your humble younger brother remain behind?'

'If you go with us', said Lew Bei gravely, 'you must be polite.'

To this Chang Fei assented with evident resignation.

They were then again on horseback, followed by a few attendants, proceeding to make a third journey to call on Kung Ming. When they were about half a mile from his cottage, Lew Bei dismounted and began to walk. To his agreeable surprise, he ran across the younger brother of Kung Ming. He immediately bowed to him, asking: 'Is your Honoured brother at home?'

'He returned just last evening,' replied Kung Ming's brother curtly. 'General, you can see him to-day.' Having said this, he walked away without more ado.

'That fellow has no manners,' observed Chang Fei, looking annoyed. 'Surely, he might accompany us to the cottage. Why should he walk away like this?'

'Every man has his own business,' said Lew Bei, depreciating the remark made by Chang Fei. 'It is unreasonable to expect others always to oblige us.'

At last, the three men with their attendants arrived at the cottage. Lew Bei knocked at the gate, and on seeing the boy said to him very politely: 'May I trouble you, boy of the Saint, to announce that Lew Bei has come to pay respects to the Master?'

'Although Master is in to-day, he is taking a nap in the Grass Hall,' answered the boy, quite unmoved.

'Since that is the case', said Lew Bei, 'please wait and make the announcement later.' At the same time he told his sworn brothers,

[1] That is Lu Vang, the famous statesman who helped King Wen ultimately to found the *Chow* dynasty, and is the same person mentioned by Lew Bei in his letter to Kung Ming (see *ante*, p. 236) and compared by Sze Ma Fay to Kung Ming (see *ante*, p. 230).

Kwan and Chang, to wait outside. Then he walked slowly into the cottage, following the boy. As he saw Kung Ming lying asleep on a sofa in the Grass Hall, he stood respectfully in the yard. For a long time Kung Ming did not wake up. As Kwan and Chang had been standing outside all this while without hearing anything, they went in. Finding that Lew Bei was still standing in the yard, Chang, quite angry, said to Kwan: 'How conceited that fellow is! Knowing that Elder Brother has been standing in the yard, waiting to see him, he still sleeps soundly and won't wake up. Let me go and set fire to the cottage at its back. You will see whether he will wake up or not.'

Kwan restrained Chang repeatedly. Lew Bei ordered them to remain outside. Looking towards the Grass Hall, Lew Bei saw Kung Ming was making a move, as if he were to rise; but he only turned his face to the wall and fell asleep again. At this moment the boy seemingly wanted to make the announcement; but Lew Bei stopped him, and waited for another hour in the same manner as he had been doing. At last, Kung Ming woke up; but, before he rose from the sofa, uttered the following lines there and then composed:

> The Greatest Dream [1] who could know in advance?
> Of life predestined I discern the chance: [2]
> A Spring nap in my Grass Hall [3] gives content; [4]
> The sun outside the window slowly went.

Having orally composed this poem, he turned round and asked the boy: 'Has any worldly guest been here?'

[1] This means life. It is a familiar saying of the Chinese that life is like a dream—a view which is largely derived from Taoist philosophy.

[2] The 'chance of life' is reflected in the next two verses.

[3] The hall where the hermit 'Sleeping Dragon' had his habitual nap. 'Grass' means rustic, that is, humble.

[4] This verse together with the next means, as I would interpret them, that, in the saintly eyes of the hermit, the truly wise man seeks from life no more than being able to have a tranquil and regular repose and all that it implies; for life, however spectacular it may be, slips away slowly but surely like the sunshine outside the window.

The Chinese hermit, it may be mentioned, is not necessarily a man who lives in solitude, but one who sees life either like a dream or 'but a walking shadow, a poor player that struts and frets his hour upon the stage' (Shakespeare: *Macbeth*, Act V, Sc. V, Ls. 24-5) and consequently disdains to 'fight for fame of vulgar sort' (see *ante*, p. 230) finding his happiness in passing his time by the stream or under the woods, or in listening to the songs of birds or the music of running brooks, or in watering his plants or trimming his flowers, or in keeping 'appointment with a wild duck' (words of a well-known modern English statesman) or sparrows, or in living up to the spirit of the following verses: (see *ante*, p. 235).

> 'I till my fields and love my cottage humble
> To pride my harp and books without a grumble.'

'Royal Uncle Lew is here,' answered the boy. 'He has been here some time.'

Kung Ming then rose from the sofa, saying: 'Why didn't you announce this before? I am going to get dressed.' After saying this, he went into his room, and remained there quite some time. At last, he came out in his hermit attire. His extraordinary figure made a deep impression on Lew Bei. He was eight foot high, his face looked like jade, and his whole appearance resembled that of a saint.

Lew Bei made a respectful bow to him, saying: 'Master, I am a descendant of the Imperial Family of *Han*, but a very ignorant man. Your illustrious name has long been sounding like thunder in my ears. I have been here twice to pay you my respects in person; but as you were out, I left a note behind. May I ask whether you have read it?'

'I am a simple man of the wilderness of *Nan Yang*, to whom love of idleness has become a second nature,' replied Kung Ming. 'The honour that you, General, have kindly done me by your repeated visits makes me feel quite ashamed of myself.'

When tea had been served and they began to talk, Kung Ming said: 'The letter I read last night shows that you, General, have your heart with the country and the people. But, unfortunately, I am in-experienced and incompetent, wholly undeserving the honour you do me.'

'But the words of Sze Ma Fay and Yuen Chih[1] about you are still ringing in my ears,' replied Lew Bei. 'I sincerely hope you, Master, will not reject me, in spite of my unworthiness and ignor-ance, but will favour me with your enlightening instruction.'

'Sze Ma Fay and Yuen Chih are the wisest men of the world,' rejoined Kung Ming. 'I am only a simple peasant. How dare I dis-cuss high politics? They have wrongly overestimated me in their recommendation. Why do you, General, throw away a jade for a stone?'

'For a great genius like you, Master, having the ability to save the world from disaster', said Lew Bei, 'how is it possible to pass the whole life idly in the forest or by the stream? I earnestly beg you will, for the sake of mankind, favour me with your advice.'

'General, let me hear your intention and ambition,' said Kung Ming, laughing.

Lew Bei, drawing himself near Kung Ming, said: 'The *Han* dynasty is crumbling, while traitors are usurping its powers. Though it may be presumptuous on my part to say so, I desire to restore justice and

[1] The reader may be reminded that these two persons are Water Mirror and Chu Shu.

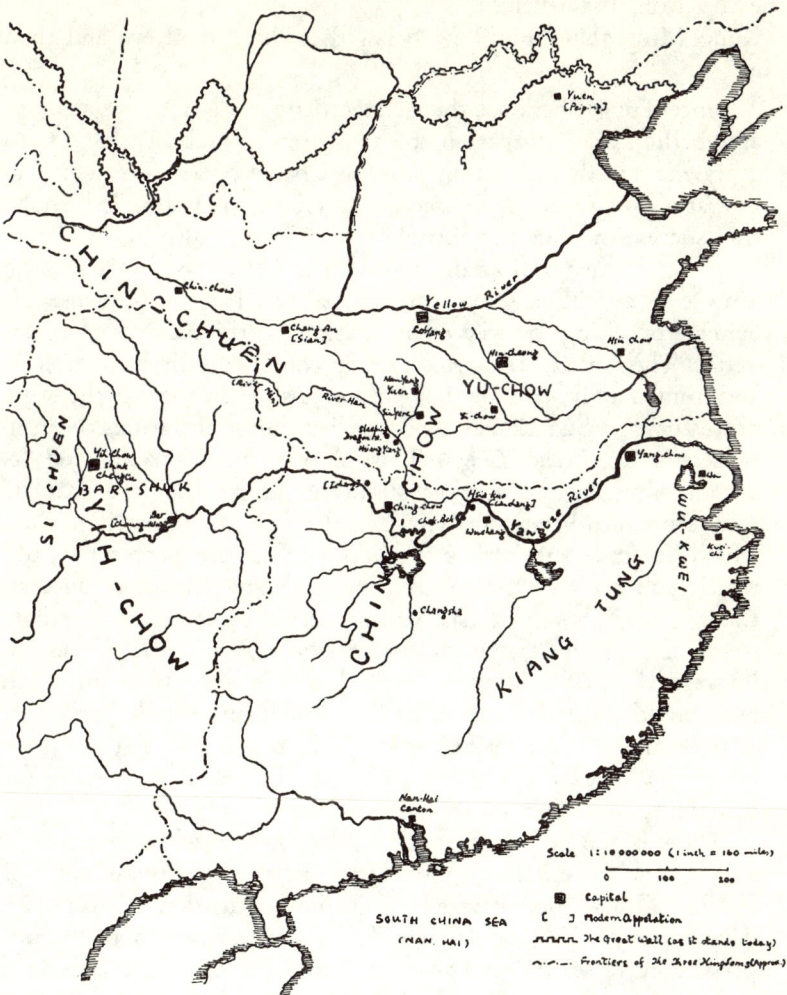

A geographical sketch of the principal places referred to in
Fragments from the 'Three Kingdoms'

righteousness to the Empire. But as my ability is limited, I have so far accomplished very little. It is only you, Master, who can save the situation. Pray, help!'

Kung Ming glanced at Lew Bei with a thoughtful eye and then said:

'Since Tung Cherk set the ill precedent in his abortive attempt at rebellion and usurpation, men of power or ability have risen everywhere with wild ambition. Tso Chau's power was not equal to that of Yuen Shao, but succeeded in eliminating him. This shows that success was due not entirely to destiny but also to the proper handling of men and affairs. Now, Tso Chau has under him an army over a million strong, and, moreover, has the immense advantage of acting, by way of usurpation, in the name of the Emperor. This means that you cannot contend with him directly and immediately with any hope of success. Then there is the other powerful man Sun Chuan, who has, for three generations, been in possession of *Kiang Tung*.[1] This place is impregnable, and its natural advantage is further strengthened by the fact that its people are firmly attached to its ruler. Therefore, it is a place which you may only utilize for aiding you in your enterprise, but which you cannot attempt to seize with any chance of success. *Ching Chow*,[2] however, has, on its north, the river *Han*, on its south, the South Sea, on its east, the border of *Wu Kwei* and, on its west, the road leading to *Bar Shuk*.[3] This is the place on which one should keep one's eyes, and of which one should make use as the starting point for expansion. This means not that the place cannot be held by its present occupant, but that it is destined for you. Have you, General, the intention of taking it?

'There is another place, that is, *Yih Chow*[4] on which one should also fix one's eyes. It is a most strategic place with vast tracts of fertile soil still uncultivated. It is like a kingdom in paradise. Thanks to it, the glorious founder of *Han* succeeded in his imperial enterprise. Its present ruler, Lew Chang, is a weak-minded and indolent person. Though the place is rich in natural resources, he does not know how to develop them for the benefit of the people, whom he has in fact neglected. Consequently, all able men with ambition are yearning for a worthier master. Now, General, you have these qualities: You are a direct descendant of the *Han* Imperial Family; your fame for benevolence, righteousness, and

[1] Land east of the Yangtze River. See *Dictionary of Phrases*.
[2] Somewhere between Hankow and Ichang.
[3] Szechuen, with its adjacent territory.
[4] Szechuen in present days.

sincerity is world-wide; you are earnestly enlisting the services of all brave men of the land, and would seek a worthy man as a thirsty person would seek water. You are therefore just the man whom able men with high ambition would desire gladly to serve.

'When you have secured *Ching Chow* and *Yih Chow*, you should, while strengthening all their strategic points, befriend the various tribes in the west, cultivate the sympathy of the people in the south, form an *entente* with Sun Chuan, without, and improve your own administration, within. When all these are done, wait for changes in the general situation. As soon as the opportunity arrives, if you dispatch from *Ching Chow* a general of the highest grade with an army to descend on *Yuen Loh*, [1] while you yourself head an army from *Yih Chow* to swoop down on *Chin-Chuen*, [2] you will be welcomed with open arms by all the people you may encounter. Thus great things may be achieved and the *Han* dynasty restored.'

At the end of the speech, Kung Ming ordered his boy to fetch a map and have it hung on the wall. Pointing to the map, he said to Lew Bei: 'This map shows the fifty-four districts of *Si-Chuen*. [3] General, in your attempt to found an empire, though, in the north, Tso Chau has the advantages of time afforded by Heaven, and, in the south, Sun Chuan has the advantages derived from the Earth, you have the advantages of co-operation due to the harmony of Men. [4] To conclude, you should, first of all take *Ching Chow* as the starting point, and then take *Si-Chuen* as the stronghold, thus establishing yourself as a power equal to either of the other two. It is then and only then that you will be able to have the chance of conquering the central part of the Empire.'

This illuminating speech was to Lew Bei like a revelation. Exceedingly delighted, he withdrew himself a few steps aside, and, with hands clasped together, made a special sign of respect to Kung Ming, expressing his appreciation and gratitude in these words: 'Master, your most instructive speech has so enlightened me that I feel as if I were able to see the sky with all the cloud and mist swept away. I am most grateful to you.' [5]

[1] Loyang and its adjacent places.
[2] Kansu and Shensi in present days.
[3] West of Szechuen.
[4] Here Kung Ming was quoting Mencius; see chapter on Philosophy, *Sayings of Mencius on Politics*, No. 4.
[5] Compare this to the remark made by Goethe after reading Shakespeare: 'And when I had reached the end of the first play, I stood like one who, blind from birth, finds himself suddenly blest with sight by a beneficent Providence.'; *Criticisms, Reflections, and Maxims of Goethe*, p. 42. Trans. by W. B. Rönnfeldt.

What Kung Ming said on that occasion showed that even before he quitted his cottage to join Lew Bei in the task of empire-making, he had well known that the empire was destined to be divided into three kingdoms. A truly great man of all ages! [1]

After thanking Kung Ming, Lew Bei continued: 'Though my reputation is insignificant and my virtue scanty, I hope you, Master, will not reject me for that, but will help me in my task. I will follow all your instructions faithfully and with the highest respect.'

To this Kung Ming replied: 'I have so long enjoyed the pleasure of the plough that I have lost all interest in worldly affairs.'

'Master', said Lew Bei with great emotion and humility, 'if you do not offer your services, what will be the lot of the people?' [2]

Deeply moved by Lew Bei's appeal and absolutely convinced of his sincerity and earnestness, Kung Ming said: 'General, I am willing to offer my life [3] to you and the country, and will serve you with all my heart.'

Lew Bei feeling grateful at once sent for his two sworn brothers to pay their respects to Kung Ming. The latter asked all of them to spend the night with him in the cottage. Next day his younger brother returned, to whom he addressed these words: 'I am indebted to His Imperial Highness Lew for the honour he has done me in having called on me three times. It is my imperative duty to give up my rustic existence and offer my services to him. Continue your farming life here, my brother, and do not neglect the fields. When I have accomplished my task, I will retire and spend my remaining days here with you.'

As every tale must end, so must this, but it is only a fragment of a long story.

---

[1] These words are the comment of the author of the 'Three Kingdoms', but they are also an historical fact. No Chinese statesman has caught the imagination of the people so vividly as Kung Ming. The story of 'Three Calls on Kung Ming' or 'Three Visits to the Cottage' is known to everybody in China, and is a very popular play for the stage.

[2] This phrase has since become historic and immortal. It is the last word that prevailed upon Kung Ming. It is now a well-known classical allusion, employed as a supreme appeal to an eminent man for the offer of his services to the public.

[3] And he eventually did, so that one can readily understand why he hesitated so much in giving up his hermit life for the position of the Prime Minister of an empire in the making, or rather to be built.

CHAPTER 9

ART

HAVING included Literature in this volume, to leave out Art would be treating her like Cinderella. As factors of civilization and culture of a nation, Art and Literature are sisters. Art is of course the elder. The first cave dweller who made his shelter, the first man of the Stone Age who made his tools, nay, even Eve, when she covered her body for the first time, must have invoked the genius of Art that lurks in the instinct of man. Literature, however, was born, only when civilization reached a stage that mere gestures and noises were felt no longer adequate to convey inner and finer sentiments.

Beauty is so essential to Art and Literature that to say a thing is artistic or a composition is literary is equivalent to saying that it is beautiful. However, the Chinese have a saying: 'The beautiful have in most cases a life that is thin (i.e., sad)', and it is an English proverb that 'There is no rose without a thorn'. It is perhaps for this reason that Art and Literature have both suffered a fate, from which, if Mercy had been more vigilant, they might have been spared. There can be no greater injury done to Art and Literature than the expressions 'the art of war' and 'war literature', as if killing and destruction could ever be associated with the fair names of Art and Literature. If this abuse were to continue, might we not one day hear spoken 'the art of murder', 'the art of suicide', and the like, or hear called an 'aggression' pact or a death sentence, literature? In the name of all that is beautiful, may there be mercy on these two innocent creatures! Robert Louis Stevenson, though he has invented a 'suicide club' in his *New Arabian Nights*, has not yet dared to call the practice of its members an 'art'. Only De Quincey has ventured to use the expression 'Murder as a Fine Art'. But were he alive to think it over, might he not experience the same consternation as when he saw a Malay swallowing a quantity of his precious drug 'enough to kill half-dozen dragoons, together with his horses?' [1]

Art is never destructive; science may be. It is Art that has created the world; it is Science that has been employed to destroy it. Art not only stands for beauty, but also speaks for intelligence, kindness, and peace. No one who genuinely loves art, like one who is able to see in 'a primrose by a river brim' something more than 'a yellow

[1] *Confessions of An English Opium-Eater*, Pt. II.

primrose to him', [1] can ever be dull, and no artist who wishes to paint well can, with his brush in hand, ever be cruel-minded. It was said of an eminent Shakespearean actor that every time he played the role of Richard III, he believed that he felt like that Plantagenet king; because it was his business to appear like a monster. But an artist who paints a group of children must try to feel like their parent. In other words, whatever he may try to paint, he must treat his subject kindly and with love. Cruelty or violence can never be tolerated by Art or in Art. People sometimes wonder how Jane Austen could have written such calm literature as *Pride and Prejudice* and *Sense and Sensibility* in the stormy days of the Napoleonic War. The explanation is that her heart might have bled for those who suffered, but her mind, true to Art, was at peace with the whole world. This is how I think of Art.

Music in ancient China was ranked in importance as an art of government. '*Li* (rules of correct conduct and good manners or propriety) regulates the mind, music harmonizes the sound, government maintains order, and punishment repels evils. *Li*, music, government, and punishment are the same in their ultimate object, and when the people are united in one harmonious whole, peace prevails. . . . The highest music is in harmony with the universe. [2] . . . Music being synonymous with happiness—(the two words being the same)—is something that cannot be dispensed with. When a person is happy, his happy feelings are revealed in his voice as well as in his actions. As a person cannot be without happiness and happiness cannot be without external signs, such signs, unless properly guided, would tend to disorder. Our ancient sage kings, in order to prevent such disorder, invented music, so that a person giving vocal expression to his feelings may not overstep the proper limits and is so guided that such expression will elevate him to virtue and not lead him to vice. That is why music, when listened to by the Ruler and his ministers in the State Temple, creates among them a harmonious spirit of co-operation; when listened to by the elders and the young in the village, it creates among them a harmonious spirit of mutual regard and respect; and when listened to by parents and children and brothers and sisters in the family, it creates among them a harmonious spirit of mutual affection. Music in a word creates harmony of body and soul.' [3]

It may seem strange in this twentieth century, when what is called music finds its place in the music-hall or the cabaret, to hear that

[1] Wordsworth: *Peter Bell*, Part First, 12th stanza.
[2] *Book of Li*, Bk. XXXVII, Title *Music*, No. 19.
[3] *Ibid.*, Bk. XXXIX, Title *Music; Hsun Tze*, Ch. 20, Title *Music*.

PHEASANT HUNTING
Painting of Ming Dynasty (A.D. 1368-1644)
Old Palace Museum Collection

music once played such a great role in history. But one must not forget that in three thousand or more years ago there could be very little law·and still less what is called sport in the modern sense of the term, that is, organized sport. Music, as it can rouse pleasant feelings among all classes of people, literate or illiterate, must have been a very useful agency in bringing them together for relaxation and creating among them a communal feeling, and, as it appeals to the ear, the heart, and the soul, must have been also a very powerful means in fostering mental discipline. Indeed, one has only to enter a church in order to appreciate the importance that the ancients attached to music. No religious service is performed without some form of music, and hymns are always sung in chorus. Julius Caesar must have had good reasons, in his observation about Cassius, for using the words: 'He loves no play. . . . He hears no music.'[1]

Writing (i.e., calligraphy) to the Chinese is an art just as painting. Any one who has been to China must have seen scrolls of writing, by eminent men ancient or modern, hanging on the walls of Chinese homes side by side with scrolls of painting by Chinese artists. Any one who is conversant with Chinese painting will agree that the Chinese artist who paints well can also write well. It may be said that no Chinese would aspire to be a good painter without first trying to master the brush in writing. The two are sisters to each other. We are told that it was not until the *Tang* Dynasty (A.D. 618-906) that painting was considered as a distinct art from writing. Hence pictures of that period have no writing on them, and often do not even bear the signatures of the artists who painted them. Since then, however, writings are always found in pictures, painting and writing being very much associated together. Sometimes poems are written on the picture to form part and parcel of it, and those who distinguish themselves in the one branch of art seek fame also in the other. Of persons celebrated in both, names can be readily mentioned by the score; for instance, Soo Tung Po, of the *Sung* Dynasty, Chao Mung Fu, of the *Yuan* Dynasty, and Tung Chi Chong, of the *Ming* Dynasty, whose names are familiar to European lovers of Chinese art.

Writing and painting are equally prized by the Chinese, neither having a claim of superiority over the other. Indeed, there is a story about a man of the *Tang* Dynasty named Ou Yang Shun, showing how a man could be enraptured by fine writing. One day he set out on a journey, in the course of which he saw by the roadside a stone engraved with the script of a famous writer of the *Tsin* Dynasty (third century A.D.), known as the *Sho Ching Bei*. He admired the writing so much that he could not go away very far without coming

[1] Shakespeare: *Julius Caesar*, Act I, Sc. II, Ls. 202-3.

back to look at it again. Finally he slept under the stone for three nights before resuming his journey.

Handwriting is considered as an expression of one's inner self. It is generally believed that no man who has not some special quality in him, though he may spend a lifetime in the practice of writing, can ever become a writer of eminence, and that, conversely, a man who has some special quality in him, though he may not have devoted much time to the practice, always reveals in his writing some characteristic which will show that he is not a common soul. The man of learning, for instance, is bound to produce in his writing a note of beauty or elegance which cannot be acquired merely by long practice. Practice may perfect one's writing in its technique, but cannot give it that quality which makes writing sublime. Sometimes we say that there is the 'book spirit' in a man's writing. This means that his writing, though imperfect or faulty in its technique, has something in it which shows that he is a man of letters.

Writing is often practised, not only as a matter of art, but also as a means of attaining calmness of mind. There is a well-known story about Marquis Tseng Kuo Fan, philosopher and statesman of the *Ching* Dynasty, who made the practice of writing a form of mental exercise. During the Taiping Rebellion, he was Commander of the Government troops against the rebels. One morning when he was just engaged in his daily exercise, a sentinel presented himself, saying: 'Sir, the enemy is at our gate.' To this he replied: 'Say that again when I have finished my writing!' This sounds like the story of Drake with his game of bowls in face of the Armada.

In writing, every stroke of the pen must be certain. Any hesitation would be fatal. It must have force and vitality and yet be natural, graceful, and easy. Defect in force may be due to lack of practice, defect in grace commonly arises from strokes that are technically called 'vulgar' or 'fiery'. Vulgarism may be due to eccentricity or inferiority complex, while what is called the 'fiery spirit' is often due to egoism or excessive self-confidence. One secret in the practice of writing is, as we are told by a great scholar, that at first we must try our best to imitate the old masters, but afterwards we must try our best to break away from them.

What has been said about writing applies equally to painting. For instance, the lines that form bridges, the curves that create mountains, and the strokes and dots that make trees or plants are governed by almost the same principles as those that govern writing. Of course, in painting the painter must, above all, have ideas and conceptions. The Chinese artist always tries to interpret nature rather than imitate it, and hopes to rise above it. Soo Tung Po, a great

poet of the *Sung* Dynasty, once paid a compliment to Wang Wei
of the *Tang* Dynasty, saying: 'His poems contain pictures and his
pictures contain poems.' There is a well-known poem of the *Tang*
Dynasty, which may be rendered as:

> 'On a thousand hills no bird has ever been.
> On ten thousand roads no human trace is seen.
> By an icy stream with snow in rustic cloak,
> An old man fishes solely in a lonely boat.' [1]

One can see that there is a picture in that poem. Conversely one
can, of course, see poems in pictures. In the words of the English
poet, there are 'tongues in trees, books in the running brooks'. [2]
That the Chinese as a people are great lovers of jade is too well
known to require affirmation. I myself have seen a man wearing
more than half a dozen odd pieces round his waist, and he does not
seem to experience any discomfort even when he goes to bed with
them. One may therefore be tempted to ask what makes the Chinese
so fond of jade. 'Superstition' some would utter; possibly because
they have been told that jade has the power of driving evil spirits
away. Such a crude explanation is no more correct than saying that
the study of the Bible is merely to keep the devil at a distance. Jade
is historically associated with virtue, and for that reason valued
above other precious stones. In the philosophic work of Hsun Tze,
whose name has been mentioned more than once, there is a dialogue
between Confucius and a disciple about jades. The Master was
asked whether the reason that the virtuous man valued pure jade
more than jade-like stones was because the former was rare, while
the latter were plentiful. To this the Master answered: 'Certainly
not. A virtuous man does not lower the value of things, merely because they are plentiful. Jade is compared by the virtuous man to
virtue: It is so pure and refined in nature and so rich and exquisite in
composition that it is compared to perfect virtue. Hence the saying:

> "There may be glittering transparency in a jade-like stone, but
> it has not the purity that is in jade."

That is why it is said in the *Book of Odes*:

> "The man of virtue to the inward mind
> Like precious jade is purity refined".' [3]

---

[1] *Tang Poems*; Standard Ed., Bk. V, p. 4.
[2] Shakespeare: *As You Like It*, Act II, Sc. I, L. 15.
[3] *Hsun Tze*, Ch. 30; The Ode appears in the *Book of Odes* (Mow Sche), Title *Kuo Feng*,
Chin; Bk. VI, No. 3.

This is the true explanation of the love of jade. If the wearing of jade serves as a reminder of virtue, whereby evil temptations are kept away, it may in this figurative sense be said to possess the charm of repelling evils; but this is not superstition.

Apart from this there are well-known historical incidents that have brought jade into great prominence. In the time of the *Warring States* (481-205 B.C.) a man named Ho of the State *Cho* presented to the King a stone which, according to his opinion, or rather conviction, contained the finest jade. His opinion was, however, contradicted by the jade experts of the day, and, as a result of his determined way of pressing his opinion, he was condemned as a madman and lost one leg as punishment. On the accession of the King's heir to the throne, he made his appearance again with the same stone and with the same persistence. As a result, he lost his other leg. When the next heir came to the throne, the poor man, with his arms round the stone, wept bitterly at the foot of the Hill of *Cho*. The new King, being informed of this, sent someone to see and ask him what he was crying for, saying: 'There are many like you who have lost their legs through punishment. Why are you alone so grieved?' In reply he said: 'I grieve, not because of the cruel punishment that has been inflicted on me, but because of the fact that the finest jade has been taken to be a common stone and an honest man condemned as a madman.' The King, on receiving the report, ordered the stone to be cut and discovered the finest jade ever seen, which was accordingly named 'Ho's Jade'. [1]

This jade was afterwards secured by State *Chao* in about 255 B.C. When this became known to the King of *Chin*, he offered fifteen cities to *Chao* for the exchange of the jade. As *Chin* was then very powerful, *Chao* did not think it wise to reject the offer; but it was a question of who would carry the jade to *Chin* and ensure the performance of the bargain. The Prime Minister of *Chao* recommended a man named Lun Sheung Yu, who he said was a scholar and brave man. Lun Sheung Yu was accordingly commissioned as an envoy to *Chin*. On his arrival he presented the jade to the King of *Chin*, who was greatly impressed with its beauty, and told the envoy of *Chao* that in due course he would receive the fifteen cities as promised. Day after day passed without any news from the King, and Lun Sheung Yu began to suspect that *Chin* had no intention of performing its part of the bargain. He therefore requested an audience of the King. When he was received in audience, he told the King that there were certain features of the jade which he wanted to point out to His Majesty. The jade was accordingly sent for and handed to him for

[1] *Han Fei Tze*, Ch. 13 (Bk. IV).

demonstration. As soon as he had the jade in his hand, he walked near a stone pillar of the palace seemingly to obtain a better view of the jade. Then he loudly shouted to the King of *Chin* some words to this effect: 'Sir, you have solemnly promised to give fifteen cities in exchange for this jade; but you do not seem to have any intention of honouring your words. I quite realize that I am here defenceless and surrounded by armed men. But if anyone should move a finger to harm me, I will smash the jade and my head also against this pillar, and you will earn the odious name of deceiver for nothing.' The palace guards naturally wanted to seize him; but the King was so alarmed by this threat, and so impressed by his courage, that he restrained his warriors and allowed the representative of *Chao* to retire with the jade until the document for the exchange of the cities was ready for execution. A few days later he was summoned to the palace, and, when asked to produce the jade, he calmly told the King that it had been sent out of *Chin* and was on its way to *Chao*; because, in his opinion, a solemn promise once broken was not likely to be faithfully kept again. The palace guard naturally again threatened to seize him; but the King felt that, as *Chao* had such a courageous man, it could not be despised. He therefore simply dismissed him not without, of course, great disappointment. Hence we have the allusion 'Kwei Chao', meaning the safe return of a thing borrowed. This historical incident shows how a covenant between States would be respected even in the time of the *Warring States*, when morality was considered to be at its lowest ebb at least according to the Chinese standard. The King of *Chin* might have harboured an intention never to give away fifteen cities for the jade; yet he felt that to flout cynically a covenant solemnly made would be too great an infamy.

The jade ultimately fell into the hands of *Chin*, when it succeeded in absorbing the Empire of *Chow* and ended the period of *Warring States* (221 B.C.). It was this jade that was made into the Grand Seal of *Chin* by order of the First Emperor, with the words: 'By command of Heaven to reign for ever' engraved on it. This was the first time in the history of China that the State Jade Seal became the emblem of Imperial authority, and, from that time onwards until the *Ming* Dynasty, a sort of divinity attached to it, its possession being deemed essential to the lawful title to the throne. For this reason on the fall of the *Chin* Dynasty (207 B.C.) the deposed Emperor was required to hand over the Jade Seal to *Han*, and during the period known as the *Five Generations* (A.D. 907-959) it was the possession of the Jade Seal that determined the legitimacy of the claim of the Rulers. For the same reason, when Huang Mang temporarily usurped the throne of

Han (A.D. 8), and in subsequent cases of usurpation during the period called the *Three Kingdoms* (about A.D. 190-260), for instance, *Wei* in A.D. 220 and *Tsin* in A.D. 265, the possession of the Jade Seal was deemed indispensable. Theatregoers in China must be familiar with the play called 'The Palace Breaking'. The scene marks the final stage of usurpation, where the dethroned Emperor was forced to surrender the Jade Seal and confess his guilt as having been an unworthy Ruler. It recalls Richard II in Shakespeare, [1] where the deposed monarch exclaimed: 'Here, cousin, seize the crown,' and Bolingbroke replied: 'I thought you had been willing to resign.' For the scene shows that the usurper would not seize the Jade Seal, but insisted on its being handed over to him voluntarily.

The reference to the Jade Seal as the emblem of Imperial authority brings me to the field of Bronzes. Lovers of Chinese art must be conversant with the history or legend of the Nine Tripods, which were no doubt the most important bronze works of ancient China. All traditions agree that they were cast in the reign of Yu the Great (2205 B.C.) from metal sent as tribute to him from the nine provinces of his Empire, but opinions differ as to their designs. Some say that they were carved with the maps, and the pictures of the products, of the nine provinces, others that they were carved with the images of the evil spirits of storm, woods, and wilderness. Anyhow, during the period known as the *Three Generations* (2205-246 B.C.) they were recognized as the emblem of Imperial authority. History tells us that they were removed by Emperor Chung Tong of the *Shang* Dynasty in the year 1757 B.C. to capital *Sheng* in Honan, and by Emperor Wu of the *Chow* Dynasty in the year 1108 B.C. to Loyang.

As with the jade that I have mentioned, there are several interesting historical incidents connected with the Nine Tripods. In the year 606 B.C. King Chong of *Cho*, in the prosecution of a successful military campaign against a turbulent State, reached Loyang. When he reviewed his troops near the frontier of Empire *Chow*, the Emperor Ting, who thought it wise to keep on good terms with him, commissioned a special envoy to bring him a message of goodwill. On receiving the envoy, King Chong inquired about the sizes and weight of the Nine Tripods. Realizing the true meaning that underlay the question, the Imperial representative replied: 'Sir, it is virtue and not the Tripods that matter. When the *Hsia* Dynasty had virtue, metal in the form of tribute from various quarters was sent to the Emperor, whereby the Tripods were cast, but when Emporer Chieh of the said Dynasty had no virtue, these Tripods passed over to the *Shang* Dynasty, where they remained for over 600 years. In turn they

[1] Act IV, Sc. I, Ls. 181 and 190.

passed over to the *Chow* Dynasty through the vice of Emperor Tsou. This shows that these Tripods, when associated with virtue, are weighty and immovable, even though they may be small, but, when associated with vice, are light and capable of being taken away, though they may be large. The Dynasty of *Chow* may temporarily be weak, but it rules by the dictate of Heaven. For that reason the sizes and weight of the Tripods should not be questioned.'[1] This answer quieted the ambition of the King of *Cho*, and the danger to the Empire of *Chow* was averted. However, the possession of these Tripods remained a source of temptation to ambitious States in those troublous days. In the year 336 B.C. *Chin*, which was growing more and more powerful among the *Warring States*, sent an ultimatum to the then Emperor of *Chow* for the surrender of these Tripods. The Emperor, being much distressed over this, consulted his trusted minister Yen Shu, who said he could obtain military assistance from *Chi*, then another very powerful State. He accordingly set out for *Chi* and, on seeing the King of *Chi*, said: '*Chin* has treacherously made a demand for the Tripods from *Chow*. The people of *Chow* are greatly distressed over this, and feel that, if these Tripods were to be given up at all, they should be given to *Chi* rather than to *Chin*, because *Chi* is a great power. Now to save a State in danger is a virtue and to secure the Nine Tripods a handsome reward. We hope you will help us.' The King of *Chi*, being moved by this appeal, intervened with an army of 50,000 men, whereby the situation was saved. When he afterwards made a demand for his reward, the Emperor of *Chow* consulted his resourceful minister again. The latter appeared very calm and said something like 'O.K.' to his Imperial master. He set out once more to *Chi*, and, on seeing the King, thanked him on behalf of the Emperor for his timely intervention. Thereupon the King asked when the promised reward would be delivered to him. In reply the envoy of *Chow* said that the Emperor was quite ready to deliver the Nine Tripods, but wished to know by which route *Chi* proposed to take delivery of them. '*Via Liang*,' said the King. 'But this is impossible,' replied the envoy; 'because, once these Tripods are in the territory of *Liang*, the people of *Liang* will never let them come out again.' '*Via Cho*, then,' rejoined the King. 'This would be worse,' replied the envoy; 'because *Cho* has coveted them for a long time.' 'Then, how are these Tripods to be conveyed to me,' asked the King. To this the envoy replied: 'When these Tripods were obtained by the *Chow* Dynasty from the *Yin* Dynasty, each of them was conveyed to *Chow* by 90,000 men.

[1] *Jaw Chuan*: History of *Spring and Autumn* (722-481 B.C.), Title '*King Cho asked about the Tripods*'.

Nine Tripods, therefore, would require 810,000 men. The task is simply impossible.' [1] This is the gist of the dialogue, and *Chow* was saved a second time. However, the latter part of the dialogue must not be taken too literally. The moral of the allusion to the number of men involved in the conveyance of the Tripods to *Chow* is that, the misrule of *Yin* had so alienated the people that, when the founder of the *Chow* Dynasty appeared as the Saviour, the people of *Yin* willingly transferred their allegiance to *Chow*; therefore it is not the mere acquisition of these Tripods that makes one the acknowledged ruler of the Empire, but virtue and righteousness. The intervention of *Chi* in saving the Dynasty of *Chow* being a matter of duty, *Chi* was not entitled to any claim for reward, and the very demand for the Tripods, emblem of Imperial sovereignty, would itself amount to usurpation.

As Empires rose and fell, so the Dynasty of *Chow* had its end. These Tripods like the 'Ho's Jade', eventually fell into the hands of *Chin* in about 255 B.C. in the reign of Chiu Sheung. According to a legend, when these Tripods were being carried to *Chin*, one of them dropped into the River *Se* in the province of Anhui. Attempts were made to salvage it; but, just as the lost Tripod was raised above water, an angry dragon darted out and bit in two the rope attached thereto, in consequence of which all attempts at salvage were abandoned in fear of offending the spirit of the water. Since then there is no record of these Tripods. This legend, too, must not be taken too literally. It is, I believe, no more than a parabolic way of describing the poetic end of a thing intimately bound up with the rises and falls of dynasties. To say simply that such a thing has been lost would argue a dearth of poetic diction or imagination. But it is no fairy tale, of which China, being a land rich in philosophy, art, and poetry, is sure to have many. Indeed dull must be the life of a people whose history does not furnish one. Still less is it superstition. To regard legends or tales like this as superstitions would be to ignore that they provide a fruitful source of inspiration to art and poetry, and that tales like Aesop's Fables and Cinderella have their permanent value either in the morals they teach or in the pleasures they impart.

So far as we know, there was no bronze work prior to the *Shang* Dynasty, and historians consider the period before then as China's Stone Age. Even during the *Shang* Dynasty the Stone Age was not quite over. Hence the term 'Gin Shih', which literally means 'Metal and Stone', that is, Bronze and Stone Age. From *Chow* to *Han* it may be said to be the Bronze Age, which also ended with

[1] *Records of Warring States*, Bk. I, p. 1, Ed. *Sze Bu Bei Yao*.

Han; for since then bronze was in great demand for other purposes than making ornaments and utensils, and at times the use of bronze by private individuals was even forbidden, because it was commandeered by the State.

As necessity is the mother of invention, the scarcity of bronze, coupled with the progress of material civilization, must have hastened the period of pottery and porcelain. Pottery was of course the forerunner of porcelain, the latter being considered the highest achievement of the former, and differing from the former mainly in such characteristics as translucency and vitrification. Pottery must have appeared in China at a very early date, even before the *Han* Dynasty; but porcelain, according to the opinion of Chinese experts, was not invented until the *Wei* (A.D. 220) or even the *Tsin* (A.D. 265) Dynasty; because the word '*Tschi*', Chinese word for porcelain, is not even found in the *Ancient Dictionary of Words* compiled in the *Han* Dynasty (206 B.C.), and it did not appear to be used until the *Tsin* Dynasty, though, from the *Six Dynasties* (A.D. 266-618) onwards, it has frequently been used in literature. As to porcelain factories, the earliest known to history is the *East Ou Factory*, built in Chekiang in the time of *Tsin*. Another old factory, later in date but greater in fame, is the one built in Kiangsi, about A.D. 583, now known as *Kingtechen*, referred to in Longfellow's *Kéramos* in the following lines:

'O'er desert sands, o'er gulf and bay,
O'er Ganges and o'er Himalay
Bird-like I fly, and flying sing,
To flowery kingdoms of Cathay,
And bird-like poise on balanced wing
Above the town of King-te-tching,
A burning town, or seeming so,—
Three thousand furnaces that glow
Incessantly, and fill the air
With smoke uprising, gyre on gyre,
And painted by the lurid glare
Of jets and flashes of red fire.' [1]

For practical purposes we may say that pottery flourished in the *Tang* Dynasty (A.D. 618-906) and porcelain in the *Sung* Dynasty (A.D. 960-1127). There is a well-known story connected with a type of porcelain called '*Chai Yau*'. Just before the commencement of the *Sung* Dynasty Emperor Chou Si Chung (A.D. 949) ordered some porcelain to be made, and, on being asked what colour he would have, he wrote down these words: 'The colour of the blue sky when the

[1] Longfellow: *Kéramos* (1878), lines 302-13.

clouds disperse after rain.' The porcelain made under this order, we are told, was 'as blue as the sky, as clear as a mirror, as thin as paper, and as resonant as a musical stone of jade'. No specimen of this porcelain, unfortunately, is left to us, inasmuch as even in the *Ming* Dynasty there was a saying 'a broken bit of *Chai Yau* is worth a thousand pieces of gold'.

This chapter cannot end without a word about the Chinese artist and Chinese art as a whole. The Chinese artist, as I have said in connection with painting, always tries to interpret nature rather than imitate it, and hopes to rise above it. He may be grand in his conception and is yet patient in his execution. Nothing is too great or too small for him: he may paint a river of a myriad miles and yet will try to be faithful even to a blade of grass that grows out of his brush. He aims at perfection and is yet conscious that he may fall short of his aims; therefore he succeeds. He may be confident in himself and yet feels that there must be others who can do better than he himself; therefore he triumphs. He may be bold in his design, and yet will not go to the extreme; therefore his creation is in harmony with life and the universe. He is never fashionable and is indifferent to popularity; therefore he becomes a great master. His mind is at peace with the whole world; therefore what he produces is the embodiment of harmony and affection.

Chinese Art as a whole is not created by the bayonet, but by the desire of those things which make perfect beauty: peace, virtue, righteousness, and love, which are the corner stones of Chinese culture and civilization.

FISHING IN THE SNOW
Painting by an unknown artist of the Five Dynasties (A.D. 907-960)
forming part of the Chinese Art Exhibition in London in 1935
Property of Chinese Government

CHAPTER 10

CONCLUSION

SAY not that East is East and West is West;
For they are whole-blood brothers none the less.
They are not twins; because the East is older,
And it in certain ways is also wiser. [1]
May they have concord as the proverb [2] says!
'Twill bring mankind so many happy days.

[1] 'Dans l'histoire comme dans la poésie, dans les manifestations religieuses comme dans les spéculations philosophiques, l'Orient est l'antécédent de l'Occident. Nous devons donc chercher à le connaître pour nous bien connaître nous-mêmes. . . . A mesure que les connaissances sur l'Orient se développeront, on verra se révéler comme un monde nouveau, une civilisation merveilleuse que l'antiquité n'avait pas même soupçonnée. On sera surpris de voir ce qu'étaient les anciens en comparaison de ses vieux peuples de l'Orient, et on sera de plus en plus frappé de la vérité de cette allocution d'un prêtre d'Egypte à Solon (conservée par Platon dans son Timée): "O Athéniens, vous n'êtes que des enfants! vous ne connaissez rien de ce qui est plus ancien que vous; remplis de votre propre excellence et de celle de votre nation, vous ignorez tout ce qui vous a précédés; vous croyez que ce n'est qu'avec vous et avec votre ville que le monde a commencé d'exister." . . . Nous ne craignons pas d'affirmer que l'étude des civilisations de l'Orient est désormais d'une nécessité absolue pour quiconque veut écrire sur les origines et la filiation des peuples, des langues, des arts, des religions, de la morale, de la philosophie, en un mot, sur l'histoire toute entière de l'humanité. Nous ne craindrons pas d'affirmer encore que la plus grande partie des livres publiés depuis la découverte de l'imprimerie (et ils sont nombreux), dont les sujets se rapportent plus ou moins directement à ceux qui sont énumérés ci-dessus, sont à refaire, parce qu'ils partent tous de données plus ou moins inexactes, de bases plus ou moins fragiles, de systèmes plus ou moins faux, parce qu'ils n'ont tenu aucun compte de ces importantes civilisations qui ont eu et ont encore une grande influence sur le développement général de l'humanité. C'est comme si tous ceux qui ont créé des systèmes d'astronomie avaient négligé ou dédaigné de tenir compte des astres les plus

rayonnants du système du monde!'—G. Pauthier: *Les Livres Sacrés de l'Orient*; Introduction, pp. vii and ix.

Translation: 'In history as in poetry, and in religious manifestations as in philosophic speculations, the East precedes the West. We should therefore try to know it in order that we may well know ourselves. In proportion as knowledge of the East develops one sees revealed, like a new world, a marvellous civilization that the ancients had not even suspected. One will be surprised to see what the ancients were in comparison with these old peoples of the East, and one will be the more and more impressed with the truth of this allocution of an Egyptian priest at Solon (preserved by Plato in his Dialogue, the *Timæus*): "O Athenians, you are only children! You know nothing of what is older than you. Contented with your own excellence and that of your own city, you think that it is only with you and your city that the world has commenced to exist." . . . We are not afraid to affirm that the study of the civilizations of the East is henceforth an absolute necessity for anyone who wishes to write about the origins and the filiation of peoples, languages, arts, religions, moral, philosophy, and, in a word, the whole history of mankind. We shall not be afraid to affirm, moreover, that the greater part of the books published since the invention of printing (and they are numerous), the subjects of which relate more or less directly to those enumerated above, have to be rewritten; because they all proceed from notions more or less inexact, from bases more or less fragile, and from systems more or less false; because they have taken no account of these important civilizations which have had and still have a great influence on the general development of humanity. It is as if all those who have created systems of astronomy had neglected or disdained to take into account the most brilliant stars of the universe!'

[2] 'When concord prevails among brothers, life is delightful.' *Book of Odes* (*Mow Sche*) Bk. IX, No. 2, Title *Chang Di*. See *ante*, p. 178.

INDEX

and modesty, his, 65, 71–3; jade associated with virtue, on, 249; *Jiun Tze*, on, 38–9, 72; contrasted with *Siao Yun*, 39–40; knowledge, on, 135; *Li* (moral rules of correct conduct) on, 35; 'Master for all ages', as, 66; philosophy on *general subjects*, 134–136; *politics*, 130–4; poverty and humble conditions, on, 94–5; prayer, on, 49; 'Recompense injury with kindness', on, 79–83; spiritual beings, on, 48; teachers, on, 86; teaching, his method of, 64; temple of, 51; tolerance, on, 81–2; truth, on, 88; truthfulness, on, 86; uprightness, on, 87; virtue, on, 67, 87–8, 178; perfect, 74, 81, 100; wealth and honour, on, 92, 94; will, on, 135; wisdom, on, 48; young, on treatment of the, 89; younger generation, on, 129; youth, his rule for the, 85.

Contentment, 108
Courage, 18, 59–60, 87, 178
Creed, 46
Crime, 108, 109, 143

Danger, 68, 154, 200
Death, 49, 50, 53, 55, 87, 92, 108, 132, 151, 154–5
Deceit, 60, 106
Democratic, 96, 101, 103, 147
Dicey, 180
Dickens, Charles, 206
Dispute, 106, 116
Divine duty and right, 145
Divorce, 181, 196
Duty, 46, 48–9, 53, 66, 67, 68, 72, 73, 76, 79, 87, 131, 134, 171, 175, 178, 185

East and West, 21, 22–3, 25, 195, 200, 257
Edward VII, King, 93, 102
Eloquence, 98, 108
'Equal love', doctrine of, 27, 114
Equality and fraternity, human, 100
Evil, 22, 58, 81, 87, 89, 107, 116, 156
Extra-territoriality, 19, 70,
Extreme, 42

Fairy tales, 256

Faithfulness, 86
Falsehood, 60
Family, 163–86; father and mother, 172; medium of love, etc., as, 186; parental power, 163; parents and children, 165–76; peace, as factor of, 186; Roman system, differs from, 163–4; sacredness of parental relation reflected in novels, 172–4; social unit, not, 163; system misunderstood by others, 175–6; wife, position of, 177–180, 182–3; husband and, 178–9; woman, the Chinese, 172, 180–1
Fault, 71, 86, 88, 108, 135
Feelings, the seven, 26
Filial piety, 53, 54, 67, 85, 153, 166–72, 174; its counterbalance, 172; how misunderstood, 175–6
Forbearance and forgiveness, 81, 82
Force, 20, 161
Form, 31–3, 46
Frederick, the Great, 25, 118
French Revolution, 138, 160
Friendship, 199–210; basis of, 201; bosom friend, 209; breach of, 202; Chinese, 208; choice of, 205; duties of, 206; indispensability of, 199; meaning of, 200; poems on, 199, 208; test of, 208; way of maintaining, 207

Gaius, 32
Generosity, 19, 58, 82, 129, 207
Gentleman, 37, 42, 109, 119, 162
Gibbon, Edward, 32
Giles, Prof. Herbert, 20, 21, 25, 30, 68, 69, 94, 180, 207, 211
God, 47–8; Chinese word for, 49–51, 91
Goddess of Mercy, 206
Goethe, 136, 152, 170, 209
Golden Rule, 21, 70–2, 74–9
Goldsmith, Dr. Oliver, 28, 32, 41, 52, 58, 64, 86, 103, 106, 135, 136, 183, 187, 191, 207
Good, 22, 59, 81, 82, 83, 89, 108–10, 132, 143, 156, 157
Government, 116, 130–4, 137–8, 146–8
Gratitude, 170
Gray, Thomas, 26, 29
Great task, 92
Great Learning, The, 60–1, 63–4